CAPTIVE

CAPTIVE

*A Mother's Crusade to Save Her
Daughter from a Terrifying Cult*

Catherine Oxenberg
with Natasha Stoynoff

GALLERY BOOKS
New York   London   Toronto   Sydney   New Delhi

G

Gallery Books
An Imprint of Simon & Schuster, Inc.
1230 Avenue of the Americas
New York, NY 10020

First Gallery Books hardcover edition August 2018

GALLERY BOOKS and colophon are registered trademarks of Simon & Schuster, Inc.

For information about special discounts for bulk purchases, please contact Simon & Schuster Special Sales at 1-866-506-1949 or business@simonandschuster.com.

The Simon & Schuster Speakers Bureau can bring authors to your live event. For more information or to book an event, contact the Simon & Schuster Speakers Bureau at 1-866-248-3049 or visit our website at www.simonspeakers.com.

Interior design by Bryden Spevak

Manufactured in the United States of America

10 9 8 7 6 5 4 3 2 1

Library of Congress Cataloging-in-Publication Data is available.

ISBN 978-1-9821-0065-0
ISBN 978-1-9821-0067-4 (ebook)

NOTE TO THE READER

This is a memoir based on my experience with Nxivm and subsequent years of research into the organization. Certain names and identifying details have been changed. Certain quotes have been reconstructed from memory, to the best of my ability.

For my India.
My love for you knows no bounds
and my hope is that you will recognize this book
as a testament of that unconditional love.

CONTENTS

CAPTIVE

Prayer to Persephone

Be to her, Persephone,
All the things I might not be;
Take her head upon your knee.
She that was so proud and wild,
Flippant, arrogant and free,
She that had no need of me,
Is a little lonely child
Lost in Hell,—Persephone,
Take her head upon your knee;
Say to her, "My dear, my dear,
It is not so dreadful here."

—EDNA ST. VINCENT MILLAY

PROLOGUE

Malibu, California, May 30, 2017

It was a question no mother should ever have to ask her daughter. But I had no choice—her life was in danger. I needed to get to the truth, and fast.

India was on the tail end of a five-day visit home from New York. We were driving along the Pacific Coast Highway to a doctor's appointment when I asked her point-blank:

"India . . . have you been *branded*?"

Words I never thought I'd hear come out of my mouth. Not in a million years.

Sitting next to me in the passenger seat, my daughter looked gaunt and sleep deprived. Her golden blonde hair had been falling out in clumps, and, at twenty-five, she hadn't had her period in a year—the reason she was seeing the doctor that day. Adding to that, my lighthearted, free-spirited daughter had grown distant and burdened in recent months, to the point where I barely recognized her.

A few weeks earlier, to my horror, I had discovered why.

A friend called to warn me that India was involved in a secret master-slave sorority in which women were put on a starvation diet and, in a secret ceremony, held down naked and branded on the pubic region with a searing-hot cauterizing iron—like cattle.

"You've got to save her!" my friend urged.

My head spun. *What? Not India!* In my mind, I could hear the women's screams and smell their burning flesh. I prayed my sweet daughter had not gone so far as to allow someone to barbarically mutilate and torture her, but I feared the worst.

I clutched the steering wheel as I awaited her answer.

"Yes, Mom," India admitted hesitantly. "I've been branded. But why is that a problem? It was a good experience for me!"

My heart broke. *No, no, no!* I gripped the wheel tighter and forced my eyes to stay on the road. How had I failed to notice she'd fallen so deeply into such a dark and evil world? I knew if I became judgmental, I'd push her even further away—beyond my help. So I tried to appeal to her sense of logic.

"Darling," I said as calmly as I could, "if you can convince me how being branded can be a *good* experience, please, go ahead."

India fell silent. She seemed confused as she struggled to answer me. Finally, she looked at me with childlike sincerity through her weary eyes and said: "It's a good thing because it's . . . character building."

I wanted to scream. It was as if someone had tampered with her brain so she couldn't think clearly or had replaced her with an imposter—like in that 1950s science-fiction horror movie *Invasion of the Body Snatchers.* Her words and phrasing sounded preprogrammed, drilled into her head by a deviant master.

I answered slowly, reasonably.

"But India, the fact that you think mutilating your body permanently is character building is *proof* that you're brainwashed."

Again she looked bewildered and shook her head.

"I'm not brainwashed."

"You *are.*"

"I'm *not.*"

"Angel, you're being manipulated by a psychopath."

"Mom, I'm not."

There was no getting through to her. Nothing I said could break the spell she was under.

A few hours later, she'd be on a plane to the cult's headquarters in Albany, New York, to take part in the next victim's branding ceremony the following week.

I'd lost her, I was sure I'd lost her. And I felt like I was losing my mind.

But there were two other truths I was immediately certain of in that devastating moment.

I was going to do whatever it took to save my daughter from the clutches of this vicious cult and get her back. And I was going to take this cult down. Not just for my daughter's sake but also for the countless other sons and daughters in this country who get lured into these exploitive, abusive traps every day.

I was a mother with a mission; I was on a crusade.

And I was not going to rest until our children were safe and the last enemy was down.

INDIA AND ME: OUR SEARCH FOR MEANING

From the second she was a little speck growing inside me, India and I were a magical, mystical team—an intertwined force of nature and spirit to be reckoned with.

When I conceived her in the fall of 1990, I was traveling through Europe obsessed with hunting down murals of the Archangel Michael. India's father-to-be, Bill, wasn't the spiritual type, but I dragged him along, waxing eloquently about angels as we explored villages and biked through the Alps.

A few weeks into my pregnancy, Bill swears that one night he had a vision of the Archangel Michael telling him we were creating an especially "conscious being" together, and it was our destiny to protect her.

"Um, are you *hallucinating*?" I said, laughing over the phone.

By that time, Bill and I weren't together anymore—our briefly crossed paths had uncrossed—and the idea of being a mother on my own was daunting. But . . . there was that vision he'd had. The Archangel Michael, I knew very well, had led God's army to vanquish evil forces and banish them from heaven.

He was just the strong, valiant, protective hero a single mother and child could use. *He's watching over us*, I decided. And so, I embraced my fate as a cosmic mother and guardian.

India arrived into the world on June 7, 1991, by my own hands.

My mother drove me to the hospital at three in the morning, and during labor I begged and screamed for drugs, but my midwife was having none of that talk.

"You wanted a natural birth," she said in a cheerful, singsong voice, "and that's what you're gonna get! Do you want to touch her head?"

"*Nooooo!*" I whimpered, but I instinctively reached down and felt her. And then, without thinking, I slipped my fingers under India's tiny armpits and gently pulled her out of my body.

At 4:36 a.m., one became an inseparable two.

My mother cut the umbilical cord, and I named my daughter India Riven Oxenberg. My best friend growing up was named India, but I was duped into believing that *riven* was Celtic for "priestess." By the time I found out it meant "heartbreak," it was too late to change it.

For the first seven years of her life, India and I were inseparable— I took her everywhere with me, be it a film set for work or a spiritual trek for enlightenment. From as far back as I can remember, I'd been an ardent *seeker*.

In 1999, our little family of two grew to five after I married fellow actor Casper Van Dien. India inherited younger stepsister Grace and younger stepbrother Cappy. Over the next four years our brood expanded further after daughters Maya and Celeste were born, and then we made seven.

But when we were alone, India and I were still the original, inseparable duo.

I continued on my path for self-improvement and illumination, often taking India with me to dance with shamans and practice with yoga masters and meditate with gurus.

As far as I was concerned, India was already *there*. She was highly spiritual but grounded, with her own internal guidance and wisdom that she followed. I was in awe of her, actually.

When she was around ten and struggling at school because of her severe dyslexia, I asked her if she wanted to do a guided visualization with me. We were the only ones home that Saturday afternoon—Casper had taken the other kids to see *X-Men*—and she said yes.

She sat down, closed her eyes, and I told her to concentrate on her breath. I took her through some guided imagery, but she had trouble visualizing what I described. I thought about one of her favorite books, *The Little Engine That Could*.

"Keep trying," I told her gently, "just tell yourself you-think-you-can."

"I think I can!" she said. "I think I can!"

Pretty soon, her mantra turned into "I *know* I can!" and she burst into tears of joy. We hugged, and she looked at me in amazement. "I can feel my body vibrating with energy. I feel so free and happy," she said. "Like I'm brand-new!"

It was her first experience with repetitive, positive reinforcement, and she sure took to it.

The next day, the two of us slipped out to a Unity Church together, just us, and when the minister announced the theme of that day's sermon—"I Can!"—we looked at each other with mouths agape. India was blown away and felt elated after we left the service. But a few days later, she wanted to know, "Mom, why doesn't the joy stay? Why does it go away? The happiness feels like a light switch that turns on and off."

"Darling," I said, sitting down. "You are experiencing the greatest and most common of all human challenges," I told her, "the desire to find happiness—and *keep* it."

India, it seemed, was a seeker, too.

PART 1

Losing India

1

THE GURU AND GOLD SASH

As always, India and I were excited to set out on a new adventure together.

We made our way along the Venice Beach boardwalk early one morning in May 2011—past the maze of street performers, mystics, artists, funky shops, and bikinied girls on roller skates—until we reached our destination: a modern-looking duplex a block from the ocean.

It was our first day of a five-day "personal and professional growth" seminar called Executive Success Programs (ESP)—a course, I was told, intended for people looking to bolster their business acumen and develop their communication skills; entrepreneurs who wanted to be successful and make money, but in an ethical, humanitarian way.

"It's *conscious* capitalism," an acquaintance of mine, who'd been urging me to sign up for months, told me. "And it's the best thing I have ever done. *Truly life changing.*"

A business seminar, life changing?

Hmm. I'd heard *that* line before.

At fifty, I was a veteran of the self-help, self-improvement, self-realization genre. In an effort to overcome a tenacious, life-threatening eating disorder that I'd struggled with from age sixteen up until my midthirties, I tried every kooky idea out there that promised to heal my body, enlighten my mind, and, hopefully, save my life.

In no particular order, I'd been rolfed, rebirthed, chelated, Deeksha-ed, magnetized, fêng shui-ed, baptized, ozoned, watsu-ed, and hypnotized. I'd meditated, chanted, 12-stepped, past-life-regressed, fasted, rehabbed, and sweated in lodges. I'd listened to Jungians, herbalists, angels, yogis, shamans, astrologers, Apache medicine men, Buddhist monks, Chopra, Robbins, Kabbalah, the maharishi who hung out with the Beatles, the constellations, and even my own dreams.

I drank a Peruvian tea that makes you hallucinate and vomit; I ran across hot coals and floated in sensory deprivation tanks; I flung myself off a sixty-foot telephone pole in the middle of a winter blizzard in Oklahoma.

I did everything I could to try freeing myself from the addictive clutches of a disorder that held me in its grip. Subsequently, self-help became a way of life. A badge of honor.

Did any of them help? Some did, some didn't. It always seemed that the more they cost, the less effect they had.

What my experiences did do for me was make me skeptical about anyone or anything that promised to have The Answer and guaranteed to *truly change your life*. My life and I were just fine now, thank you very much. I'd recently entered a new decade and made peace with my past and with myself. I was done looking for that one magical, miraculous recipe that would make me perfect.

Life didn't work that way, I'd learned. And human perfection was an oxymoron.

My sweet India, on the other hand, was a young woman on the threshold of seeking, trying, questioning, and experiencing everything life had to offer—as one should be at nineteen.

Back home after a year studying entertainment media at Bay State College in Boston, she was head over heels in love with her high school sweetheart, Hudson, and embarking on a new business venture with a friend: a gluten-free baking company called Scrumptious Soul.

India was a born entrepreneur and foodie. As a little girl, she watched the Food Network as passionately as other kids watched cartoons. At six, she was whipping up those premixed, chemical-filled Easy-Bake Oven cakes (that Mom ate dutifully with a smile), and by seven, she'd graduated to artfully arranged vegetable and *burrata* platters (that Mom devoured!).

When we'd attended the ESP introductory meeting three months earlier, she'd been in the happy throes of creating her company and shooting a pilot for a potential TV series about their mobile bakery truck called *Food Angels*.

I was helping her launch this dream career of hers, so the opportunity to take a course that would hone India's business skills (and in a *humanitarian* way!) sounded like a good idea.

India and I sat in a rented conference room with a small group of other wannabe entrepreneurs, ready and eager to hear how to be successful businesswomen with heart.

Mark Vicente, a high-ranking member of ESP, began by explaining that the program was based on a revolutionary, patent-pending "technology" called Rational Inquiry, created by a scientist and philosopher named Keith Raniere.

"As we develop, we form beliefs about ourselves and the world, often innocently making associations that are inconsistent with reality," said Mark. "Our technology allows you to uncover, reexamine, and integrate these mistaken perceptions. We offer you the tools for removing errors of cognition and for creating consistency . . ."

Right around there, I started daydreaming—then perked up when I heard Mark say that this guy Keith had an IQ of 240, which apparently was in *Guinness World Records*. Really? Was that even possible? I'd never heard of anyone breaking the 200 barrier, not even Einstein. And this Raniere guy obviously wasn't a devotee of physicist-cosmologist Stephen Hawking, who said a few years earlier that "people who boast about their IQ are losers."

Mark continued to boast:

"He's been recognized as one of the world's top three problem solvers. He has an estimated problem-solving capability of one in four hundred twenty-five million with respect to the general population."

Whatever that meant. If he was the third best problem solver in the world, I wanted to know who the first and second were! Still, number three was pretty impressive. Mark Vicente was known and respected in the entertainment industry, so I assumed he wasn't making up this shit. He'd cowritten, directed, and produced the 2004 indie hit *What the Bleep Do We Know!?*—a spiritual, existential documentary about quantum physics and how consciousness shapes the material world.

After Mark's pitch, a handful of current ESP devotees got up in front of the room and proselytized about how much better their lives were because of the program. A pretty brunette, who I would later find out was Sarah Edmondson, an accomplished Canadian actress in her late thirties, stood up to give a charismatic close, avowing that "ESP is the key to success and happiness." With Mark, Sarah was the co-owner of the Vancouver ESP center, and she was hosting this introductory course with him.

Again I heard the term *life changing*. It was about more than just business, they stressed; it was about learning tools that would improve all of mankind.

What tools, you ask? So did a bunch of us in the room, including me, who couldn't make heads or tails of what they were saying. Mark was expounding some kind of lofty, noble ideology, but it wasn't clear how they or we were supposed to achieve it.

Apparently, we'd have to wait a little while longer to find out. None of those details could be divulged in the slightest until *after* we made an initial down payment on the very special, time-limited $2,400-per-person discount rate that would end imminently.

It was all very top, top secret because their material was "proprietary," Mark said with a reverential tone, and people were always trying to steal it and copy it.

"You do *not* want to miss this *deal of a lifetime*," one of the coaches urged us.

Oh, pleeeeease, I thought, trying not to let any of them see me roll my eyes.

I turned to India, assuming she would have seen through the snake oil tactics as well.

"This is for me," she said resolutely. "I want to do this, Mom. And I want you to do it with me."

Later, I would wonder desperately what attracted her so powerfully. I think it was their talk about creating more joy in the world and improving mankind. Ever since she was born, India was good and kind to her core and drawn to help others. She was the family mediator who rushed to diffuse anger and find common ground when a squabble was brewing among siblings and parents. With her light touch and disarming sense of humor, there was an artistry to her diplomacy.

She couldn't stand violence or to see anyone get hurt, and acted as warrior and protector for those who were. In those instances, her touch could be bolder. When she was nine and at summer camp with her younger stepbrother, Cappy, she saw him being picked on and pushed around by a group of bigger, older bullies. She marched straight up to the bullies, unafraid, and demanded, "Leave my brother alone!" The boys scampered away.

Around that same time, she also showed a wisdom and empathy beyond her years. I took her with me to Italy when I was shooting *The Omega Code* in 1999, and, as usual, little India had an impact on everyone she met, in the most beautiful way.

We were filming in the Castello Orsini-Odescalchi, a fifteenth-century castle just north of Rome (Tom Cruise and Katie Holmes would marry there a few years later in what would become Scientology's most extravagant and highly publicized wedding of all time), and the director invited India to be an extra in one of my scenes. They made a big to-do: the costume person took her out to get a new dress, and they did her hair and makeup in the trailer, sitting right next to me. She loved it!

India always had a luminous, ethereal quality about her, but as soon as they put her under the lights, she looked . . . magical.

"Remember, angel face, don't look into the camera," I reminded her in a whisper before the director called "Action!"

She looked at me like I'd just said the most asinine thing in the world to her.

"I *know* that, Mom!"

As the camera rolled, I watched her out of the corner of my eye; she knew exactly where to go and what to do. I was so proud! She was a natural. Later, as Linda the makeup artist powdered her nose in between takes, India looked at her seriously.

"Linda, even though you're smiling," she said, "and I heard you tell someone with my rabbit ears that you're happy, you don't have to lie about your feelings. Kids always know the truth."

Linda looked at her, stunned. She had indeed been going through a difficult time all week but was trying not to show it.

"But it's okay," India continued. "Don't worry. You may not be happy now, but you will be—soon."

Linda nearly fell over backward. Everyone was amazed at how precocious and compassionate India was.

So back to the ESP introductory meeting: I imagine their promise of creating a better, more ethical workplace and happier world appealed to India. Whatever it was, I put aside my skepticism, took out my credit card, and checked and signed some paperwork they'd handed me without much scrutiny.

What appealed to *me* was spending time and sharing a new experience with my daughter—that, I was always interested in.

—

WHEN WE ARRIVED at the beach house three months later on that May morning, we still had no idea what to expect. As well as being excited, we were both also slightly disheartened. A week before, India's bakery business and TV pilot had fallen through. And a screenplay that my husband, Casper, and I had written about my grandfather, *Royal Exile*, hadn't interested producers as I hoped it would. The time for both of us to learn new business skills was perhaps more apropos now than ever.

The scene that unfolded inside was just as bizarre as the madcap mystics and circus performers on the boardwalk. The loftlike living room was set up like a minimalistic lecture room, with a few couches and rows of folding chairs and not much else. It was as if the ESP troupe had slipped into town the night before and transformed someone's home into a pop-up self-help venue.

Standing at the front of the room, an army of barefoot ESP coaches greeted us. They wore green, orange, and yellow sashes around their necks, and they grinned from ear to ear. And when I say they grinned, I mean *grinned*. I'm talking face-splitting, vaguely unnerving, over-the-top smiles—as if they were trying desperately to convince us: we're the happiest, most successful people on earth. I felt like I was standing before a choir of Tom Cruises.

The attendees included a few celebrities and some high-profile people already attached to the organization. Emiliano Salinas, the

son of former Mexican president Carlos Salinas de Gortari, was
there—he held a high-ranking position in the group and wore an
elite green sash around his neck. Each color signified a level in the
group's hierarchy. "Like a martial arts dojo," explained one coach.

Beginners started off with white, and then you got stripes added
to the bottom of your sash as you moved up in the color group. The
next color was yellow, which you received once you became a coach.
Then came orange and, finally, green, which meant you were a senior
proctor. I have a vague memory of a blue and purple sash, too, but
at some point, their system got very fuzzy to me, so I can't be sure.
Gold was the highest sash color you could wear, but later I would
find out that only Nancy Salzman, the organization's second in command, was deemed worthy of one.

With Salinas was his new girlfriend, Polish-Mexican actress Lud-
wika ("Mika") Paleta, who was taking the course for the first time.
She sat with her arms crossed and projected that cynical I'm-not-
going-to-buy-into-any-of-this-BS attitude.

We spotted actress Rosario Dawson, and India went over and
struck up a lively conversation with her. India had always been a care-
free spirit who could chat with anyone; she was never overly impressed
or intimidated by people she didn't know. I was more reserved and
envied her confidence in that way, and was glad when I saw a good
friend of mine in the small group: British actor Callum Blue.

We glommed on to each other like allies and took up permanent
residence in the back row while India took a seat near the front.
That's when I noticed for the first time that Callum had a big, beautiful blue tattoo of the Archangel Michael's sword running up and
down his left arm.

"He used to stand at the end of my bed when I was a child—ten feet tall, with a sword of light," Callum explained.

"Throughout my life, I always felt protected by Michael," he said.

I was starting to feel left out; these visitations from Michael were a dime a dozen with my family and friends, but he was playing hard to get with me.

———

MOMENTS LATER, WE were asked to remove our shoes and put away our cell phones—they were officially banned from the house for the duration of the course.

Then a hush fell over the room: Nancy had arrived.

She was short, bespectacled, and overcaffeinated, and went by the ancient Roman title "Prefect." Of all the smiling going on, Nancy had mastered it the best—or rather, the worst. Her wide, pasted-on grin was so inauthentic to me that it looked like a Halloween mask set off eerily by her gold sash and bobbed hair.

She stepped to the front of the room, and all the coaches put their hands together and bowed to her.

Creepy, I thought.

Even creepier was our instruction that we, too, were to bow to the Prefect every time she entered or exited the room—and every time we left the room ourselves. At the beginning of each day, coaches instructed everyone to huddle together and repeat in unison their mantra: "We are committed to our success!" This was accompanied by a synchronized hand clap.

And, we were also told that we'd have to bow for the founder and creator of ESP, the genius problem solver Keith Raniere. Only his name wasn't Keith anymore. We were now instructed to call him "Vanguard." Apparently, he didn't need no stinking colored sashes, because he never wore one.

We wouldn't have to worry too much about bowing to him, though, because we wouldn't be meeting him. Vanguard, it seemed, was as elusive as the Wizard of Oz. He did all his brilliant thinking back at ESP headquarters in Albany, and no student got to meet him until they had graduated from the first level of classes.

But although he wouldn't be with us physically over the next five days, he would most certainly be there in spirit. He would be talked about, thanked, and glorified in almost everything we did—God forbid we should forget Vanguard for one second.

"We must always remember to pay tribute to Vanguard," Nancy said with reverence. "Without him, these great teachings wouldn't exist."

Just like a god, I thought.

I couldn't help myself; I had to see what kind of power trip this guy was on. I whipped out my iPhone, hid my hands behind Callum, Googled "Vanguard," and snuck a peek.

Up popped a site for a comic book character of the same name: a gigantic, muscle-bound alien superhero with tiny antennae on his head. His job was to guard Planet Earth.

Oh, man, I thought. *This guy is living out his childhood fantasy.*

I showed Callum, and we both laughed. Back then, it was just funny and nothing to take seriously.

—

AFTER ALL THE bowing was done, our next step was to recite in unison the mission statement written out in big block letters on a giant poster board at the front of the room. It was to be regurgitated daily until we knew it by heart.

I silently read the twelve points on the board as the others said them out loud. It was a word salad of platitudes and obsequious beyond belief:

Success is an interior state of clear and honest awareness of who I am, my value in the world and my responsibility for the reactions I have to all things.

What did that even mean? And then there was this gem:

The methods and information I learn in ESP are for my personal use only. I will not speak of them; nor will I give to others knowledge of them outside ESP. Part of being accepted into ESP is to keep all the information confidential. If I violate this commitment, I am breaking a promise and breaching my contract, but more, I am deteriorating my internal and integrated honesty.

And the statement ended with us making a vow to bring in more students:

I promise to share and enroll people in ESP and their mission for my own benefit and to make the world a better place to live.

My hand shot up in the air.

"I have a problem with that," I said to Nancy and her foot soldiers. "I didn't sign up to recruit people."

There was an uncomfortable silence in the room.

"And furthermore," I continued, "the idea that I can't share this experience with my family is simply unrealistic."

Apparently, the reserved Catherine had left the building. Nancy cocked her head like a parrot, and the coaches looked both surprised and mildly annoyed at me but kept their smiles intact. I guess no one had ever challenged the mission statement before.

"You already agreed to all of it," said one of the smiling, yellow-sashed ones. "When you signed the nondisclosure agreement."

The wha—? And then I remembered: the paperwork I had quickly filled out and signed months earlier at the intro meeting. Wow, that was sneaky. And it didn't sit well with me at all. I'd been tricked into signing a legal contract, and now they wanted to bind and gag me to secrecy? That was preposterous and fundamentally wrong to me.

Much later, I'd understand exactly why. This kind of extreme exclusiveness was the first wedge a group like this placed between you and your life outside the group. It was the first stage of imprinting upon you that loyalty to ESP overrode anything else in your life.

And that, I would learn, was the beginning of being inducted into a cult.

—

EACH DAY WE began at eight in the morning, broke for lunch, and finished around ten at night. We didn't get a break for dinner, and by the end of the day, I was famished.

What India and I expected to be a course about business was more of an intensive facilitated group therapy. We learned a technique called "mirroring"—a type of NLP (neuro-linguistic programming) in which you built rapport and influenced business associates by copying their body language. Nancy's background was as an NLP practitioner, and it was something I'd already learned from numerous seminars by Tony Robbins, the self-help guru. The technique was performed without the other person's knowledge, and that always struck me as highly manipulative—was it even ethical? I wondered. I could see India's profile from where I was; she was listening intently in the front row.

We learned something called a "takeaway," which was standard salesman-pitch stuff, and we learned how to avoid libeling or slandering someone—which would end up being the most valuable tool I learned that week. The information was couched within a lesson about how to speak honorably about people and make judgments without committing "verbal violence" against them. You could pretty much say anything about anyone, they taught us, as long as you prefaced it with the phrase "in my opinion." It was a tool to build better communication skills, said Nancy. (And one I was grateful for years later, when I would use it against them while at war with ESP.)

For a program supposedly based on ethical business practices we spent an inordinate amount of time learning about how a con man runs a scam and how to pinpoint and identify the telltale signs and markings of a con artist at work.

Other than that, most of what we learned had nothing to do with business.

In the mornings, we cycled through a number of "modules":

weirdly constructed question sets full of hokey terminology that put me to sleep. If you nodded off in this class, you received a very unique kind of scolding:

"Catherine! You're falling asleep because you're disintegrated! Which is why you need to pay even closer attention!"

Translation: I wasn't *evolved* enough yet to absorb the highly evolved principles they were talking about. It was the worst insult they could give you, and they gave it out frequently that week. Telling someone she was "disintegrated" was cultspeak for calling her stupid in front of the entire class. Pretty soon I noticed that a lot of students stopped asking questions or making comments for fear they'd elicit the D word.

Even though Nancy was there in the flesh, she introduced the modules to us using cheaply produced videos in which she was the only star on a TV screen. In the videos, she asked us a series of tedious questions, which she compensated for with overanimation. Then we broke into small groups to come up with the answers.

My daughter and I weren't allowed to be in a small group together, they told us that first day. The group talks could get emotional, the coaches explained, and they insisted it was best for us to be separated. India seemed to agree, giving me a "like I really want to watch my mom bawl her eyes out over some childhood memory" look.

But I was frustrated by this rule. We were doing this together to share an experience; that was the whole point of it! I didn't like being disconnected from her like this. I'd noticed earlier the wedge they tried to create between students and their outside lives; obviously, this applied to family as well. Looking back, it was easy to see what they were doing: separating you from your real family so that you'd think of the group as your new family.

One module was called "Honesty and Disclosure," and I remember it well because it posed one of the more interesting questions: if you were in Nazi Germany and hiding Jews in your basement, and the Nazis came to the door searching for them, what would you do? Would you give them up, or would you lie to save their lives? The real question was: When is it ethical to lie for a higher purpose?

When discussion time within the groups was over, Nancy would return to the front of the classroom with much fanfare to give the "debrief."

Each group would report the answers its members came up with, and Nancy, or Prefect, would smugly "correct" them, providing them with the *right* answer. No group ever got it right on its own, I noticed.

After the modules, we moved on to what they called "exploration of meanings," or "EMs," an umbrella term for a Socratic line of questioning that's more experiential than the modules. It's a one-on-one process done with a coach that is meant to unhook the emotional charge around painful memories in one's life and dismantle phobias. The same one-on-one process done in a classroom setting where other members witness it is called a "sourcing."

(For the sake of simplicity, I'll refer to both "sourcing" and "exploration of meanings" as "EMs.")

But before we even got to that, I was already having an emotional charge of my own—and not a good one. Somewhere between the sashes, the bowing, the groveling mission statement, and the hokey handshake they showed us to use, I snapped. Like an allergy, I had a violent reaction to the structural rules and rituals these people were presenting, and, from the back row, I became the rebellious, obstreperous teenager I had never been.

I refused to call Nancy Prefect. (Callum and I came up with our own nickname for her early on: Gold Sash.) I refused to bow to anybody, I refused to learn or do the silly handshake and clap, I refused to say the mission statement (I mouthed the words and, under my breath, said "Blah, blah, blah, *blahhhhh*"), and I refused to wear the white Level-One sash I'd been given. Just the *thought* of putting it around my neck made me choke. I kept leaning back and letting it casually slip off my neck and slither down the back of my chair until it reached the floor in a heap. (I found out later that Keith had requested patents on many of their weird rituals, accessories, the methodology, and terminology—including the sashes, and even the handshakes and hand claps.)

Emiliano Salinas always seemed to be conveniently lurking nearby when that happened, and he would pick it up for me and put it back on my neck. After the third or fourth time my sash fell, I'm sure he was onto me. But at least he wasn't a dick about it.

In fact, speaking of . . .

Another of the peculiarities I noticed that first day was how the male sash wearers in the room all had a vaguely "beta male" quality about them—a description Casper used when he attended later. They gave off a subservient energy that was disturbingly deferential to Nancy, who reveled in her power.

I was the opposite of deferential.

As Nancy debriefed, I raised my hand every ten minutes like a disruptive heckler with Tourette's, yelling out "I have a problem with that!"

And I truly did. I was trying to be open minded for India's sake, but most of what Nancy was saying continued to rub me the wrong way. I made horrendous comments that had Callum doubled over in tears of laughter.

When Rosario Dawson had to leave in the middle of day two because of a death in the family, I quipped a little too loudly to Callum, "Lucky Rosario!" He almost fell off his folding chair.

I was shocked at my behavior, and I'm sure Callum was, too. He was British, after all, and to a born-and-bred Brit, being rude is a cardinal sin. The funny thing was, my actor buddy was born on the wrong side of the tracks and grew up in a strip club with a gangster dad. And here he was, acting the perfect gentleman (except when I had him guffawing) and pretty much channeling his role as the duke in *The Princess Diaries 2: Royal Engagement*.

Meanwhile, I'd been taught the strictest rules of proper etiquette and was descended from a royal pedigree (Mom is a bona fide princess, and second cousin to Prince Charles of Wales), and I was acting like a common, haggis-tossing hooligan!

And there was India up front, behaving like the well-mannered dream I'd brought her up to be, looking over at me quizzically. It was like we'd done the *Freaky Friday* switch, and I was the immature adolescent.

The only, *only*, other time I'd ever behaved this outrageously in a class setting was the time India was in preschool at the prestigious and progressive Waldorf School and her teachers were putting on a Christmas nativity play for the kids.

Again I sat in the back of the classroom, teetering on a tiny kindergarten chair, while India was up front acting like a little lady. I was fine until the teachers put on their woolen, felt hand puppets and proceeded to enact the biblical nativity story, not as Mary, Jesus, and Joseph but *as a family of insects*. It was their version of a New Age nativity play; it was an Insect Revival!

One look at those insects huddled in the manger, and I lost it. I laughed so hard, I couldn't walk and had to get down on all fours to crawl out of the room as snot poured out of my nose and dripped down my face. Not my finest moment.

Other than that day and this one, I was Miss Manners all the way. Which is why the way I was acting made no sense to me.

Could it be an absurd, delayed reaction to my strict upbringing? My father adopted the motto of a generation that believed children should be seen and not heard. If my siblings or I were disobedient or voiced an objection, we were punished. I loved him, but my father had a fierce temper, and for my own survival, I taught myself to be quiet and stay out of his way.

The one and only time I did muster up enough courage to defy him to his face was when I was sixteen. I spoke back, and he grabbed me by the throat and threw me up against a wall. You can believe I never tried that again. (The following year, I did tell him to go fuck himself, but it was over the phone, with an ocean between us to keep me safe.)

And now, everything in my nervous system was urging me to

fight back in that ersatz classroom against those smiling sash wearers, no matter what the consequences.

Why? *Why?*

Later on, I'd figure out why: although I wasn't aware of it consciously, my subconscious knew very well that it was under siege; it knew I was being infiltrated and indoctrinated by a system of pure subterfuge. My gut was trying to tell me that my daughter and I were being lured into a trap.

Nancy, of course, corrected me with the *right* answer as to why I was being so combative in class.

"You, Catherine," she said, pointing at me from the front of the room, "have a *defiance* issue. We'll have to work on that."

It was a word Nancy would use for me many times over the next five days, but once again—I had a problem with that.

She may have considered me defiant, but what she was witnessing wasn't defiance at all. It was the wisest, strongest, truest part of me rising up to do battle—and for very, very good reason.

2

LOVE BOMBING AND EPIPHANIES

And then, something unexpected and inexplicable happened to me.

Somewhere around day three, I wrote in my journal: "Hated the process. At the same time, *couldn't wait to get there.*"

We began EM-ing in class and broke up into small groups again. One coach was assigned to each group to work one-on-one with each member and go over answers we'd given when filling out a questionnaire on our first day. The questions included:

What is the worst thing that's ever happened to you?
What have you done that you're most ashamed of?
What is your greatest fear?

The questions were designed to expose our weaknesses, and they did. Within fifteen minutes, students were making confessions and having tearful breakthroughs and revelations left and right like an explosive fireworks display—including me.

Nancy was coaching my group. When it was my turn, the first thing she tried to dismantle was the emotional charge around the memory of my father throwing me against the wall at sixteen.

"Had you known then that it would be the worst thing he'd ever do to you, would that have lessened your fear in that moment?" she asked.

"I suppose so . . ."

"And you survived it, and you are alive, right? So you survived the worst."

"Right."

"Men get terrified when they lose control of their children, Catherine. You were taking control in that moment, and that scared him. He was acting out of his own insecurity. Can you see that?"

"I never thought about it that way . . ."

"Your father yelling at you or grabbing you by the throat has nothing to do with who *you* are. And it doesn't mean he doesn't love you or that you are not lovable."

I could feel a tug-of-war taking place inside of me: the kind of internal fight that ensues when a person tries to make a deep-rooted change. I'd held on to a specific perception of the incident for many years, and now Nancy was inviting me to reexamine it and dismantle it through a new lens—*her* lens. I felt a struggle, and then gave in to it.

Her explanation humanized my father and helped me understand his own struggle, lessening the resentment, fear, and grief I'd previously linked to the memory. Looking at him through this new lens, I actually felt compassion for him. I was even able to thank him for inadvertently being a powerful teacher for me in his school of hard knocks.

"He was an antagonist for most of my life, but I developed a lot of strength, resilience, and self-reliance because of him," I told the group, who all nodded in understanding. "I started supporting myself financially at seventeen. I became adept at dealing with difficult people."

Suddenly, in that room, I felt safe surrounded by these encouraging, empathetic people I barely knew, which was unusual for me. It was a soothing feeling, like a warm, gentle waterfall—and completely unexpected.

Nancy asked me what I'd like to work on next, and I told her about my phobia of auditions. For decades, I'd get so overwhelmed by anxiety before walking into an audition room that I'd often end up not going in at all.

"Why don't you want to walk into that room?" she asked.

"I don't know. For some reason, I just don't feel safe."

"Do you remember the first time you felt that way?"

I closed my eyes and took a deep breath . . .

—

SUDDENLY I WAS four years old at a family gathering north of Florence, Italy.

My grandfather on my mother's side, Prince Paul of Yugoslavia, owned a beautiful summer residence, Villa Demidoff, built by Francesco de' Medici, the grand duke of Tuscany, in the fifteen hundreds. It was a palatial home filled with antiques from my grandfather's Russian heritage. In the gardens, I used to climb onto the thirty-five-foot-tall, half-man, half-mountain sculpture *Colossus of the Apen-*

nines by the Italian artist Giambologna, a disciple of Michelangelo's. My sister and cousins and I would dare one another to run into the grottos at the back of the sculpture, which were filled with bats, and were warned by our parents not to swim in the lake out front because it was filled with venomous snakes.

In the villa, family and friends had gathered after dinner in the living room: my mother; my sister; my cousins; aunts and uncles; Princess Marina, the Duchess of Kent; and my grandmother, Princess Olga of Greece and Denmark.

My uncle was sitting in the antechamber, and as I ran by him, he grabbed me by the waist and pulled me onto his lap. I didn't understand what happened next, but even at four, I knew it was wrong. He started rocking me back and forth. I wanted it to stop, I wanted to get away, but instead I froze.

I looked across into the living room; no one noticed what was happening to me. I could see my younger sister and cousins gathered around my grandfather. He was dunking sugar cubes into his coffee cup using a little gold spoon and distributing the cubes into the palm of each child's hand. *"Faire un canard,"* he called it—French for "to make a duck." He lined the children up in a row, like his little ducklings, eager for coffee sweets. In my mind, I imagined I was standing next to my cousins enjoying a coffee-soaked sugar cube, not frozen on my uncle's lap.

—

WITHOUT ANY PROMPTING, that memory rolled seamlessly into another:

I was in my early twenties, at an audition for a big part in a Blake Edwards film, and it was the first time I experienced debilitating anxiety during an audition.

I'd grown up on the *Pink Panther* films, and director-producer Edwards was an idol of mine. His 1982 film *Victor Victoria* had recently won an Academy Award and a Best Actress nomination for his wife, Julie Andrews (*The Sound of Music*). I was still wet behind the ears and new to the profession. I'd made my acting debut two years earlier, playing Lady Diana in the highly rated TV movie *The Royal Romance of Charles and Diana,* and had just been cast as Amanda Carrington on the hit ABC-TV series *Dynasty.* This was one of my first auditions for a feature film, and if I got the part, working with Edwards could be a career maker.

I met with him alone in a studio lot office in Culver City, and he gave me some pages to read—we call them "sides" in the film biz—from his new screenplay. As I started to read, both my hands suddenly started to tingle, and I couldn't move my fingers. I looked down at them; they were like two frozen crab claws pinching the pages, as if rigor mortis were setting in. I tried to concentrate on delivering my dialogue, but the tingling and numbness began to creep up my arms, sweep across my chest, and spread up to my neck. I had no idea what was happening—I felt embarrassed that he might notice and scared that something was terribly wrong with me. Most of all, I felt like a freak. *Why is my body doing this to me, and why now, of all times?*

As they say in show business, "The show must go on," so I did. But I sped up my reading pace, worried that if the paralysis reached my jaw, I wouldn't be able to enunciate or even breathe. After I was finished, I quickly thanked Mr. Edwards and rushed out of the room, thinking I needed to get to a hospital and fast.

But as soon as I left the audition room, the paralysis went away as mysteriously as it had taken hold.

Amazingly, I did well enough to almost get the part—*almost*. Edwards called me the following week to tell me that the final decision was between me and another actress, and to let me know that he and Julie would be in Switzerland in the coming weeks at the same time I was vacationing there.

"Come visit us for tea at our chalet in Gstaad!" he insisted. "We can discuss the part some more before I make my final decision."

His chalet, called the Fleur de Lys, was sumptuous. When I got there, I was ushered into a spacious living room with a stunning panoramic view of the Swiss Alps, where the director and Julie Andrews were waiting for me.

Maybe it was the thin mountain air, but I immediately turned into the world's most obnoxious fan. I was starstruck.

"I can literally recite all the lines from *The Pink Panther Strikes Again*," I gushed. Then I went into the infamous "Does your dog bite?" scene, acting out all the roles: Peter Sellers's Inspector Jacques Clouseau, the old hotel clerk, and even the dog.

"Does your *duuug biiiite*?"

"No."

"Nice doggie—ouch! I thought you said your *duuug* did not *biiiite*?"

"That . . . is not my dog."

Somewhere in the middle of my barking, I noticed the polite, tolerant smiles on their faces. Of course: they probably had rabid fans acting out for them "Does your *duuug biiiite*?" about a hundred times a day for the last decade. I felt like an idiot.

We made chitchat, and they were very gracious, until Julie left the room to answer a phone call, and Edwards leaned in toward me.

"Before I work with my leading ladies," he said, "I like to go off with them alone for a weekend to get to know them really well."

I froze, just like I had when I was four. And in five seconds, a lifetime of admiration I had for my childhood icon shattered into a million pieces. I panicked, flushing from head to toe, and felt like I was suffocating. How could I get out of there without making him angry and losing the film role?

I stood up and stuttered some lame excuse and rushed out of the room and out of the chalet without even saying goodbye to Julie. I was mortified, and agonized about whether I'd accidentally done something that led him on in some way. (I know now that victims of sexual harassment and assault often blame themselves at first.)

I consoled myself with one bright side: at least I hadn't gotten down on all fours when I did my dog impression.

It was the first time a powerful man in the industry propositioned me, but it wouldn't be the last by far. Each incident after that would harm me not only as a woman but also as an actress, chipping away at the love I had for the craft until there was barely anything left. It happened a lot, but I never got used to it. This kind of sexual harassment in the film industry has been around since movie cameras were invented, I'm sure. We were the only industry that proudly originated our own pet name for it: the casting couch.

After my experience with Blake Edwards, I became plagued with terrible anxiety before auditions. Sometimes it got so bad, I had to take a tranquilizer beforehand to survive them. I had to monitor my dosage carefully, so that the effect would be somewhere between paralyzed and slurring.

—

"SO NOW," NANCY prodded, bringing me back to the present, "why were you so afraid to go to auditions after that? Why don't you want to walk into that room?"

I looked down at the floor, barely able to talk.

"Catherine?"

I thought of the room where my uncle had touched me inappropriately and the room at Edwards's chalet, and realized something.

"Because"—I looked up at Nancy—"every room I walk into could potentially be a room I would be abused in."

Not until that very moment had I ever linked together the abuse at four, my incident with Edwards, and my subsequent angst before auditions.

"You formed a belief about men in power hurting you," Nancy observed.

I continued to connect the dots:

"I feel as though the memory of my father grabbing my throat is woven in there, too," I said.

Nancy nodded.

"Maybe my body started to shut down at the audition with Blake Edwards because my subconscious sensed he was a predator?"

More nodding from Nancy.

"The anxiety after that—it's like I've been suffering a form of PTSD," I said.

I took another deep breath and exhaled, bursting into tears. My little group cheered me on in support, and, again, I felt a wave of relief wash over me. All week, we in the class would bravely bare our souls and reveal our flaws and imperfections to one another—our version of emotional boot camp. Like soldiers in the trenches, we formed very special, intimate bonds.

Did I overcome my audition anxieties after that day? I'll never really know the answer to that because I haven't auditioned since then.

Did I feel fantastic after Nancy led me through a mosaic of memories until I reached a moment of connection and understanding? Yes! I felt elated! I found reason for my fears, I thought, and that gave me a sense of relief.

"Human beings are meaning-making machines," Nancy told us. That's why it felt so good to make the associations I did during my EM-ing. Afterward, I felt empowered and exhilarated. And that day, I was the EM-ing rock star of the class.

"Good luck to any of you following Bruce Springsteen here," said one of the coaches, Nippy (who later married Sarah Edmondson), patting my back as I dried my eyes.

I went home that night exhausted in body but euphoric in spirit.

So it didn't occur to me to ask Nancy or any of the coaches while they were zigzagging around in my brain if they were licensed therapists. It didn't occur to me to wonder why most of the exercises we did in class had nothing to do with business skills.

And it didn't occur to me to remember that I'd been down this road before.

Did I suddenly have amnesia? After a thirty-year history in the self-help world, I should have known this was the same-old, same-old, just repackaged. It had only been two days earlier that I was the Defiant One! Instead, I was once again getting hooked on a heady cocktail of neurotransmitters that was the chaser for each poignant revelation.

The ESP program was so carefully calculated, so devious, and such a well-oiled machine that my subconscious had now been distracted and disarmed. As the ancient Chinese general, military strategist, and philosopher Sun Tzu once said: "The supreme art of war is to subdue the enemy without fighting."

—

AT THE END of the five days, we had a graduation ceremony.

Callum had been chosen to do a "live" EM in front of the class, as a shining example of a student who gave his all during explorations. He went to the front of the room and, before starting, warned Nancy with a chuckle, "I'm a really good actor, you know."

Nancy took him through some heart-wrenching experiences with alcoholism and difficult childhood memories, like the time his mother introduced him to his "real" father when he was five years old.

"But . . . I thought the man we visited in prison was my dad?" he asked her.

"No, dear, that was your imaginary friend."

Callum had the entire class laughing and crying, and for a moment, I had to remind myself this was real life, not acting class. If I was the Bruce Springsteen of the class, Callum was our Daniel Day-Lewis.

When his EM was over, he was drained. "Go take a walk outside on the beach," Nancy told him. "Give yourself time to integrate."

After Callum left the room, we all wiped our tears, and Nancy announced proudly to the class that she'd just cured his alcoholism.

Little did she know that as soon as he walked out the door, Callum went straight to the nearby pub to celebrate his "integration" with a few beers. He'd faked his entire EM, he told me later! After a few ales, he returned just in time for the official ceremony.

The coaches lined up in front of the room, with Prefect center stage. Then, one by one, we went up and bowed our heads (even though I'd vowed not to), and Nancy ceremoniously placed our newfangled sashes around our necks. Our old ones had been taken away temporarily and transformed to reflect our progress. Callum and India now had one stripe added to the bottom of their sashes, to symbolize that they'd finished the first five classes. Mine had three red stripes across the bottom—the most you could be awarded.

Me? The highest honors? Callum and I were dumbfounded, and then one of the coaches explained:

"You've been awarded the honor of Best Recruiter in the class because you signed up more recruits than anyone else!"

Callum and I looked at each other again and went into hysterics. After my dramatic protest on the first day refusing to ever, ever recruit for them, I'd gone ahead and beat everybody at it. Earlier that day, I'd signed up my husband and his two kids from his first marriage, Grace, thirteen, and Cappy, sixteen, to take the five classes we'd just completed—that's how I'd become a three-striped family recruiter!

Before we left that day, the coaches went into overdrive pressuring the class to sign up for the next five classes of Level One. As it turned out, the entire level consisted of three sets of five classes, fifteen in all. So while we were all whipped up in a frenzied, vulnerable state of bonding and emotions on graduation day, they tried to trap us into more.

Callum was for sure bailing and urged me to do the same.

"It's a *cult*, dummy!" he said.

I laughed, and imagined myself dressed up in those shapeless, pastel prairie dresses worn by the many young wives of polygamist Mormon sect leader Warren Jeffs, who was about to be convicted for sexually assaulting two of the girls—one fifteen years old; the other, twelve—and sentenced to life in prison plus twenty years. *Now* that's *a cult*, I thought. This group was just . . . way, way too happy and dogged.

"You're just a sore loser, because you only got one stripe!" I teased.

A trio of coaches came over and zeroed in on India and me like heat-seeking missiles.

"You've seen such remarkable gains so far," they said. "It only gets better from here on out. You two showed so much promise in class—we've never seen so much potential!"

They were like a cheerleading squad on steroids. Something felt off to me about their effusive flattery, but I couldn't put my finger on it. Later, I'd learn from cult experts the term "love bombing":

the overly affectionate and ego-boosting attention that cult members lavish upon you when they are trying to build you up and lure you in. It's an aggressive, predatory, and manipulative seduction meant to make you feel special and irreplaceable. In the world of romance, it would be like dating a sociopath-narcissist.

Little did we know that, in a sense, we were.

After the love-bombing stage comes the "devaluation" stage. But I'll get to that later. For now, India and I were still in the honeymoon stage of being seduced.

India was intrigued to go further, and I was curious to know why. We hadn't shared our experiences in class together during lunch breaks or at home—she didn't want to hear about mine and didn't volunteer about her own process.

And because we were never in the same group, I had no idea if she was having epic breakthroughs like me or not. I glanced over at her group from time to time, but hadn't overheard or seen any emotional outbursts from her.

Which was getting more and more frustrating for me.

I'd had this fantasy of watching her bloom in front of my eyes with new revelations about herself—or, at least, of hearing about it from her! But it was not to be. I wanted to respect her privacy, so I didn't pry.

But I wondered later if this was part of the group's divide-and-conquer strategy. We'd embarked on this journey to share an experience, and, against my best efforts, my daughter and I were in our solitary orbits.

When it came time to decide whether to sign up for more or not, I finally asked India: "What are you getting out of this?"

She was quiet for a moment, because she knew she wasn't sup-posed to speak about other people's experiences outside of class—what went on in that room was sacrosanct. Then she told me about a moment in class that had moved her profoundly. An older man had broken down crying as he opened up about his childhood abuse for the first time in his life.

"He pulled up his shirtsleeves, Mom," India said with tears in her eyes, "and showed us long lines of scars up and down both his arms. They were from his mother. She used to abuse him when he was little."

I saw how she'd bonded with her groups, and I could understand that. I was making friends myself. I met Sasha and Katie those first few days, and Katie would become not only my seminar buddy but also one of my dearest friends outside of ESP.

Perhaps India didn't need bursting fireworks or cathartic break-throughs the way I did. Maybe she was such an empathetic spirit and felt so deeply for others, she shared in their healings as if they were her own, and that made the process meaningful and intimate for her.

We signed up for the rest of Level One, and now, with Casper and the two other kids signed up too, I'd be able to talk to someone about what happened behind ESP's closed doors. Screw their confi-dentiality agreement!

—

THE FOLLOWING MONTH, in August, I flew to Albany on my own to take the continuation of Level One after Nancy offered to give me some emergency, one-on-one EM-ing. I was freaking out after a botched eye surgery and having panic attacks that I'd ruined my eyesight forever.

"Come to Albany, and I'll do some work with you," Nancy suggested, "to get you less panic-stricken about the fact that you've blinded yourself."

The ESP headquarters was a plain brown-brick office building on the outskirts of the city, off a large highway. Inside, it was sparsely furnished like the house in Venice, but even more drab and generic: a few couches, a few tables, some office chairs, and a handful of private coaching rooms off to the side. Everything was in a dishwater-brown color.

The only décor I remember was the framed headshots of Vanguard and Prefect on the wall, displayed prominently like religious icons—side by side, as if they were Jesus and Mary: Keith with his long hippie hair and Nancy with her neck wrapped in her beloved gold sash. Both of them smiled for the camera as though they were posing for cheesy prom shots. I was mesmerized by how awful these portraits were.

—

MY FIRST DAY there, Nancy helped me with my panic attacks. And then she asked me to choose a fear I'd like to work on.

"Public speaking," I told her. "When I have to talk in front of a live audience, I feel disoriented, like I will lose my balance. I can't stand being in the spotlight."

"What are you afraid of?"

"Feeling exposed."

A memory popped into my head that I hadn't thought of in forty years.

I had to deliver a monologue at school, and, feeling the first stirrings of my feminist self, I had chosen to deliver an excerpt from the classic sociopolitical comedy *Lysistrata*, by the Greek playwright Aristophanes.

First performed in Athens in 411 BC, it's a story about how the women of Greece decide to withhold sex from their husbands and lovers in order to force them to negotiate peace and end the Peloponnesian War—a natural choice for an eleven-year-old girl to pick, of course. What was I thinking? Where did I even find it?

I got up in front of the class and began:

"Then submit, but disagreeably: men get no pleasure in sex when they have to force you. And make them suffer in other ways as well. Don't worry, they'll soon give in. No husband can have a happy life if his wife doesn't want him to."

I was passionate! I was bold!

And as I walked back to my seat after my rousing performance, I discovered that the fly on my trousers had been open the entire time. There I was, my first triumphant feminist manifesto, and the whole time I was flashing a bunch of sixth-grade boys like a cheap porn star. The shame and humiliation were almost too much to bear.

"So what if your underwear was showing," Nancy asked, back in the present. "What was so bad about that?"

"I felt exposed," I said. "Men will think I'm inviting attention."

"Catherine, you've assigned far too much significance to the power of your undergarments," Nancy pronounced. "You can make a simple, human mistake like forgetting to zip up your fly and not have it mean Armageddon."

—

EVERY DAY WAS an emotional whirlwind of crying and confessions, leading to yet another catharsis or two, or more. I was the rock star of EM-ing, they said. Later on, I would ask myself: How much of what I was doing was a purely hedonistic pursuit?

While in Albany, I stayed at the home of Sara Bronfman, the daughter of billionaire philanthropist Edgar Bronfman Sr. She and her younger sister, Clare, were the heirs to the Seagram fortune. They, Keith, and Nancy all lived in the upscale Albany suburb of Halfmoon.

Sara was a proctor when I met her, and she and Clare had both been deeply involved in the ESP world since 2003—both had served on the executive board and had prominent roles in the company.

Sara stayed somewhere else while I was a guest in her home, but I met her at the office near the end of my stay and thanked her. She was cool and distant, and I was beginning to notice something about the ESP devotees: while the process itself was highly emotional, and there was a lot of smiling and persistence coming from the coaches, they were also strangely emotionless, as if they'd deleted feelings from their operating systems.

Sara's coolness made me self-conscious. I started babbling about how I'd been a "disintegrated" houseguest ever since I was ten years old and stayed at the stately Sussex mansion of Antony Lambton, the 6th Earl of Durham. It was very *Downton Abbey*.

"I slept in a different bed each night to test them out, like Goldilocks," I told her, "and then I got found out because I had lit a fire in the last bedroom and left embers as incriminating evidence. My mother was so mortified that she had me apologize to every member of the staff. I remember the lineup of twenty-odd servants, like a firing squad . . ."

Sara didn't look amused at all or the least bit interested, and I felt ridiculous for having told her the story—it was completely irrelevant.

I left Albany with one epiphany unrealized: a sighting of the infamous Vanguard. Even half-blind, I assumed I'd catch a glimpse of the mysterious Oz in the office at some point during the week, but, no, he was a no-show.

I was beginning to wonder if Keith Raniere existed at all. The only concrete evidence of his reign was that framed portrait on the wall: a repackaged, generic Jesus with a photo of the middle-aged, gold-sashed Madonna on the wall beside him.

The scratched glass sparkled and the cheap frame shone, as if they were Windexed and buffed on the hour.

But no amount of spit and shine could ever make this false messiah worthy enough to be anyone's idol of worship.

As I would find out very soon.

took over our house. Casper was more than happy to do it. One of his nicknames was "Disneyland Dad," and, given the choice, he'd pick a weekend of Mickey Mouse over another self-improvement seminar any day.

My mother, Elizabeth, was visiting from her home in Belgrade, Serbia, at the time. I was excited she'd be taking part with India and me, making it a three-generational Oxenberg female empowerment fest. I'd mentioned ESP to her over the last few months and was eager to introduce it to her and see what she thought.

We gathered in the living room with coffee and tea as Nancy introduced the program and began the modules, posing question sets about men, women, and relationships.

Men don't experience intimacy. Imagine the difference between sticking your finger in someone's mouth and them sticking their finger into your mouth. The first one is not an intimate experience, the second one is. That is what sex is like for a man.

Really? Whoever came up with this bullshit had obviously never experienced intimacy before, I thought. We broke off into smaller groups to discuss and then came back for more from Nancy:

Men are designed to be polygamous, and women must learn to tolerate this behavior. Men are more loyal than women. When men cheat, they go back to their wives. When women cheat, they tend to transfer affection and leave their primary relationship.

3

THE DEFIANT ONES

The hypnotic bubble I was living in began to burst two months later.

At a weekend seminar Nancy asked me to host that October, it struck me for the first time that what she and Keith were teaching was dangerous.

The seminar was called "Jness"—another made-up word by Keith, I imagined—and it was meant to be a "fantastic new women's empowerment curriculum" that Keith and Nancy wanted to introduce to the LA community. Jness was a sister program to ESP under a parent company called Nxivm. I had no idea what any of these words meant at the time.

I agreed to host it in my home after Nancy offered some enticement: the group would pay all expenses for Casper to take Grace, fifteen, Maya, ten, and Celeste, eight, to Disneyland (now demoted to the *Second* Happiest Place on Earth after ESP headquarters and its wide-grinning, ecstatic coaches) for the weekend while fifty women

That was her definition of loyalty? None of this rang true to me at all. But again I went with my small group to discuss and debate, after which we returned again to Nancy for more:

Men abide by an honor code, and women do not. This code gets passed down, like a legacy, from father to son. Women, on the other hand, are whimsical, entitled, spoiled, overemotional, childish, self-serving, weak-willed, indulgent, lack discipline, have trouble keeping their word, and are bereft of any such code.

My gut lurched in protest and anger.

What the hell was she saying? Had she really just described women as defective, useless second-class citizens? Was I in a remake of *The Stepford Wives*, and no one had bothered to tell me? I looked around the room to see everyone else's reaction. *Nada.* India was in the kitchen, setting up food. When Nancy divulged proudly to the class that it was Vanguard himself who had benevolently and brilliantly devised the entire Jness program to guide women, bells went off inside me like a fire alarm.

This is ridiculous! A program about female empowerment devised by a man? I didn't care how high this guy's IQ was; no man was genius enough to understand the inner workings of a woman's soul. The nonsense Nancy was spouting was offensive. Why not just drag us by the hair back into a prehistoric cave or something?

I was livid, and wanted desperately to raise my hand, raise hell, and call for anarchy in my own living room, like I'd done the first day back in Venice. But as hostess, propriety ruled. I'd invited all these people into my home, including two good friends, so my hands—and my aforementioned defiant spirit—were tied.

I needed a comrade in arms and searched around the room for my mother's face. On it I saw the same expression of disgust that I was trying to hide on mine. Our eyes met, and she rolled hers heavenward and frowned. I would have a lot of apologizing to do later for getting her into this.

My mother is a wise and insightful woman with a great sense of humor. But she'd never been particularly patient and definitely didn't suffer fools lightly or gladly.

—

TO EXPLAIN MORE fully: my mother, Princess Elizabeth of Yugoslavia, is the only daughter of Prince Paul of Yugoslavia and Princess Olga of Greece and Denmark.

She was born in Belgrade; grew up and was educated in Kenya, South Africa, the United Kingdom, Switzerland, and Paris; and speaks nine languages.

Her great-great-grandfather was George Petrovic, nicknamed Karađorđe (Black George) by his Turkish enemies. He was a Serbian revolutionary leader who fought against the Ottoman Empire for his country's independence during the First Serbian Uprising of 1804–1813, liberating his people from five hundred years of Turkish oppression and enslavement.

Black George was murdered by his best friend, Milos Obrenovic, who ordered Black George's head chopped off and had it delivered on a platter to the Turkish sultan. My courageous ancestor was the

founder of the Karageorgevic dynasty, from which our family de-
scends.

My mother's father, Prince Paul, is the one I wrote the screenplay about, *Royal Exile*—and the one who fed us grandchildren
coffee-soaked sugar cubes in his beautiful Italian villa. But before
that, he was thrust into the unenviable position of prince regent of
Yugoslavia after the assassination of his cousin King Alexander on
the eve of World War II. My grandfather became the first leader to
establish democracy in Yugoslavia. Long before any other leader in
the world, he recognized that Adolf Hitler was a threat. In 1939, he
warned Joe Kennedy Sr., who was ambassador to Great Britain at the
time, that after meeting Hitler, "I have looked into the face of evil."

Winston Churchill instructed my grandfather to declare war on
Nazi Germany unprovoked, which Paul knew would be suicide for
his country, so he refused. Instead, he met in secret with Hitler and
Foreign Minister Joachim von Ribbentrop at the führer's Eagle's Nest
lair in the mountains of Berchtesgaden to negotiate a nonaggression
pact. His brilliant negotiating skills secured his country's autonomy
while refusing to grant passage to German troops and refusing to
fight alongside them—a status of neutrality no other enemy of Hitler
had been able to attain.

In 1941, the British secretly mounted a military coup d'état
against my grandfather and his government, and he was accused of
being a Nazi collaborator—the furthest thing from the truth. Prince
Paul was forced to abdicate at gunpoint, and the royal family had
four hours to leave the country or be shot to death. They rushed to
the train station, made their way to Greece, where they were denied
entry, were then flown to Cairo, and eventually ended up in Kenya,

under British house arrest. My mother was four years old at the time and remembers this moment like it was yesterday.

Her family was declared enemies of the state by the Communist regime in 1947, and her father was vilified as a traitor and a war criminal for trying to save his country from the war.

Since then, my mother had worked hard to clear his name and reinstate his legacy. In 1989, she uncovered the British plot after going to the head of the Special Operations Executive, a branch of the British Secret Service, and convincing him to give her classified documents. It didn't hurt that my mother was glamorous and alluring, and that the real-life James Bond type had a mad crush on her.

In 2012, thirty-six years after he died at the age of eighty-three, my grandfather Prince Paul was finally vindicated as a national hero and the true humanist that he was. I was with my mother when his coffin was lifted precariously out of his grave in a cemetery in Lausanne, Switzerland, and brought home to Serbia for an official hero's burial.

Mom currently lives in Belgrade, where she was a recent Serbian presidential candidate, and spends her days working as a human rights activist, much like her father.

—

IN OTHER WORDS, my mother was intelligent, beautiful, educated, regal, worldly, and came from a long line of fierce, brave fighters for independence and justice—as well as being one herself. There was no way someone like her would put up with Nancy's bullshit ideas that would drag women—especially the women in her family—back to the dark ages.

As Nancy continued to talk, making derogatory remarks about women behaving like "princesses," my mother started yawning and shuffling around things, causing a minor disturbance. She was bred only partially in Britain, and her troublemaking Slavic side trumped ladylike etiquette when the occasion demanded.

Later, after all the women had left for the day, she was more vocal.

"What utter rubbish!" she said as she, India, and I gathered in the kitchen to make dinner. My mother's breakout group that day had been assigned Nancy as their coach, and she was describing to us with great pleasure how she'd launched a private revolt against Nancy's oppressive regime.

"I spent the whole day answering her as stupidly as possible," she said. "I gave Nancy the most inane answers I could think of, just to annoy her on purpose. Whatever she said to me, I answered the opposite. The whole thing was boring, and that Nancy was . . . colorless."

As Mom spoke, India was quiet. I could see she was uncomfortable to hear her grandmother mock Prefect. By this time, she'd finished the second segment of Level One and had signed up for the third.

"What did you think of the class today, India?" I asked.

She shrugged. I knew that meant she wasn't crazy about it. When she likes something, she says so, and the same for when she doesn't. Although she was the sweet peacekeeper of the family (just like her great-grandfather), India had also inherited our family's fierce DNA, and like my mother and me, there was no way she would have agreed with anything Nancy said in our living room that day. But as outspoken as my mother was that night, my daughter was the opposite.

Looking back, I'd pinpoint this as one of the first moments when India may have been following ESP's commandment: loyalty to the group above all else, even above your family.

Like my mother, I had a lot to say about what we'd heard that day, but I was too shaken up to know where to begin. It was the first time I'd seen blatant, overt signs of misogyny in an ESP-related course, and it more than unsettled me—it disturbed me deeply.

I tried to shrug it off, like India, hoping that Jness was some weird aberration from the regular program. I'd already paid for the entire course and was two-thirds of the way through, so it made no sense not to finish just because of one bad weekend, I told myself. I hadn't seen any other evidence of sexism from the people or with the curriculum thus far. For now, I'd give them the benefit of the doubt—but I would stay on high alert for more warning signs.

Maybe the ugly things I'd heard at Jness would be wiped away by the magnificence that the coaches kept promising me, over and over, was still to come.

"Just wait until you reach the Magnificence Series!" they would say. "It happens on the last segment of Level One. All the diligent work you've been doing will come together in the end, and you will truly integrate and get to pay yourself tribute!"

Tribute? *Us?* Here was something new. Because the only people receiving tribute so far—again and again and again, ad nauseam— had been the mighty Vanguard and his sidekick, Gold Sash. But now, after fifteen days of crying, fake bowing, vomiting out my secrets, and lip-synching the mission statement, I would finally be worthy of some tribute of my own? Well, it was about time, damn it.

I went to Vancouver, British Columbia, for the final five days, and my husband trailed along dutifully. Poor Casper. I'd dragged him to so many seminars, workshops, lectures, and therapies throughout our marriage that somewhere along the way, he realized it was pointless to fight me.

One time, after we returned home from a month of ashram hopping in India, he said to me, "I can just imagine how horrendous and impossible you'd be to live with if you went off and got enlightened by yourself somewhere while I was fighting vampires on a film set."

In Vancouver, I booked us a luxurious room at the Four Seasons so that we'd have a bit of a romantic getaway, and for the next five days, Casper and I immersed ourselves in moduling and EM-ing.

The coach in charge was orange-sash-wearer Wendy, who started us off with "Relationship Day," and it was freaking depressing. All she and the other coaches talked about was how emotional attachment was an expression of weakness. Wendy said she would find it impossible to be married to someone who wasn't in ESP. I looked at Casper. Would we be doomed if one of us decided this wasn't for them?

The coaches didn't mention the word "love" once; so much for putting the two of us in the mood for a romantic escape.

Casper really got into "Control Day"—it was like theater class and gave him a chance to flex his acting chops. We learned how to create different emotional states: excitement, power, high intensity, superenergized (think Tom Cruise jumping on Oprah's couch). I had little doubt when he was doing his "power state": I could hear his

Tarzan cry from across the room, and who couldn't? He had played the role of Tarzan in the 1998 film *Tarzan and the Lost City*, and reprised one of his chest-thumping, vine-swinging scenes for class, to the delight of all the women, I'm sure.

Casper was a good, obedient student—at least outwardly; I, on the other hand, had apparently acquired a reputation as "a tough nut to crack." So much so, that they shipped a special handler from command central in Albany across the country to Vancouver to break me down.

It's not that I hadn't been opening myself up to the process and having dramatic breakthroughs, because I had—lots of them. I'd been existing on a steady and heady cocktail of tears and buzzing neurotransmitters each time I had a transformative moment in class. But now I was nearing the end of Level One, and they had to take quick action so that they wouldn't lose me.

They were already losing my friend Katie. During one of her EMs this time around, Wendy's feedback was that she was "forgettable." She wasn't happy about that.

I was a high-profile student and considered a "good catch." My name and involvement had the potential to bring celebrities and dignitaries into the fold and help spread the good ESP word.

There was just one problem: I wasn't *compliant* enough. I embraced the emotional catharsis part of the program easily and willingly but was resistant when it came to bending to their will. I wasn't toeing the line.

They obviously didn't know that toeing the line to the will of others was *not* my family's tradition.

So Esther—a tall, eagle-beaked witch of a woman—was dispatched and ordered to do whatever it took to break me down and make me a "sheeple."

It was on Control Day, of all days, when a power struggle erupted, pitting me against Wendy and Esther.

Casper and I were never allowed to be in the same group together, just like India and I hadn't been. So for once, I asked if I could watch Casper's EM-ing that day. I'd regretted not being able to share more with India during class and hoped I could make up for that a little bit with my husband.

It was a way to be closer to him, and Casper had no problem with it. Wendy and Esther, though, came down on me hard for even asking.

"Why do you want to do that?" Esther demanded.

"Why are you more invested in your husband's process than he is in yours?" accused Wendy.

"Your motives are fear based," Esther said, "and you're trying to control the process."

We had two different agendas: mine was to get closer to my family, and theirs was to divide families and conquer them. I'm not sure I was aware yet of their motive, but I sure felt strongly about what I wanted and needed, and I wasn't going to let them get in my way.

"Well, that's your opinion," I shot back, close to tears and ready to come to blows with them. "I don't see it that way!"

The class watched silently, mouths agape, but I held my ground and got my way. They were going to have to find another way to string me along; trying to force me to be submissive wasn't going to work.

Finally, Casper and I made it to the end of Level One and reached the much-anticipated Magnificence Series. Sort of. Day three came and went, and so did day four. Nothing. Near the end of the last day, Wendy told us it was time to pay tribute to ourselves.

"I want each group to come up with a one- or two-word description of each person's *essence*," she instructed. When it was my turn, I stood in the center of our little circle, and the students yelled words out at me:

"Lioness!" "Sparkly!" "Exquisite!" "Nurturer!" "Captivating!" "Ethereal!"

They finally decided on combining four of them: "Exquisite Nurturer" and "Sparkly Lioness"—the latter because I was fiercely maternal. (Ironically, they didn't realize they were naming their own downfall.) Casper's was "Playful Intensity."

This was the great tribute I'd waited for? I had expected the heavens to part and the angels to sing, but it was not to be. Instead, it was like Affirmations 101.

By the end of the week, I was drained. The big tribute was a complete washout, and I'd spent so much time dismantling myself that I didn't have any energy left to put myself back together. Enough was enough. It was time to say my goodbyes, get out of Dodge, and go back home to my life.

—

HOW I ENDED up enrolled in Level Two in that state of mind baffles me.

First came the persistent love bombing about what a stupendous job I'd done and what a shame it would be not to keep going. Then came the big push with the *huge* special discount they offered: *$2,000 off if you booked in the next forty-eight hours!*

When neither of those worked, they figured out one that did. I grumbled to Sarah Edmondson, the co-owner of the Vancouver center, that I hadn't had the uplifting, transcendental finale I was expecting at the end of Level One, and a handful of them immediately swarmed around me.

"You weren't ready yet," one explained.

"You weren't able to receive tribute because you don't have enough of a foundation of self-love. There's nowhere for that tribute to land," insisted another.

"But Level Two begins with 'Mobius,' and it's all about self-love!" piped in a third coach. "It's *exactly* what you need, and then everything you've worked for and hoped for will all come together in one grand moment of enlightenment!"

The problem wasn't the program, you see, it was *me*. I had yet another deficiency I needed to fix by taking another bullshit-sounding class. That's the endless cycle they get you on.

This time the classes were almost double the price: $6,000 each. Never mind broken—these guys were going to make me broke. (Later, I would learn that the self-help business was an unregulated industry that generated up to eleven billion dollars per year.)

"Just get a new credit card and charge it!" the coaches told the class when they expressed shock at the significantly higher price moving forward. "Your personal growth should be your number one priority above everything else!"

Now they were playing the guilt card. And there was one more enticement, lest we forget: the Meet the Great One card.

"Level Two is in Albany," they reminded us, "and Albany is where you will meet Vanguard."

Oh, yeah.

Him.

4

THE GREAT OZ HAS SPOKEN

Casper and I landed in Albany in early January 2012, bundled up in parkas and boots for the wintry weather.

We were set to stay the week at Mark Vicente's home in nearby Clifton Park. He was the filmmaker who'd done the pitching at the introductory meeting eight months earlier. Mark and his wife, Bonnie Piesse, lived just twenty minutes away from headquarters in a cookie-cutter townhouse on a pretty, leafy cul-de-sac.

That's the thing about ESP: on the outside, it didn't look anything like a cult you've read about or seen in the movies. There was no creepy compound behind a fence, which would have been a dead giveaway. The hundreds of Espians in Albany were spread out inconspicuously in the suburbs, embedded into real neighborhoods. It was great cult camouflage.

Bonnie and Mark were a sweet, fun, creative couple, and we liked them immediately. Tall, with thick salt-and-pepper hair, Mark gave off a very dignified presence. Bonnie was a blue-eyed, blonde beauty from Australia—a prettier Reese Witherspoon with a sweet, melodious singing voice. She'd been an actress for many years and had a recurring role in two *Star Wars* films but had recently given it up.

We didn't see too much of them during the week because the schedule for Mobius was as grueling as the others, starting at eight in the morning and not ending until we got back to Mark and Bonnie's by eleven at night. The best thing about Mobius was that we had graduated to live coaching—which meant no more cheesy videos of Nancy!

In class, we were each given a personal mentor, and, just my luck, who did I get?

She's *baaaaaack*. I got Esther, the green-sashed enforcer who'd shadowed me in Vancouver. She was back for round two. This time she seemed intent on humiliating me in front of the entire class—obviously, one-on-one hadn't done the trick the last time. Public shaming was a time-honored cult technique, and now she was resorting to extreme measures to crush my self-esteem.

"You feel entitled, don't you?" she asked smugly, hovering over me in front of our small group as we began an EM-ing. "You're used to getting whatever you want, huh? Aren't you?"

She kept needling me, and I got more and more frustrated. This wasn't just about breaking me down for a catharsis, this was about Esther staging a big sideshow to prove her dominance. And this time it was personal; she was out for revenge after our confrontation in Canada.

She wants drama? I'll give her drama. I thought of Callum and his Oscar-winning performance in class the summer before, and I could almost hear a director shout *"Action!"*

I burst into tears, going into a ten-minute soliloquy and making up a bunch of shit about my traumatic, loveless, brutalized child-hood to prove to her that I was the antithesis of entitled. I plagiarized an entire Dickensian youth—complete with the requisite begging bowl—just to get Esther to feel sorry for me and get her off my back.

And it worked. She fell for my Method 101 performance hook, line, and sinker. So much so, in fact, that I think I saw a tear in her eye—the first authentic emotion I'd seen from a coach yet!

Over my convulsive sobs, she told the group how proud she was of me that I'd "pushed to penetrate through to my authentic self."

Although it was wasted on Esther, that moment in class might have been one of my finest performances ever. I silently thanked actor Richard Burton, my very first acting coach, when I was thirteen, for saving me from Esther's wrath. A longtime family friend and former fiancé of my mother's, Richard taught me how to mesmerize an audience when coaching me in the role of the fairy Mustardseed in William Shakespeare's *A Midsummer Night's Dream* at school.

"You are way too shy to act," he'd tell me, and then proceed to show me how to sob on cue. To this day, I often think of a line by the British historian and politician Lord Acton that he used to quote constantly, which made sense to me in class that day: "Power tends to corrupt; absolute power corrupts absolutely."

—

IN AN EFFORT to advertise their noble, nonviolent, Gandhiesque lifestyle, everyone at headquarters was a strict vegetarian. The two of us were not, especially Casper—who was on one of his crazy body-building diets and was timing his protein: four ounces every three hours. It was challenging enough to eat at restaurants with the others as they stared at us like we were a couple of bloodthirsty savages. But the long class hours, which messed up Casper's workout schedule and special diet, meant that he had to try to sneak contraband meat into the communal fridge at the office.

When one of the coaches spotted his doggie bag of sirloin one day, it caused a small uproar. He paraded the offensive bag of flesh around the room until Casper fessed up to it. He was then escorted out of the building by a procession of coaches, like a funeral march, until he dropped the bag in a trash can across the street.

I'd think about this ridiculous moment years later when I found out about the branding.

How sensitive they were about harming animals, yet they were branding women's flesh as if they were cattle. It would be laughable if it wasn't so tragic. They should have had one of those disclaimers on their front door, like at the end of movies: "No animals were harmed in the teaching of our program—only women."

Casper and I were never left alone to eat lunch by ourselves; a posse was always with us, and there was reason for that. Leaving students by themselves at mealtimes or in hotels gave them too much time to ruminate about any doubts they might have about the teachings. It interrupted the careful indoctrination process. Coaches were ordered to stick to students like white on rice and to make sure they didn't congregate and conspire against the training.

At night, we'd have tea with Mark and Bonnie in their kitchen and exchange updates about our days. They were both very busy "in service to the great Vanguard's mission to save the world." Mark spent a lot of time in the basement, knee-deep in editing a documentary that he'd been working on for four years already: *Encender el Corazón* (*"Light the Heart"*).

It was about the kidnapping epidemic in Mexico and the ethics of paying ransom for a loved one's return. Slipped in there, of course, was an interview with Keith and an introduction to his principles. Vanguard believed you had to say no to paying ransom money and refuse to be extorted and blackmailed. You had to be willing to sacrifice your loved one for a higher ideal, he said.

Applying his ideology, the film implied, would make the kidnapping problem in Mexico disappear magically.

Espians were trained to believe that Keith, the third best problem solver in the world, had the answer to every global crisis.

Though she'd given up acting, Bonnie kept up with her music. Like Mark, she steered it toward the higher good of the mission, strumming her guitar and performing her original songs at local colleges. She had an angelic, ethereal quality about her that reminded me of India.

Both Mark and Bonnie believed in earnest that what they were doing was for the betterment of mankind. They were good, honest, sincere people. Could they have guessed at that moment that, five years later, my daughter would be branded with a searing hot implement of torture half a mile away from their home? I don't think so. I think their devotion blinded them to the darker elements lurking underneath the veneer of Nxivm.

Other than giving up their glamorous Hollywood life to move to Albany "for the community" and to be close to Keith—which would make me suspicious of anyone—they seemed like a very happy, normal couple.

I couldn't say the same for two of their friends, another ESP couple also crashing at Bonnie and Mark's that week.

Casper and I were staying in the guest room across from the couple. One night, I bumped into the wife in the hall coming out of their room and I got a glimpse through their open door. On the floor next to the king-sized bed were two pillows and a pile of blankets made up like a bed.

Seeing my confusion, the woman volunteered cheerfully, "I'm sleeping on the floor."

"Why? Bad back?"

"No." She smiled. "I'm doing penance. For being defiant to my husband."

My jaw nearly hit the floor.

"What? He told you to sleep on the floor?"

"Oh, no, no. *He* didn't," she said sweetly. "It was my coach who gave me my penance!"

"And your husband is okay with that?"

"Of course!" she said, nodding. "He supports whatever I need to do for my personal growth."

We stood for a moment in the hallway together, between the two rooms, and I wanted to take the woman by the shoulders and shake her. I didn't understand; she seemed so *gleeful* about being punished. And she was acting so normal about it, as if all husbands and wives did this.

It all made sense when I found out later that the woman had been mandated to take the Jness eight-day intensive, a more intense version of the program that had made my mother revolt and gripped me with chilling images of *The Stepford Wives*. Mark, too, was taking a very new, complementary course for men called Society of Protectors (SOP) that aligned with the same teachings. (Within the year, he'd start leading it as well.)

For the rest of our stay, I went to great, almost comical lengths to hide the other couple's sleeping arrangement from Casper—racing up the stairs and rushing ahead of him to make sure their door was shut. My husband supported my doing whatever I needed to do for my personal growth, too, but I was seriously worried he could buy into the whole subservient-wife thing, and I didn't want him getting any ideas.

I'd done the three-day seminar, and this woman had done the eight-day-intensive: that was only five days' difference between me sleeping on the floor or not!

I went to bed that night confused. If these programs were supposed to teach people how to think more effectively, as Mark had preached to India and me a year before, why did it sometimes seem as though they weren't thinking for themselves at all?

—

BACK AT HEADQUARTERS, there was no sign of Keith. Around day four, we were alerted that our lucky day had arrived: it was time to meet the great and powerful Oz.

By then, most devotees were brainwashed into thinking the guy was a demigod, after having bowed to his image and thanked him hundreds of times already. The insane anticipation the coaches built up about Keith was another way they strung you along. Maybe you'll see him, maybe you won't.

Our big meeting with the man who held the keys to the kingdom was an invitation to watch him play volleyball one Monday night. He played regularly with a group of Espians, and it was considered a privilege to watch him play, the coaches told us in hushed voices.

A bunch of us piled into a car near midnight and drove out to a gym in the suburbs. Casper thought the whole thing was overkill, watching some guy play volleyball, but he perked up when they invited him to join Keith's team. (I was not invited.) Here was a chance to get a workout and flex his pecs! Casper was a good athlete, known mostly for his enthusiasm—he'd won awards for his enthusiasm. He wasn't a regular volleyball player, but he'd played one in a movie, *Kill Shot*, more than a decade earlier, which is almost as good.

As for me, I was conflicted about meeting Keith. I was still disturbed about what he'd concocted for the Jness program, but I was curious to meet him after the endless hoopla.

We weren't the only spectators when we arrived. A gaggle of women of all ages from the ESP community were lined up in folding chairs along the perimeter of the court, watching Keith direct the players.

I rubbed my eyes and squinted. Was that *him*? Maybe my vision was still blurry from the botched surgery I'd had months earlier. I blinked and looked again.

There he was: a short, stocky, nerdy-looking guy wearing Coke-bottle glasses, Velcro sneakers, a headband, short shorts, and striped tube socks circa 1975. He looked fiftyish and unremarkable in every way.

This was the almighty Vanguard?

Casper dashed onto the court, and the men began to play. The female fan base at courtside jumped up out of their chairs and cheered every time Keith made contact with the ball, which wasn't so often—especially because he kept stopping the game.

What we didn't know was that Keith had made up his own rules for the game, just as he'd dreamed up his own words in the English language and invented his own warped moral doctrine. Keith had to be the Conceptual Founder of everything he did.

So every ten seconds, he stopped, irritated and slightly impatient, to correct my husband on the rules. Casper's footwork was wrong, he was moving out of bounds, he wasn't supposed to hit like that. Everything Casper was doing was incorrect because the official volleyball rules and choreography had been Vanguard-ified.

Casper tried to be a good sport and follow Keith's nonsensical instructions, but fifteen minutes into the game, he leapt high into the air to take a shot and accidentally rammed his elbow into another player's head—and not just any player, but the best player on Keith's team. The guy crumpled to the ground, knocked out cold with a concussion. You might say Casper made a *Kill Shot*.

The rest of the players—all nonviolent, non-meat-eating pacifists—were horrified by such uncouth, aggressive barbarianism. They didn't understand he was just being enthusiastic. I couldn't help but think: *That's what happens when you pit a real man against a team of beta males.*

Keith gave someone a nod; Casper was escorted (for the second time that week!) off the court. He went to the sidelines to check on the guy he'd knocked out, and Keith took that moment to come over and greet his fans.

The women rushed to him, fawning.

One blonde in particular reached him first, threw her arms

around him, hugged him full body, and kissed him on the lips like a lover. I'd noticed her when we first arrived but didn't know who she was. Someone whispered, "That's the actress from *Smallville*," but I'd never seen the TV show, so I didn't recognize her—her name was Allison Mack.

After he finished kissing Allison, he tended to the others. One by one, he gave each a tight, extended hug and a kiss on the lips—long, lingering, deep kisses, with plenty of penetrating eye gazing. It was bizarrely intimate.

Just as bizarre was what *wasn't* happening. Here was Casper—a hunky Hollywood celebrity in a gym in suburban Albany, New York—with dozens of female groupies in the room, and none of them gave him a single glance. Not one! I had never seen this happen before; he might as well have been invisible. Keith had a Svengali hold on people that eclipsed everything and everyone else.

Now Vanguard headed toward me. Casper watched from the other side of the gym, eyeing us like a hawk. Keith came up close, too close—I could smell his bad BO—and fixed his Casanova stare on me. That's when I saw . . . this Don Juan was cross-eyed! He leaned in, lips puckered, and I put up my hand like a crossing guard that tells kids: Do Not Cross This Line. As if I was going to let a stranger who'd just French-kissed the entire cheerleading squad and thought women were "entitled, overemotional, self-serving, weak-willed, and indulgent" kiss me?

Never going to happen, my friend. I stuck out my hand.

"Hi," he mumbled, giving me a moist, limp handshake.

Keith was soft-spoken with a high-pitched voice, like a ten-year-old choirboy. In other words, he was no James Earl Jones.

We made small talk for about ten seconds. I don't even remember what we said; that's how memorable it was. And then it was over. Seven months of building him up as mankind's salvation, the missing link, the fulcrum of humanity, the holder of all secrets, and I get this cross-eyed messiah? It was a total lunch-bag letdown.

Vanguard went back to his fans, Casper came over, and we plotted our escape. We looked over at Keith, who was again deep-kissing all the girls.

"He's having sex with all these women," my husband blurted out.

"Oh, come on," I said. "What woman would want to get naked with this guy?"

We tried slipping out of the gym inconspicuously, but that was impossible with Elvis still in the building. We got the stink eye from a bunch of them for making such a blasphemous exit. But we didn't care. Between Casper's volleyball mishap and my anticlimactic meeting with the Oompa Loompa boy wonder, all we wanted to do was get in our rental car and run for the hills.

—

AFTER WE RETURNED home from Albany, India emailed me a photo of a mural she'd seen on a brick wall while stopped at a light on Beverly Boulevard:

Cheap Lobotomies: Call 323-906-XXXX

It was so her wacky sense of humor, and I laughed.

But as a woman who believes that the universe sends us signs,

I wish I had paid more attention to that one. Had I taken it as an omen, I would have realized that India and I were unwittingly enrolled in a lobotomy procedure of sorts, only it was far from cheap.

But I didn't pay heed, because, on the surface, everything still looked fine.

The leader of the program creeped me out, sure. Mobius was humiliating at times, yes. But my final days were about self-love, reclaiming my innocence, and self-forgiveness, so when I finished, I was drunk from love bombing myself. I was sure I'd improved my "love state," and I left that program on a high.

India was happy, too—very much so. As we entered the new year, she was excited, busy, and growing up before my eyes. This year she would turn twenty-one.

She was working as a freelance photo assistant and a model, recently nabbing lucrative campaigns for JCPenney and Nike. We went on a family outing to Macy's to see the display of her floor-to-ceiling lingerie ad, and she looked stunning. ("Ooooooh, India, you're naked!" Maya and Celeste squealed. "Why are you in your underwear?!")

And she attributed her success, she told me, to a new confidence and assertiveness she'd acquired because of her ESP classes.

So it seemed India was attaining exactly what we'd hoped she would gain when the two of us embarked on our journey together a year before.

But it was the sweet before the bitter pill, as they say.

The day when we first signed up for ESP, they promised us it would change our lives, and they would keep their word: it *would* change our lives. Just not the way that either of us could have imagined, and definitely not for the better.

5

TWO ROADS DIVERGED

ESP was starting to spread in Los Angeles—not like wildfire but enough to graduate from its previous pop-up venue and merit its own new center in Venice, still close to the carnival-like atmosphere of the boardwalk.

Early that year, India had enrolled me in a yearlong program, "Ethos," a few weeks before my underwhelming meeting with the mighty Vanguard. Again I was hoping that she and I could find a way to travel this bumpy trek through the bizarre world of ESP together.

"Ethos" was an ongoing, twice-weekly class in which, I very soon discovered, those same old Level One module videos of Nancy were being rehashed over and over; nothing new was offered. The repetition was essential, the coaches emphasized, so that the material would sink in as deeply and as irrevocably as possible.

"In order to *fully* integrate," they explained, "you need to do each module three times at the very least—if not *more*—because the concepts are so, so complex and so, so advanced!"

If you didn't agree with a concept, here was a chance to simply redo that module over and over again until you convinced yourself that you did. And if that sounds to you like indoctrination and brainwashing, you'd be right.

But here's the rub: every time a new student joined the group, we had to start all over from the beginning of the first module—so we stayed stuck, frozen in time, in the world of modules one and two. The repetition was like a *Groundhog Day* nightmare loop in which each class seemed to consist of the same questions, the same heated discussions, followed by the same debrief every time.

To the newbie, it might have been provocative and new. As for me, I was like Bill Murray's TV weatherman character heading out to Gobbler's Knob yet again to see if Punxsutawney Phil the groundhog would see his shadow, when I already knew he wouldn't. I wasn't feeling more integrated, as promised, I was feeling increasingly bored and suffocated. Once I knew the debriefs by heart, I started tuning out and daydreaming—waking up just in time to give the perfect answer to the module, thereby impressing the new kid.

India loved it, but the whole setup seemed like a money scam to me. I forced myself to go for a while because I'd prepaid for a year of classes, and I hated wasting money or bailing on a commitment. Also, in the beginning, I enjoyed driving to and from class with India. But after a few months, she began going early and staying late, so even that was taken away from us. I started tapering off until, finally, it got to the point where I had to either stop or chew off my arm.

That didn't stop them trying to recruit me for more, though.

Once you'd signed up for Level Two, the coaches started badgering you to become a coach, too—their urgings were a constant chorus on a broken record set on endless repeat.

"The work really only *starts* when you join the stripe path," they'd say smugly. That was Keith's wonky phrase meaning that you'd signed up to be a coach; you were "on the stripe path." It made no sense to me, but as I said, he labeled things at whim. He ruled a kingdom with its very own language. Creating his own jargon for the program made members feel like they were part of their own community, with outsiders unable to understand them.

The coaches impressed upon the students that, because they'd been given the greatest tool ever offered to mankind, they owed it as a debt of gratitude to pay the teachings forward for the good of others. Recruiting new students wasn't enough anymore: you had to teach this crap, too.

"That's never going to happen," I told them. "Don't even bother with me."

My refusal to commit further to the cause, I'm sure, was frowned upon, and forevermore put me in the category of lightweight dilettante to the higher-ups. India, however, had been toying with the idea of becoming a coach since they began luring her a few months earlier. The topic came up only once between us, and I uncharacteristically gave her my unfiltered opinion. I usually try hard to not give my kids unsolicited advice and allow them the freedom to explore without me interfering or robbing them of the dignity of their own process. But in this case, the words slipped out before I could rein them in.

"If you really want my opinion, India"—which she didn't—"I think this program should be used as a tool, not a lifestyle. Becoming a coach means it will consume your life."

India was quiet. She clearly felt very close and anchored to the group members after having shared so much with them. I felt that way about the people I'd met, moduled with, and EM-ed with, too. But for India, those feelings went deeper. She loved the sense of community she'd found with Espians and had even been socializing with the coaches, attending regular Humanities Events—Keith's term for group hikes and potluck dinners. (He not only made up words but was also a walking malapropist.) I suppose the insinuation was that when Espians hung out, they were evolving humanity somehow through their very convergence. My daughter was hardly ever home. Her schedule was jam-packed with Espian classes and events.

"They're like an extended family," she said to me around that time.

It was also around that time that I began to notice something ever-so-slightly odd about India's behavior. When we spent time together, she was with me, but . . . she wasn't. We'd go for walks on the beach, and the whole time, she'd be on her phone, three feet ahead of me. I couldn't keep up with her, and it felt like she was leaving me behind.

As she grew closer to this false family, she began distancing herself from us.

—

AROUND MARCH OF 2013, India nonchalantly let it slip in conversation that she'd become a "shadow coach": a coach in training. This time it was me who was quiet.

I started noticing subtle changes in her then. She was showing signs of becoming secretive, distracted, and unreliable—showing up late for appointments or not helping out at home when she'd promised she would.

Not coincidentally, this was all occurring around the time I'd filled out paperwork to pass her custodial bank account to her. My father had left her an inheritance—a hefty six-figure sum—to be given when she turned twenty-one. The Espians must have gone into overdrive to pull her deeper into the fold, knowing she'd soon have access to and control of all that money. India was sweet, generous, and now wealthy—a perfect target to become one of their cash cows.

She wasn't quite acting herself, and I was worried.

Pulling her aside one day, I asked, "India, what's going on with you?"

She shrugged.

"Are you upset about something? Do you not feel well?"

"No, nothing like that. It's just . . . I don't want to show that I'm happy here because I'm afraid then that I'll never leave."

I looked at her, confused. In hindsight, this was the first time I didn't recognize the words and thoughts coming out of her mouth as being her own. They didn't ring true to me; this did not sound like her.

"I don't understand," I said. "You're free to leave anytime you want. Are you pushing me to kick you out and make the decision for you? India, I love you too much, and I am not going to participate in ruining our relationship to help make the decision for you. We have always had a wonderful relationship, and it means too much to me to compromise it in any way, and there is no reason to ruin it because you don't want to make the decision to move out. You don't need to create a problem where there is none."

Still confused, I called up Nancy to see if she could offer any insight.

"She's just individuating," Prefect explained knowingly, referring to the natural phase young adults go through when they are trying to find themselves and leave the nest.

The explanation was reassuring. Problem was, Nancy was wrong—and she knew it.

Instead of trying to find her individuality, India was in the process of losing it. Everything that was strikingly unique about her was about to be erased as she transferred her loyalty from one family to another. That first thin wedge, slyly slipped between us on day one of ESP, had now formed a chasm.

—

MY DIVISION WITH the group increased that same month.

Inspired by my experience writing *Royal Exile*, I'd begun a blog on my website two years earlier and loved the creative outlet that writing gave me. In March I posted on the vulnerability in relationships and quoted something Nancy said to me once in passing:

"Men traditionally initiate with women, asking them out, and women generally are the ones who get to reject or accept men's advances. It is a very vulnerable place to be in—to be in the position of being rejected—over and over again."

I posted the blog and then proudly emailed a copy to Nancy, thinking she'd be pleased. Within minutes my phone rang. It was Nancy's daughter, Lauren—also a high-ranking, green-sashed member of ESP.

"Anything that comes out of my mother's mouth is *proprietary*!" she shrieked. "You are infringing on our *material*! *Take it down!*"

"I'm sorry," I said, trying to explain. "I thought she would appreciate the tribute."

With all the bowing and thanking she expected, I'd never known Gold Sash to turn down a little tribute.

When I hung up the phone, I was shaken. It took me one minute to move to pissed off.

Had Lauren just threatened me? I owned my own experiences! Why should I censor my one area of free expression because of them? What if they started to claim everything I wrote belonged to them? It was absurdly Big Brother of them.

Fuck that.

Not only was I not going to take down the post, I wasn't going to remove the quote *or* her name. It would stay up there for at least a year, until I subbed in a well-known psychotherapist instead, who gave me an identical quote (by then, I'd found out that Nancy's previous experience was as a registered nurse—more like Nurse Ratched in *One Flew Over the Cuckoo's Nest*, I imagine—not a therapist). So much for ESP's unique, patented material.

—

IN MAY I flew to Mexico City to take the next class, Family Values—which ended up having no value whatsoever.

Attempts to establish a stronghold in Europe had fallen flat, but ESP garnered a big following in Mexico. Go figure. I was always looking for ways to improve my parenting skills and had heard abou

this class, but it had been discontinued in the States and exiled to Mexico, like the defunct dolls banished to the Island of Misfit Toys in *Rudolph the Red-Nosed Reindeer.*

I stayed in a luxurious mansion belonging to a wealthy patron of ESP. Its security rivaled Fort Knox, as did the security for the ESP center: a modern white triplex with a back patio situated in a busy part of the city. Bulletproof vehicles were parked on the street in front, and armed guards milled about. Because of the crime and violence that roiled Mexico, anybody who owned anything worth stealing lived behind fortress-sized walls and employed bodyguards. In fact, just minutes before I arrived, one of the students had been held up at gunpoint en route back to the center from lunch.

Inside the clinical and sparse office, the mood at times grew just as threatening.

My new nemesis, Nancy, had flown in to be head trainer for the week and brought Wendy (one of the battle-axes from Vancouver) and a gaggle of other high-ranking staff in tow. Other than them, I was the only female American in the room—the rest of the coaches and students were locals. The group was composed of Mexico City's elite, wealthiest, high-society types. The children of four former presidents of Mexico have been involved with ESP, and, sure enough, there was Emiliano Salinas with his actress girlfriend Mika Paleta, canoodling in the corner on the first day.

I was shocked to see how different Mika's attitude was this time. Gone was the resistant rebel I saw at my first class. Now she sat on Emi's lap the entire week and embraced him—*and* ESP—lock, stock, and barrel. The flames of romance had obviously quieted her skepticism, and I'd lost a potential ally in dissension!

The main arc of the week's discussions was how to apply the ESP principles to parenting, and topics included the concepts of shame, punishment, conscience, and consequences. Which on the surface sounded intriguing until we explored underneath—then everything started to remind me of an Opus Dei–like storyline in a Dan Brown novel, in which supplicants self-flagellate with cat-o'-nine-tails. All that was missing were the hair shirts.

But the archaic, self-flagellating program wasn't my main discomfort—though I could see why this course had been discontinued in the States. The threatening mood I felt in the room had more to do with some of the men.

"There is a healthy, *good* kind of shame," the coach in my breakaway group told us on the first day, as we attacked that topic. "We call it 'at-cause' shame." This was another one of Keith's wonky terms for "blame-free."

"I don't agree," I piped up, to get the discussion going. "I don't believe there's such a thing as healthy shame. My definition of what you're referring to would be 'remorse,' and—"

The coach cut me off instantly, berating me for not immediately accepting the doctrine he'd just provided.

"You're wrong!" he yelled. "You don't know what you're talking about!"

I was taken aback. He might as well have tacked on "you ignorant woman!" The coach's name was Raton, which translates into English as a kind of rodent, appropriately enough. He was a total jerk. I confronted him later and told him to back off, and he did, with apologies. But still, I was shocked he would talk that way to a student, and I gave him a wide berth, avoiding him for the rest of the week.

We moved on to the topic of penance, not normally covered in this program. Thanks to an overenthusiastic Mexican coach, we got some bonus material! She talked about how taking on penance for your children's transgressions would help them build a conscience. I struggled with their *Lord of the Flies* premise that children were little savages who needed to be civilized, versus my experience with my own children: they each seemed born with a strong innate sense of conscience.

The coach in class told the story of how she used this technique to teach her young sons to be intolerant of violence. After she'd caught them fighting and hitting each other one day, she picked up and held a heavy rock for thirty minutes in front of them. Instead of punishing them, she punished herself. The boys were devastated to see their mother suffering because of their own actions, taking on the penance that was really their own.

I fantasized about what penance I could take on the next time my children fought. Maybe cleaning the cat box indefinitely? Or using public transportation? When I got home the following week, I settled on the latter. The kids went into convulsions—of laughter. The joy they derived from the image of their posh mom on a bus made the whole trip worthwhile.

Nancy avoided me the entire week like the plague. I had intended to confront her about the blog bullshit, but she was protectively escorted out of the classroom during breaks and immediately after each class was over by two devoted subordinates. She was having trouble breathing because of Mexico City's high altitude and the toxic smoke in the air released by the active, erupting volcano nearby.

When she wasn't gasping her way through a module, Prefect was hooked up to an oxygen tank in the room next door. Her usually colorless face looked a paler, extraterrestrial blue. I was having constant nosebleeds from the pollution and the altitude myself.

Inside the classroom, a whole other level of toxicity continued.

On the second or third day, we got on the topic of abortion. The coach in my group (not the rodent) asked if we ever thought it was ethical to have one: "What if a woman was raped, for example, and got pregnant?"

My group that day was dominated by overly macho Latin men— not the ideal scenario for debating a woman's right to choose. These men had probably never changed a diaper, never mind squeezed a baby out of their bodies. I, on the other hand, was a woman who'd squeezed out three beautiful babies and also had two abortions. Even though terminating the pregnancies was extremely traumatic for me, and I've lived with the emotional consequences of my choices every day, it's not a decision I'd ever want taken away from me or from any woman.

One of the macho guys in my group inflated his chest:

"There is *never* a reason to terminate a life—the end!" he said, eyeing the women in our group with contempt, in case one of us had even considered it. One of the women, who we found out later had been raped, burst into tears. Now it was my turn to lose it. I wanted to both vomit on the guy and punch him.

"That's *bullshit*!" I yelled.

Our ensuing argument escalated into a melee when the coach threw another stick of dynamite into the already heated discussion: according to ESP teachings, there are no ultimate victims in this world.

"Are you telling me that women are responsible for their own rape?!" I cried again, exasperated.

Oh, no. It was much worse than that.

"We actually believe that the victims are the abusers."

Which, looking back, was pretty ingenious of them. They did indeed teach this belief in their classes, and in fact, it was even part of their twelve-point mission statement. And by doing so, they set up the cult members for abuse while at the same time convincing them they couldn't possibly be victims. The women who ended up enthralled by and in thrall to Keith would not be capable of admitting they were victims after indoctrination like this.

Hearing that, I had to remove myself from the room before I did some violence of my own. I stormed out onto the patio and shoved a wad of Kleenex up my nose. I was bleeding again. So much blood was coming out of me I was starting to think I had stigmata of the nose—in keeping with the self-flagellation theme of the day, of course.

What was going on? I'd never seen such chauvinistic attitudes expressed so overtly from the men in ESP before. If anything, they were normally as docile as lambs. At the time, I wrote it off as a cultural thing, but I started to put together the pieces much later when I talked to Mark Vicente about it.

Espian men in Mexico had been signing up for the newly rolled-out men's course, SOP (Society of Protectors) in droves. It was promoted as the counterpart to that misogynistic course I'd unwittingly hosted less than a year earlier, Jness. While the men thought they were being trained to become honorable, noble protectors of humanity, they were actually being molded to serve as mindless soldiers in Keith's perverse army—the sole goal of which was to protect Vanguard and his harem.

There was an even darker, uglier agenda to it all.

"It was turning us all into assholes," Mark told me years later. He had been one of the three leaders of the course for many years. "It was turning us into misogynists."

At the end of Family Values Week, Emiliano and Mika hosted an elegant cocktail party on the terrace of his penthouse apartment. His place was sealed up like a fortress, and the heavy metal front door looked as impenetrable as a bank vault. Anyone considered high profile was a kidnapping risk there.

I sipped champagne on the roof as my nose bled, and the volcano in the distance growled and began to smoke.

I couldn't wait to get home.

—

THAT SUMMER WAS the beginning of a turning point for both India and me, but on roads leading in opposite directions.

Maybe it was in reaction to and in protest of the hostile guys in Mexico, the lingering effects of the misogynistic rhetoric of Jness, and even my fight with Nancy for creative freedom, but when I got back to LA, I picked up two ultra-female-positive and girl-friendly books for some scintillating and political summer reading: *Vagina,* by Naomi Wolf, and, I'm embarrassed to admit, *Fifty Shades of Grey.*

That summer, the book was a global phenomenon, and all the women at my tennis clinic were reading it and getting titillated, calling it "mommy porn." My curiosity finally got the best of me, and I bought a copy. Man, it was badly written—and yet I couldn't put it down. Shakespeare it wasn't. But a lot of women (including me) were so desperate to get turned on that we were subjecting ourselves to what seemed like hundreds of pages of . . . drivel.

More than a hundred million women read that book in a compressed period of time that year and got fired up about it, which made me wonder about the "hundredth monkey" effect I'd heard about. It's a hypothetical phenomenon that explains the dynamics of evolution, suggesting that when a critical number of members of a species understand a new idea or exhibit a new behavior, it spreads spontaneously to other groups.

Perhaps I was feeling the zeitgeist of that. But all I can tell you is, the book had me buzzing and thinking. The plot was inconsequential to me; I was interested and moved by what the story was doing to women all over the world as a collective.

There was something women needed, and they were reading this book out in the open, boldly and unashamed, to get it. It was a new kind of sexual liberation and strength, and an idea was percolating in my mind about a female-empowering project I could create to support it.

I was excited and filled with energy and wanted to discuss everything with India, but she'd whisked herself away to Albany to take another bunch of classes and then stayed on there to celebrate her twenty-first birthday with the Espians. That saddened me. My sweet daughter had come of age, and she'd chosen to observe this milestone with them. This sense of them versus us kept growing stronger and stronger.

When she got home in July, the first thing she did was break up with her boyfriend, Hudson, whom I adored. They'd been dating since they were sixteen, and he'd always been a strong, devoted, solid presence in her life. Hudson was such a gentleman, he reminded me of a knight—he had an old-fashioned, chivalrous air about him.

When India told me about the breakup, I burst into tears. She seemed strangely unemotional about it, which I found odd. He'd been the love of her life for five years, and her emotional response was detached—almost robotic. It reminded me of Relationship Day back in Vancouver, when the ESP coaches taught that emotional attachment was an expression of weakness.

I'm sure that was especially true when the attachment competed with your loyalty to the group. I've learned since that members were often persuaded to sever relationships that "weren't supportive of your personal growth and the mission."

Hudson had never been a fan of self-help courses, and he definitely did *not* like ESP. And in India's case, it would have been a critically important time to pull her away from any attachments that would get in the way of her money, now that it was officially hers. A future with Hudson, marriage, children, a life outside of ESP—those things would not support the mission.

Soon India was off again, this time for ESP's annual Vanguard Week (aka V-week)—a ten-day camp the Espians held at a YMCA in upstate New York every August in honor of Keith's birthday. Yes, it was a ten-day week. That's because Keith had to tinker with everything, even the Gregorian calendar, and in his kingdom, a week had ten days instead of seven. I would find out later he actually hated the number seven, which is fitting because it's considered a holy number!

I assume that India had met Keith briefly before, but this was her first V-week, where she'd be more exposed to him. Like me, she thought he was creepy, and she tried to avoid him, but it wasn't so easy to do confined to a small campus.

According to Bonnie, throughout the week, Keith would see her from across the room and call out, "Oh, *Innnnndddddeeeeeaaaahh-hhhh!*" and she'd roll her eyes (like grandmother, like mother, like daughter), hide shyly behind her mane of golden hair, and then slip out the back door.

In the beginning, she wasn't attracted to him. And why would she be? She was young, innocent, and radiant. He was an un-attractive, paunchy, middle-aged gnome with BO and a bad retro 1980s haircut.

But he had his eye on her; he had his eye on the prize.

By the end of that year, India would graduate from shadow coach to official coach, but she didn't tell me about it this time—not even nonchalantly. I caught a peek of her yellow sash—the color for a new coach—draped across the back of a chair in her bedroom.

My heart sank.

I imagined she felt good and strong at that time, finding a mis-sion for herself and thinking her work there would better humanity. I felt strong and good, too, filled with the stirrings of a purpose to help women find a certain kind of liberation they were seeking.

She and I were so very alike in our motives and goals, both pas-sionate about helping people and making the world a better, more just place—much like our ancestors before us. The difference be-tween our two noble pursuits was that mine was to free women; hers would, unbeknownst to her, imprison them.

Mine was guided by my inner truth; hers was unknowingly mis-guided, based on the lies of a madman.

6

SEX, LIES, AND VIDEOTAPE

I was tired of the madman's lies—or any man's, for that matter.

For the first time in my life, I was feeling bold enough and ready enough to seek out a career—and a life—that would help women free themselves from restrictions or harm and find the answers they needed within themselves, on their own.

As life imitates art, I started with myself.

By January 2013, I was deep into the research for my new passion project: a documentary called *Sexology*.

After my ugly, infuriating encounter with the men in Mexico, followed by my proactive, profemale reading list, a surge of creative energy unleashed inside of me, and the documentary idea downloaded one day like a high-voltage current. I'd been yearning for more of a creative outlet, and here it was.

My project would be about women, sex, and female energy, and my idea was to travel the world with my friend, actress Gabrielle Anwar, and explore the meaning, force, and relationship of all three.

After a year dismantling myself piece by piece with ESP, it felt invigorating to put myself back together and begin work on a project to help women, including me, find self-power and wholeness.

As part of my research, I finally read the book I'd bought the summer before: Naomi Wolf's *Vagina*. The old me wouldn't have even said that word out loud, let alone walk around toting a book with *Vagina* emblazoned in giant red letters on the cover. But that was the point of my project: to boldly go where many women, including me, had not gone before. Much to my kids' dismay and groaning, I bought dozens of copies of Wolf's book and stacked them by the front door to hand out like party favors, thrusting them into the hands of every unsuspecting female who crossed our threshold.

In February, India and I flew to Albany together for a class called "Human Pain"—for sure the least enticing name for a workshop in the history of self-help. But I was promised that it was a "beautiful" program. If "Mobius" was about self-love, this one was about deepening one's connection to self and increasing empathy by awakening one's conscience.

The trek there was always a pain in itself because it took an entire day—two flights with a stopover wherever. But for once, I was happy for the lengthy haul, as it gave me some time with India to myself, which I hadn't had in months.

By now, I was swept up planning the film's production and putting together a shooting schedule for the fall. I wanted to include India in the project as much as possible, if she was willing.

"Darling, maybe you could be a part of the production team?" I asked as we flew east.

"Sure, Mom, sounds great," she said, busy typing on her laptop.

"I'm not quite sure what's on my schedule then with my other com-mitments, but . . . if I can juggle it . . . sure."

My friend Katie was with us again, so she and I chatted away excitedly for the rest of the flights. Katie owned LA's most promi-nent casting workshop but became so enthused about *Sexology* she planned on taking a sabbatical to roam the world with me as one of my producers. We had a lot to discuss!

After arriving in Albany, we unloaded at Bonnie and Mark's and set up camp for the week.

Also sharing the house was that actress Allison Mack, who gave India her bed to use for the first couple of days. Allison spent a lot of time in the kitchen cooking up vats of low-calorie vegetarian food, which she stored in Tupperware for the week. "Wow, that's a lot of vegetables," I said one day, wandering into the kitchen to find Alli-son at the stove and the countertops overloaded with mountains of produce.

"I'm chunking," she said. (Keithspeak for time management, I assumed.) "I'm preparing my meals for the entire week."

I tried to make more conversation with her, but . . . she was one of those people who rubbed me the wrong way, right away. I was allergic to her. She had one of those giant Nancy-like smiles, but it was all shine, with no sincerity behind her eyes.

Vacuous, I thought. *She's a Gold Sash in training.*

At headquarters, I caught quick glimpses of Nancy in passing—we still hadn't spoken since before the blog incident, and she was still avoiding me. There was no sign of Keith, either; so far, we'd never seen him there. Not once. This time another wizened battle-axe by the name of Karen Unterreiner acted as head coach for the seminar.

At first, as with many of their classes, I liked "Human Pain." I could relate to one of the concepts Karen began with, which was that we needed to feel loss in order to feel more love. My father had passed away nearly three years earlier, and I had found that grieving his loss had, in fact, opened my heart to him. I felt more love for him now than I'd ever felt when he was alive.

But in true Espian fashion, things suddenly turned weird.

"The gateway to growth is through pain," Karen said, adding that the pursuit of comfort and satiation (Keithspeak for self-care perceived as self-indulgence) were weaknesses of character and should be frowned upon.

"We need to proactively choose pain to develop our capacity to deeply love."

It was a messed-up concept, if you asked me, and I could already foresee problems with it. Couldn't this set the foundation for someone to confuse pain with pleasure, and vice versa?

Although I'd gotten a sneak peek of the concept of penance back in Mexico, this class was specifically intended to teach that theory. Karen told us that if we broke a commitment, our punishment or penance should be harsh enough—even unbearable—that we'd be forced to keep our word.

"Learning to honor your inner word is your ultimate value," she said.

Inner word? What was that? More Keithspeak.

Karen was very excited to assign the class some hands-on homework. She divided us into small "conscience groups" and for the first time ever, India and I were put in a group together! I couldn't believe it. I was excited we'd finally be able to share in an ESP experience—until the nature of the assignment was explained.

The goal was to practice keeping a commitment of our choosing. If we failed, the entire group had to do penance. For example, if you promised to stick to your diet and then cheated, everyone in the group had to take a three-minute freezing-cold shower or run a mile or some other punishment previously decided upon. Sure, the penance sounded doable. But if you kept cheating on your diet, it got worse—the icy shower became ten minutes, and the jog became three miles. Keep in mind that everyone in the group had to do penance for *all* its members, so if you had a group that couldn't keep their hands off the chocolate éclairs, everyone could end up running a marathon and taking cold showers all day.

To keep from getting to that point, you upped the ante a different way: by adding what they termed "collateral."

Their version of collateral was almost like a "deposit." You handed over, say, $100 to your "accountability buddy," and if you failed to follow through on whatever your task was, you lost the money.

Each time, the amount of money in your collateral was raised, until you couldn't afford to break your word one more time.

In a conscience group, everyone lost their collateral if you didn't complete your task.

"You must learn to collateralize your word," Karen told us (Keithspeak for adding leverage to your conscience).

Damn, these people were hard on themselves. The whole thing sounded dreadful to me. I didn't want to be responsible for other people running in a blizzard at three in the morning!

I refused to participate, and, thankfully, India wasn't so into the assignment, either. Because when I really thought about it, pairing us together for something like this was downright devious. I was already feeling that new distance between us because of ESP, but to throw manufactured punishment and resentment into the mix for a class assignment? That could have destroyed us.

Years later, when I found out about the inhumane penance the "slaves" like my daughter were forced to endure if they or someone in their "slave cells" failed at an assignment, this class made sense. It was indeed laying the groundwork for worse pain to come. Being branded by a flesh-searing implement, India would tell me four years later, was a "good" and "character-building" experience for her.

I wondered what she thought about the love-pain-inner-word-penance philosophy, and I asked her, not really expecting an answer.

"I think it's very moving," she said, "and quite beautiful."

I could see why she would. My daughter was so generous and altruistic, she would find the idea of taking on pain or sacrificing her own comfort to help someone else learn or evolve an honorable undertaking—especially if it meant the end result was for the good of all civilization.

But India was such an empath already and sensitive to other people's hurts, she didn't need anyone to teach her about that. She was so caring and obliging, I worried people would take advantage of her.

Indeed, experts would tell me later that cults often targeted idealistic personalities, like India, who wanted to make the world a better place. By promoting their groups as humanitarian, they are able to recruit them. Which is the ultimate irony, because often, they end up convincing good, kind people to do harmful deeds in the name of humanity.

—

CLARE BRONFMAN INVITED us to stay at her place for a few nights, but I ended up bowing out after just one. She'd put India in a bedroom downstairs next to hers and relegated me to an upstairs bedroom in Siberia that had no heat. The billionaire heiress couldn't afford heat for the second floor? I wrapped myself in long johns, hat, gloves, earmuffs, and even put on my boots to keep from freezing to death.

It was all part of the Spartan ESP lifestyle that Clare had adopted, and I guess I wasn't cut out for it. My pursuit to be warm and comfortable was a "weakness of character."

"I am so-oooo indulgent," I mumbled to myself that night, over and over, through gritted, chattering teeth.

India stayed at Clare's another few nights on her own, and I was concerned. All week, Clare had been trying to convince India to move to Albany full-time, live with her, and work as her personal assistant and gofer—at minimum wage, no doubt. Clare was notoriously cheap, and I'm sure she assumed anyone would find it an honor to be her lackey. There was one instance where she commanded her assistant to fetch her a meal twenty minutes away in the middle of a terrible blizzard, even though the terrified assistant protested that her car had no snow tires. "But what will I eat for dinner?" Clare whined.

The idea of India working as Clare's assistant sickened me, as did seeing how aggressively Clare tried to sink her hooks into India. Call it a mother's instinct, but it felt very predatory. I was beyond relieved when India said no.

By that time, I'd heard about the *Vanity Fair* magazine feature story published in 2010 about Keith and the Bronfmans, titled "The Heiresses and the Cult." The article reported that Clare and her sister Sara had taken $150 million from their trust funds to help finance Nxivm and that Keith had lost at least $66 million of it in failed commodity trades, spent $30 million to buy real estate in LA and around Albany, spent $11 million for a twenty-two-seat, two-engine Canadair CL-600 jet, and spent millions more for legal costs on behalf of himself and Nxivm.

"If Keith's so smart," I asked Esther, who was taking part in the intensive, that week, "how come he lost sixty-six million of the Bronfmans' money trading in commodities?"

"Eh!" Esther answered. "That's nothing for them! A drop in the bucket!" She went on to allege that Clare and Sara's father, Edgar Bronfman Sr.—who would pass away later that year—had rigged the market to make sure Keith's infallible algorithm would fail.

I was stunned, and speechless. Seriously? She and the others actually *believed* this?

On the flight back home, India kept busy typing as Katie and I tried to figure out the mysteries of "Human Pain."

"So . . . let me get this straight," Katie said as we flew westward. "We destroy our conscience by conditioning ourselves to do the wrong thing, right?" she asked.

"Right," I said. "And then we make doing the wrong thing feel *right* by justifying it. Right?"

"Right."

We both sighed and sat back, exhausted from trying to make sense of the word salad. This would be Katie's last course with ESP, she told me. She couldn't afford it anymore and refused to take out a new credit card, as the coaches strongly suggested, to max it out on more courses.

Katie put on a movie, and I looked out the window for a while, daydreaming.

I had no intention of using pain as a gateway to love, as they were teaching. That was not my way. I wanted to use *love* as a gateway to love, and, like most people, I hoped that love would be as pain free as possible.

I was ecstatic to get home and back to my project. That April, India helped me put together a mission statement for *Sexology*. We bought a giant poster board, and she wrote out the project's statement in giant pink letters using a thick Sharpie. Unlike the mission statement that ESP made us read aloud each day, which was about limitations, rules, and secrecy, mine was about expression, fun, and freedom:

> *This is about our aliveness, our passion, our creativity, our ability to tap into an infinite source of well-being, of yumminess . . .*

Not only was I trying to involve India in my project, I was trying to get her interested in *anything* outside of ESP. I was watching her get sucked into the organization's vortex, and I started to feel quietly desperate about it. I started pitching India for jobs left, right, and center, and frantically talking her up to my friends and coworkers who might have positions available that she'd be interested in.

Without India knowing, I orchestrated a summer job offer for her through a friend as actor Pierce Brosnan's personal assistant on the film *The November Man*. It was to shoot for three months in Belgrade starting that May—an ocean and worlds away from Albany, New York. I called up the line producer in Serbia to say entre nous that I'd supplement whatever salary they had budgeted for the position so they could offer India more.

When my daughter accepted the job, I was over the moon. She packed her bags to stay with my mother for the summer in her fifth-floor penthouse apartment in a bustling, happening part of the city. My mother knew something was up, and she knew to keep India as busy and having as much fun as possible when she wasn't working. In true Slavic grandmother fashion, my mother welcomed her grandchild into the bosom of the motherland and devised her own loving agenda to keep India there forever: by introducing her to as many eligible Serbian beaus as she could. It was my mother's own version of *The Princess Diaries*.

"Maybe she'll get engaged to someone here and stay!" she said.

It seemed like *everyone* wanted India.

Sure, sure, I thought—anything to keep her away from Albany.

During the summer, my mother would send frequent reports about India's activities. She was going out with the crew and partying at the nightclubs, having a great time. Next to the hardship of spending long days on a film set with one of the most handsome men in Hollywood, India's biggest worry for those three months was probably how she'd remain a new vegetarian in a country that considered pig's feet the *najbolji deo*—"the best part" of any meal—and had a national meat dish named after her very own ancestor, Black

George, called Karageorge schnitzel: pork cutlets stuffed with cheese and ham, and then breaded and fried. Every restaurant had it on the menu. Karageorge schnitzel looked like a giant, textured salami; hence its naughty nickname, "the maiden's dream."

But, you know, sometimes a schnitzel is just a schnitzel.

With India far away in our homeland with my mother, I breathed a sigh of relief. She was safe there.

—

MEANWHILE, CASPER AND I went back to Albany soon after India left for Europe to attend our third set of Level Two classes, "Characterization," and, essentially, to break up with Keith. At this point, we were both nearly at our end points with ESP. The more confident I grew about being a woman in my own body and helping other women do the same, the less effect ESP had over me.

As for Casper, he'd gotten into a scuffle with the Albany group a few months earlier and was hesitant to go back at all. He'd gone on his own for a "Society of Protectors (SOP)" weekend seminar—that women-hating class that was making all the men assholes, Mark told me later. During the first day's talk about being "honorable, noble protectors of humanity," the lead coach said something to the effect of: "And you know, *our job is to protect Keith!*"

That was the wrong thing to say to Casper, who had no respect for a guy who didn't put up his dukes and fight his own battles. He looked at the coach like he was nuts.

"I'm not going to fucking protect Keith," he fumed. "Are you serious? He can protect himself!"

After that, as Casper described it later, the room got a little unhinged.

The men swarmed him, and he thought for sure someone was going to throw a punch. He was ready if they did: although Casper wasn't a martial artist, he'd played one in the TV series *Mortal Kombat: Legacy*—just as good. But as quickly as the room heated up, the aggression evaporated.

For all their talk of protecting, they didn't have any real fight in them in the end, it seemed. They were still beta males, just flustered ones. Not only did we notice that the men seemed more feminized the longer they spent in ESP, but also we observed that, conversely, the women became more masculine.

Nancy, Clare, Esther, Wendy, and even Nancy's daughter, Lauren, all gave off a bit of a butch vibe to Casper and me—especially to my husband, who fancied himself a female sex appeal whisperer.

"None of those women," he declared to me one day (after careful examination, I'm sure), "has an iota of sensuality."

When we arrived back in Albany that May, I was still in the middle of a silent cold war with Nancy, so she sent Mark to do Keith's bidding with me. They'd all heard through the ESP grapevine that I was working on what could be a groundbreaking project about female sexuality.

I saw Allison Mack there again, though not in any classes. She seemed to be a permanent fixture, but I wasn't sure what she did. During a break from class, we chatted a bit in the lobby. She asked me about *Sexology* with mock interest, and when I told her a little about it, she gave me the same vacuous smile as before, then cocked her head à la Gold Sash and said, "You should talk to Keith about this!"

Just then, Mark approached. He'd been primed by Nancy and sent to ambush me in the lobby to get Keith in on the *Sexology* action.

"You know, Keith is a master of tantra," he informed me, looking uncomfortable with his mission. Oh, Lordy, was there anything this guy *wasn't* a master of? "He'd love to talk with you about sexuality on camera. Are you open to doing a roundtable with him?"

In an effort to improve the organization's image, Keith had been conducting roundtable chats with high-profile ESP members to post on the website. Mark had been running around doing damage control all year after the *Albany Times Union* had published a scathing exposé about ESP and Nxivm. I'd heard about the article only recently but hadn't read it yet. But I knew that the last thing I wanted to do was talk to the Oompa Loompa boy wonder about sex. The thought of it made me throw up a little in my mouth.

I felt cornered. I told Mark I had to make a call and would get back to him. I raced out into the parking lot to find a private spot to call my partner Gabrielle Anwar. She'd know a way out of this. Just as I was about to dial, I was cornered again—this time by Esther. She'd followed me.

"Catherine," she said, slightly out of breath. "I'm glad I caught up to you. I hear you're doing a project about sex."

"Yes, Esther. It's a docu—"

"Catherine," she cut me off. "Listen to me. You *have got* to help the Espian women."

"Help them? Help them how?"

"None of them are having orgasms."

Oh, God. Bad enough I had the image of Keith performing tantric sex in my head, thanks to Mark. Now I had to be tormented by visuals of the manly Espian women not getting off? This was cruel. And it was the second time that year Esther had rendered me speechless. Now came a third:

"You know, Catherine," she said, still very serious, "the only way to true enlightenment is by having sex with Keith."

Oh, would this day never end?

"Ya know, Esther? I'll have to get back to you on all this."

I weaved my way farther into the parking lot, leaving Esther behind, and hid behind a car. It had come to this. I dialed Gabrielle's number—she was in Miami, shooting the TV series *Burn Notice*—and I hoped she could find an out for me regarding Keith. She didn't disappoint.

"Absolutely not!" she yelled into the phone from the set. "Under no circumstance should you get in front of a camera with that man! Look online. There are allegations of pedophilia against him there! Women have come out saying he'd raped them when they were under the age of fifteen! You *cannot* risk or taint our brand and be seen on camera discussing sexuality with him!"

What she said startled me. I knew Keith was creepy, but I had no idea people had accused him of such heinous crimes. All ESP students were dissuaded from looking Keith up on the internet and warned in advance that people have a vendetta against him and have tried to discredit him. When India and I started more than two years earlier, the worst of the bad press hadn't appeared yet. The salacious stories I did see on blogs at that time sounded so outlandish, my thinking was: *If this is true, why isn't he in jail?*

But since then, the in-depth exposé on Nxivm by the *Albany Times Union* had been published, among others. This is what Gabby was looking at as we spoke on the phone.

Even if they were just rumors, I agreed it was too much of a risk. I went back inside and found Mark to tell him so. And, like a fool, I repeated everything Gabby had told me verbatim.

"Mark, the terrible things online about Keith. Are they true?"

Mark brusquely dismissed my question with the wave of his hand.

"Don't believe anything you read. Keith has a lot of enemies— very powerful, wealthy people, who are out to get him and have spent a lot of money in an effort to destroy his public image."

Of course, Mark then went straight to Nancy, who went straight to Keith and repeated everything I'd said—especially about my concern that he'd tarnish my brand.

And here's the problem with saying no to a malignant, narcissistic psychopath like Keith: his fortes are revenge, vindication, and retaliation. He is as methodical as Hannibal Lecter. And if he wants to get back at you, he doesn't care how long it takes, he'll spend the rest of his life doing it.

Years later, I would have a sick, eerie feeling thinking about that moment when I stood in the lobby at Nxivm headquarters and said no to Keith Raniere via Mark. What if my refusal had become a defining moment for Keith, one in which he initiated a meticulous, devious, painstaking plan to capture and destroy my daughter to punish me?

Your penance suffered by one of your loved ones, remember?

What if he'd thought to himself, *That bitch is going to pay for this.*

She's worried I'll taint her brand? I'll steal her daughter away from her forever and burn my mark into her.

Then we'll see whose brand gets tainted.

What if.

———

THINGS WENT DOWNHILL after that.

It was as if high command had already put out an all-points bulletin for my methodical torture and began the assignment to tear my family apart. For good reason, I already struggled with trust issues with Casper regarding other women, and I'd talked about it and cried about it during various EMs in class, so the coaches were aware of it.

The first part of our marriage had been a bumpy ride, navigating the challenges of Casper's roving eye. We once came face-to-face in the grocery store with a woman he'd strayed with, and I screamed every insult known to mankind at her in the deli aisle. Then I turned and punched Casper in the face. Hard. He fell backward into a six-foot bakery stand piled high with cookies, cakes, tarts, meringues, pies—the works. He lay sprawled on the floor, buried in a batch of freshly baked goods.

You might say I'd hit the sweet spot.

Anyway. Casper and I had worked hard to overcome that big hurdle, and I'd forgiven him—but not forgotten.

Now, suddenly Casper's breakout groups all week consisted of young, attractive women who fawned over him and hung on his every word—which had never happened before in class (due to Keith's aforementioned Svengali hold on them).

Casper played to his enraptured audience all day, every day, very loudly. I tried to concentrate across the room, but all I could hear was my husband doing his sexy voice followed by girlish shrieks of delight that reverberated through the room.

I was getting so pissed off that I finally relocated my group to another room.

Seeing him flirt in such an overt way brought the old hurt stinging to the surface. And somehow, everything around us was encouraging his behavior and egging him on. All week, the curriculum endorsed unleashing the beast within. And then at the flip of a switch, the nonsexual Espian women were suddenly seductresses. The women in Casper's groups had gone from robots to sirens oozing sexuality. What was wrong with this picture?

I couldn't help but feel we had been set up, as if they'd all been given the command to move in and destroy.

By the end of the week, I was fuming, and Casper was confused. He didn't understand what he'd done wrong. When we left Albany, it was never to return. We skipped the final class in the series—"Ascension"—even though I'd prepaid for it. We were going to have to remain earthbound for a little while longer.

———

INDIA CELEBRATED HER twenty-second birthday in Belgrade, and that July, I sent her a plane ticket to fly straight to the Dominican Republic, where Casper and I were shooting a goofy Roger Corman film, *Sharktopus vs. Whalewolf.* My plan was to extend India's hiatus from ESP as long as humanly possible.

On set, I noticed Casper flirting again—this time with one of the actresses in the film. But as my passion for my own project continued to burn, it stopped bothering me.

After our time in the Dominican Republic, I convinced India to come with me straight to the Bahamian island of Eleuthera to hang out as Gabby and I filmed the sizzle reel (a short promotional video) for *Sexology*. India came, lay out in the sun, and starred in some of our B-roll, swimming gracefully underwater like a mermaid.

Unfortunately, we had no idea how to actually shoot a sizzle reel. After we FedExed the raw footage back to Gabby's Oscar-nominated film editor father, Tariq Anwar (*The King's Speech, American Beauty*), to put it together for us, we got a phone call.

"If you girls want me to edit this, you'll need more than one camera angle. What am I supposed to cut to?" he asked. "And I recommend having some *sound,* too. Being able to hear what people are saying is a key component of a documentary."

India had just come from a professional film set to witness Gabby's and my dismal attempts at the sizzle reel, which fell flat. I'm sure our work didn't exactly entice her to join the *Sexology* production team.

But it was now early August, and time to revisit the conversation I'd had with my daughter on the plane earlier in the year. My fingers were crossed that she'd stay on working with us on the film, but before I could broach the subject, she dropped the bombshell two days before we were to leave Eleuthera.

"So, Mom . . . I'm not coming home with you," she said. "I'm going to fly to New York to attend V-week."

I could feel her slipping through my fingers. I tried begging.

"India, we start production in mid-September, and I could really use your help and support."

Then, for the second time, I broke my number one parenting rule and tried to steer her to do what I thought was best. I'd bitten my tongue during the two weeks we'd just spent together, but now I couldn't hold back.

"Darling, aren't you worried that ESP is taking over your life?" I asked. "Don't you want to branch out and do other things?"

India shook her head and smiled sweetly.

"Mom, I really want to go. There's a coach summit afterward, too. Just think of this as the university training I didn't get. I'm investing in myself, like I would if I'd gone to college. But this is the education I want."

I was crushed. I'd put four months, a country, two islands, two movie sets, and an ocean between her and ESP, and still she wanted to rush back to them. How had they sucked her in again so easily?

By now, I'd heard rumors about what went on during those ten-day V-weeks. It started off innocently one year, with everyone kissing everyone on the mouth regardless of gender, as a taboo-breaking exercise orchestrated by Keith. But that was merely the amuse-bouche.

At some point, the antics escalated. They got dark and twisted, just like the classes. Vanguard was preparing them, just as the classes were.

Not this year, but in the years to come, I would hear that the self-proclaimed tantric sex master started bed-hopping and humping naked all over the forest, and V-week apparently devolved into an orgiastic melee. A free-for-all.

All those lucky women, having sex with Keith; they wouldn't have orgasms but they'd get enlightenment!

It was all part of Keith's plan to bend the lines of morality and see how far he could push people. He wanted to confuse them about what was right and what was wrong.

Once they didn't know the difference, he would be the one to tell them.

For he was Vanguard, creator and ruler of everything.

7

HUMAN PAIN AND BLISS

When Casper returned home from directing a film the following April and announced abruptly, "I'm done. It's over between us," and walked back out the door, I went into shock.

No matter how tough the challenges were in our marriage, I always assumed it was death-do-us-part. Maybe because I'd come from a broken home myself, I'd made a vow not to do the same to our children.

The initial shock quickly rolled into a combination of agony and desperation, slamming into me like a steel wrecking ball.

That night, I enlisted one of my *Sexology* experts to act as a mediator for us. By day, he was a Unity Church minister; by night, he moonlighted as a sex therapist. I figured that covered all bases. In a three-way phone conversation, he tried to convince my husband to work on the marriage before suddenly abandoning our family after fourteen years, and Casper vacillated. He agreed. Then five minutes later, he changed his mind: the answer was *no*.

As I hung up the phone, my heart raced to maximum throttle.

I thought it would break through my ribs and explode out of my chest. I couldn't breathe; I was in the middle of a full-blown anxiety attack.

The timing couldn't have been worse. It was midnight, and I had a six o'clock call for our first expanded, full-scale shoot for *Sexology* in a rented house in Malibu, five minutes away from my home. How the hell was I supposed to calm down and get any sleep? I tossed and turned, then as a last resort, took half an expired tranquilizer I found in the medicine cabinet—something left over from my pre-audition-anxiety days—and waited. Nothing. An hour later, I took another half, finally passing out around three in the morning.

Three hours later, Katie was banging on my door to rouse me from my stupor. I groggily got dressed, and she stuffed me into the passenger seat of her car. When I got to the set and started talking to the crew, they looked at me like I was a crazy person.

The day before, I'd called a big powwow with the entire production team to make an impassioned plea that we keep our set a drug-free environment. "We're going to ask you to refrain from drinking alcohol or taking any recreational drugs for the period of the shoot," I told them, "because we're trying to create a *sacred space*." *Namaste, Namaste*.

But there I was, incoherent and slurring, drugged out of my mind. I was so nonfunctional that Katie had to usher me into the master bedroom of the house, where I flopped, face-first, onto the plush king-sized bed. From there, I attempted to direct the day's shoot using Katie as a go-between.

"Just get me an ambulance," I slurred to Katie between takes.

"Get me to an emergency room! I'm having a heartbreak. I think I'm dying."

If pain was the gateway to love, as Karen the wizened battle-axe from "Human Pain" claimed, then I was earning major brownie points for future bliss.

But at that moment, and for the next year and a half, my life as I knew it would implode and collapse piece by piece. Casper did return a month later wanting to reconcile, and that instigated an eighteen-month roller-coaster ride in which we went back and forth and up and down, trying everything possible to save our family.

Then, in the summer of 2014, another relationship shattered: my friendship and partnership with Gabrielle. I had to let go of *Sexology* because we had artistic differences, as they say in Hollywood, and because I hadn't insisted from the outset on a legal contract between friends, I didn't protect the documentary as my intellectual property. Not only did I lose control of my passion project but I also lost a friend.

I was, however, able to salvage control of the instructional footage meant for the *Sexology* website. I transformed my dining room into an editing suite and, for the next five months, threw myself into work, feverishly splicing tape day and night. That creative work was the stabilizing force that kept me sane during the chaos my life had become.

I was so wrapped up and consumed by my own drama that year, I didn't see what was happening with India.

After spending all of 2013 trying to find ways to get her away from ESP—jobs, expensive vacations, activities to distract her—I'd

decided I couldn't spend the rest of my life trying to manipulate her, albeit with love. It didn't work, anyway; every time I did manage to distract her, they sucked her back in tenfold. She was going to have to make her own choices and figure it out for herself, I finally realized. I couldn't run interference anymore—I had to let go.

So all year, she'd flown under my radar. Because I was in my own personal hell, I didn't notice that India had descended deeper into her own abyss. Not that she thought she was in hell, because she certainly didn't; according to her, she was thriving and moving forward and upward in her world.

Maybe because our family had been torn apart, seemingly beyond repair this time, India felt a need to fall further into the waiting clutches of her other family.

She'd always been our family peacekeeper; perhaps we'd failed her with our breakup. In contrast, the ESP family seemed invulnerable. Theirs was a family you couldn't, didn't, leave; a contract and a vow you didn't break—even if you wanted to. It was forever.

Our family breakup didn't happen because of ESP, but, looking back, I could see how our involvement pushed the envelope. I had encouraged the classes as a family-togetherness experience, but a friend told me later that "the more classes you all took, the more distant from each other you seemed to get instead of getting closer."

A cult expert told me later that's one thing cults do on purpose: polarize and destroy families if the family members are not willing to toe the party line.

By the fall of 2014, India was dating Michel, one of her orange-sashed superiors at ESP, and they soon moved in together. At nearly forty, Michel was sixteen years her senior. We'd met him three

years earlier at our first class in Venice. What he lacked in physical stature, Michel made up for as an aggressive recruiter. And after hooking up with him, India went from a gentle, mild-mannered, not remotely pushy person at all to an Energizer Bunny missionary.

She systematically went through every single Facebook friend of each member of the family and sent messages to more than a thousand of our contacts, urging them to improve their lives using ESP. I found out about it when my friends started to call me up.

"Do you know your daughter is trying to recruit me for some weird cult thing?"

I sighed, apologized, and explained. "I'm hoping this is just a phase she's going through that won't last much longer . . ."

I wanted to scoop her up in my arms and tell her, "You don't have to do this," but I worried that any attempt to thwart her might have the opposite effect.

At home, India's sisters were noticing a change in her. When she visited, she went into coach mode with them. One day one of her sisters came home from school upset about a friend, and as she was telling us what happened, India went into autopilot EM questioning.

"Let's break down why you're upset," she said briskly.

She meant well, but her tone was patronizing, and her sisters did not like it one bit. All of a sudden, she'd gone from being their sister to being an all-knowing, pontificating superior doing therapy on them.

"Can't we just have a normal conversation without you doing that *thing* to me?" Maya, thirteen at the time, once snapped at her in frustration. Then to me she said, "Mom? India's in a *cult*."

The irony was, there was a time when India would have said the exact same thing—and *did* say it, when she was even younger than

Maya. Casper and I used to go to seminars to learn parenting skills and techniques to use on her and her siblings, but she always knew when I was trying out some new therapeutic jargon.

"Mom," she'd say, shaking her head and rolling her eyes, "I know what you're doing. You're doing *that thing* on me."

The kid busted me every single time; her instincts were so good then.

But now—now—she was acting like an evangelizing religious fanatic. After I got more phone calls and emails from bewildered Facebook friends, I tried to use humor to get her to ease off without making her think I was judging her.

"India, you might want to back down on your Jehovah's Witness enrollment tactics," I joked.

Her response was silence—as if she had a wall up and couldn't hear me.

My buddy Callum, who'd pegged ESP as a cult way back, was also one of India's targets. He, of all people, knew better. They'd hang out together, and whenever she inevitably tried to recruit him, he'd say, "I'm getting a Mormon vibe from you here." After numerous email requests to join the group, he finally texted her to say "Come on, enough already. You've just got to stop this. It's not okay."

But she couldn't stop. And she couldn't see that it wasn't okay.

—

BY THE END of 2014, India had been actively coaching for almost a year, which meant three things.

First, she'd entered the "devaluation" stage that came after love bombing. Once she'd joined the "stripe path," her superiors had permission to give her brutal, incessant criticism designed to break her down. They would tell India it was to help her become a better version of herself, but what they were really doing was making her submissive and suggestible, and then locking in a new persona: her cult persona—rebuilding her in their image.

Second, as a full-fledged coach, now she was required to attend and pay for Ethos twice a week and also teach it—for free. So those gobbledygook Level One modules I'd found so boring, she had now repeated hundreds of times until they were embedded in her subconscious.

And third, she was required to take (and pay for) every new class they introduced.

That year, ESP rolled out an endless stream of curriculum on a nonstop conveyer belt, one after another: new classes, new levels, new for-pay activities, from Consciousness Groups to Goals Labs— each with shiny, new Keithspeak names: Exo-Eso, the Source, Ethicist, Anima, Ultima. It was as if he'd figured out a way to target slightly different demographics using the same regurgitated bullshit, repackaged and prettied up with a different bow.

By that point, my daughter must have spent tens of thousands of dollars on class fees.

Sometime in early 2015, I got a call from our financial advisor and family friend, Hillary. She'd worked with my mother for decades, then added me, and now was India's financial advisor as well. Hillary was the one who'd coordinated the transfer of India's inheritance money when she'd turned twenty-one. She was calling now about my daughter's account, not mine, which wasn't the usual protocol. But after leaving several messages for India and not hearing back, she reached out to me, concerned. India and I had always had an open-door policy with Hillary when it came to discussing India's financials, and her statements still came to my house.

Hillary had noticed a lot of money going out to companies with suspicious-sounding names, she said, and was worried that someone had hacked into India's account. I sighed again, like I'd done with my Facebook friends, and explained the situation to Hillary.

"Is there any way to restrict how she spends her money?" I asked.

"Unfortunately, no," she said, "because she's over twenty-one."

All I could do, it seemed, was stand by and watch helplessly.

A lot of money was going out, and no money was coming *in*.

That was something India promised she was about to remedy with a brand-new job, she told me a few weeks later, at which she'd be pulling in the big bucks. She'd taken a full-time position at Rainbow Cultural Garden (RCG): an unaccredited, unlicensed, untested day care school program designed by Keith and run by Michel.

The concept of Rainbow, she explained, was to teach children from infancy to age ten up to nine languages at once, including Mandarin Chinese, Arabic, Russian, German, Hindi, and Spanish. Only languages approved by Keith were allowed.

According to the official website, they wanted to "create the leaders of tomorrow" with an "early child-development program which, through careful, progressive exposure to multiple languages, cultures, representational systems, and aesthetics, seeks to inspire and capture the miraculous, creative, learning lives of children."

Ideologically, it sounded great: teaching children up to nine languages by the time they're four. I'd grown up in Europe, where people are exposed to a lot of languages simply because the countries are all pressed against and into one another, and you were obligated to speak more than one. My grandfather spoke thirteen, my mom speaks nine—making her the embodiment of the ultimate Rainbow child—and I trail in last place at three.

But when India began telling me what her duties were, I started to get that sick feeling in my gut that was now all too familiar.

Her job was to find teachers and then train them how to interact with the infants and children according to Keith's specific guidelines. The teachers, she explained, were often foreign nannies they found on Craigslist and then paid minimum wage to talk to the children in their native tongue. Their correct title, India informed me, was multicultural diversity specialist (MDS): Keithspeak for unaccredited teacher. Or maybe his acronym for maids.

I was in no position to judge, being a college dropout myself, but I wondered, why was *she* training the nonteachers, when she had no training herself in education, or even a college degree?

And if the cost per child was up to $120,000 a year, and the nannies were making only minimum wage, where was all the money going? India herself was to be paid on commission only, so she had to target and woo billionaires (Who else could afford those fees?) to get a paycheck, and that wouldn't be an easy sell.

I wanted to ask these questions, but I didn't. She continued explaining, but the more she talked about it, the less sense it made to me, and the more alarmed I got.

"We encourage the parents to stay away from their babies and children all day while they are being taught a language the parent doesn't know," she said cheerfully.

That was the part that concerned me the most.

My immediate thought was that Keith—who'd never had a healthy connection with another human in his life, I suspected— didn't want these children to bond with their parents. But I didn't realize until later *why* he'd want to prevent this bonding and what his deeper ulterior motive might have been.

They wanted to "create the leaders of tomorrow," their website said. But in reality, I think he wanted to create the *followers* of tomorrow. He wanted to sculpt and control these children's minds to create his own army of the future that would follow his orders and agenda. And because the families of these children were wealthy and powerful, their wealth and unlimited resources would be in his clutches as well.

The thought gave me chills.

"Mom, I love working with the children," India said, "much more so than with the parents."

I didn't doubt it. If I was one of those parents, and she told me I had to stay away from my kids for however long, I'd raise hell.

"Darling, why do they teach Arabic but not Hebrew?" I asked. I'd always sensed that Keith was anti-Semitic. I'd heard he sometimes called Nancy "Hitler"—but didn't mean it as a negative. Bonnie later confirmed to me that Keith was an avid Holocaust denier.

"Keith says Hebrew isn't relevant."

I tried to hide my disgust, but I have a lousy poker face. The whole conversation and India's belief in Keith made me ill. ESP prided itself that its teachings made students more reality based in their lives. But this was the first time I looked at my daughter and thought: *Oh my God, my child's thinking is not based in reality!*

But what could I say to her?

Maybe she really was spearheading a totally forward-thinking program that was going to change the world, and I was just a backward dinosaur. My entire life had imploded that year, so who was I to make any judgments?

But if she was delusional, I also didn't want to burst her bubble too callously. Our family was going through enough bubble bursting as it was.

—

WITHOUT WARNING, CASPER filed for divorce on my birthday in September 2015, while I was in the air flying to Tulum, Mexico, with my mother.

I got the email from his lawyers as soon as I landed, and panicked. Casper's timing sucked once again, to say the least. He was in Belgium, and I was now in Mexico, and our kids were at home in LA with a caretaker, with neither of us there to help them deal with this. I called them immediately, but as I suspected, they'd already read about it on the internet and were distraught.

I was stuck and couldn't go back to them just yet.

I was in Tulum to teach a workshop I'd created and called Body of Bliss, but I was feeling anything but. In between my talks, I'd rush out to the hallway and hide in a nearby broom closet so I could burst into tears in private. I didn't want my students to see I wasn't walking the walk!

Thank God for my mother, who had been divorced three times and was a pro at it.

"Divorcing in Mexico must be a family tradition!" she said, laughing, and reminded me about my own parents' unconventional divorce there nearly fifty years before. My father had insisted that, to save money, they had to fly to Mexico to get their divorce because it was cheaper to do it there. And with the money they saved, Dad wined and dined Mom and took her on what he called "our divorce honeymoon."

They had a grand old time and went to the bullfights, and after their divorce was finalized, they took their judge to the bullfights, too! Now, that's the way to end a marriage in style.

"The best part of my marriage with your mother," my father used to say, "was our divorce!"

Mom's retelling of that story made me laugh and took me out of my funk for the rest of our two-week stay.

Tulum is on the Caribbean coastline of Mexico's Yucatán Peninsula, and it is known for its incredible beaches, warm turquoise waters, and well-preserved ruins of an ancient Mayan port city dedicated to the goddess Venus.

As it turned out, Tulum would be a magical place of healing for me, just as Mexico had lifted the spirits of my divorcing parents.

The beach house I'd rented—Casa Dos Besos ("House of Two Kisses")—was beyond enchanting. It had adobe walls and a thatched roof, and everything inside was pristine, white, and made of carved wood. The back terrace looked out to the sea and miles of white, powdery sand that looked like confectioners' sugar, and everything growing around the terrace resembled a Claude Monet painting of pastel blues, greens, and pinks.

As jagged and raw as I was feeling, Tulum smoothed out the sharp edges; I melted into its warm waters like I was being reborn.

At night, I opened my bedroom windows wide and stretched out fully on the four-poster bed like a starfish, to claim my space and my life.

Tulum had an awesome, freeing energy, and it was there that I knew I was ready to let go of my marriage. The very thing I had dreaded the most had, ultimately, liberated me.

—

AFTER I GOT home, I started writing and didn't stop.

I scribbled diary entries for the end of 2015 and the first few months of 2016 as if my life and sanity depended on it, reviewing my past failures and what I'd learned. I started writing a book, *Venus Rising,* and went into depth about what I had wanted to say with my documentary but didn't get the chance. I poured my heart into every sentence and got so immersed that it took a second call from Hillary to yank me back to the present.

This time she was calling me because her concern for India's well-being had heightened, due to an extreme increase in activity on her account.

"Are you sure she's okay?" she asked.

This prompted me to open up one of her statements, which I stared at in shock. The inheritance my father had left her was almost gone.

"Nxivm," I said. "is going through her money so fast. She doesn't spend any money on herself."

I tried to look on the bright side. Maybe after India ran out of all her money, they'd have no more need for her and cut her loose? I couldn't believe that was the best-case scenario, how sad . . .

After I hung up the phone, I went downstairs to check the pile of mail I'd been holding for India. They were all overdue bills. I'd been handing her stacks of mail each time I saw her, and now I realized they were all the same bills, over and over, that she wasn't paying.

What kind of "executive success" business program takes all your money and encourages you not to pay your bills? That ESP touted itself as a business program and then drained students' bank accounts and steered them toward bankruptcy made the scam all the more ludicrous.

By the spring of 2016, India had grown more distant than ever—she just didn't seem *present*. So much so that within a short span of a year, she'd totaled two cars in accidents, and now I was worried for her physical safety as well as her mental agility. What was going on with her that she was getting into these accidents? She'd asked me for a few tiny, loose diamonds I had from a ring so she could design a belly chain for herself, and I gladly gave them to her.

Around then, I received a third call from Hillary, reporting that my daughter had withdrawn the rest of her money and closed her account. When Hillary asked her what she was going to use the money for, India told her she was starting a new business. We crossed our fingers that this meant she was leaving the group and striking out on her own, and I waited patiently for India to tell me herself, which she did a few weeks later.

"Mom, I just wanted to let you know that I split from Michel, and I quit my job at the Rainbow school," she said as we prepared dinner one night.

"Oh, really?" I tried hard to subdue my enthusiasm.

"Yeah. I'm going to start a new business."

"That sounds great, India! Is this something . . . you're doing on your own?"

I had a split second of hope before the word salad came tumbling out of her mouth again. Keith had designed a new business just for her called Delegates, she said, her eyes lighting up.

"It's innovative and exciting! Keith is brilliant! And he's going to mentor me personally, Mom. This is an opportunity I can't pass up!"

She explained the concept as best she could.

"India," I told her, "that sounds just like TaskRabbit." She didn't hear me.

"And I'm going to develop an app for it, and I have to raise eighty thousand dollars for it and . . ."

Oh, God. Raise money? This is where the rest of her inheritance was going: as seed money for one of Keith's inane, self-serving creations.

"And there's more!" she said.

I didn't think I could take any more.

"I'm moving to Albany in September," she said, "to be a part of this new university program Keith created! I'm going to be one of the first guinea pigs—it's going to be so much fun!"

I was at a loss for words at this point and could answer her only monosyllabically. I couldn't say "Great," and I couldn't say "I'm excited for you." I couldn't say any of the things that a mother would want to say when her child was about to embrace a new stage of her life.

The best I could manage was: "Wow."

She'd dumped so much upsetting news on me, one item after another, I didn't even get a breather in there to enjoy the fact that she'd dumped Michel. She'd already traded up to Keith, which was so much worse.

Later, I would learn about two events that had happened a few weeks before our conversation and had swiftly hoovered her deeper into the ESP underworld.

First, she and Keith had taken a little walk together around the town of Halfmoon, where he lived, and when they returned, India was flushed and giddy. Whatever her previous feelings about him were, they'd been erased, and from that moment onward, she'd wear the same adoring expression on her face around him as those volley-ball cheerleaders from five years earlier.

Second, Allison Mack had recruited her into some new, top-secret, badass female empowerment sisterhood sorority—"like the Masons, but for girls!" was the pitch. "We'll be like ninja warrior women!" Allison told her.

Allison was to be India's group "master."

But I didn't know any of that yet.

All I knew so far was that the devil himself had taken India personally by the hand, and now she was leaving us to move to Cult Central.

—

THAT SEPTEMBER, SHE gave away and liquidated her possessions as if she were leaving the planet. All my daughter left behind were dozens of packets of colorless, zero-calorie noodles in the fridge in my garage—they looked like baby eels floating around in a murky fluid, like something that ends up invading the world in a horror sci-fi flick if you let it loose.

After our conversation, I saw her fleetingly over the next year. Our next extended visit with each other was in the spring of 2017.

Again I rented the enchanting white house by the turquoise waters of Tulum.

This time I gathered three generations of Oxenberg women there: Celeste, Grace, and Maya came in with me from LA, my mother flew in from Belgrade, and India flew in from Albany. This was our *own* badass sisterhood sorority.

It was our first vacation together as a family without Casper, so it was an important one. We'd all survived the wreckage of divorce, and now I wanted us to share an inspiring, magical, celebratory time together. I wanted us to feel our solidarity and unity as a family again. I wanted us to bond and heal from the last two years.

Tulum had healing powers before; I was counting on it having them again.

We went for long walks on the beach and visited the Mayan ruins nearby. My mom hired a chef to whip up fantastic, fresh meals, and the kids spent all day in the water.

And while I was there, I worked on the mission statement for my next creative project to help women: a nonprofit human rights organization I was going to establish as soon as I returned to LA.

"The Catherine Oxenberg Foundation is a human rights organization dedicated to empowering women to lead more embodied lives," I wrote.

"This can only become a reality in an environment where women are free from subjugation, exploitation, and abuse. We champion issues essential for the enhancement of female health and well-being—emotional, physical, and sexual—through the areas of research, rehabilitation, and restoration."

We all had an amazing, rejuvenating time together in Tulum, but . . . there was something off about India—more than before, I mean.

She had a weary lifelessness in her eyes that I'd never seen before, and her usual radiant luster was replaced with dark circles under her eyes. She looked gaunt. While the rest of us basked contentedly like beached whales soaking up the sun on the sand, India couldn't sit still. She was constantly jumping up, restless, in perpetual motion—going on endless runs up and down the beach. At one point, oddly, I overheard her telling my other kids, "I don't want to have children."

Why would she say this? That didn't sound like her at all.

"Mom, I'm down to a hundred three pounds!" she said, proudly, drinking some liquid concoction while the rest of us wolfed down mountains of food from the huge spread on the terrace.

I smiled, and nodded. She hadn't been that weight since she was thirteen.

"Darling, you look beautiful. I hope you don't think you need to lose any more weight."

India tried to hide the fact that she carried two phones now, but it was pretty hard to conceal when both of them beeped constantly and she was always leaping up to answer a text or a call. The fact that she couldn't get decent cell reception in Mexico made her frenzy even more frenetic.

But she felt happy and purposeful, she told me, even though she didn't look it. My daughter seemed more burdened and serious than ever before.

Even my mother noticed something wasn't right. After chatting with India out on the terrace one afternoon, she came in to talk to me in the kitchen.

"I asked India what she was doing in Albany and what her plans were, and I didn't understand her answer at all," said my mother. "It sounded like she was talking in circles. Maybe I'm just going senile."

"No, Mom, you're not," I assured her. "What she says doesn't make sense to me, either."

Something was definitely wrong—more wrong than before—but I couldn't put my finger on it.

A few days after we got home, and India rushed back to Albany, I got a worrisome phone call from India's father, Bill.

"India told me she was a hundred thirty thousand dollars in debt," he said.

Neither of us knew that the unaccredited university program she had signed up for was costing her five thousand a month.

How was she going to dig herself out of this? I hoped the money she owed was to ESP and not credit card companies.

I was trying to figure out a way for her to get out of her financial mess when another phone call interrupted me.

It was Bonnie, whom I hadn't spoken to in four years—ever since I'd left ESP for good and distanced myself from everybody involved. I'd heard she'd recently defected from the group.

"Bonnie, how are you doing?" I asked.

"Catherine, you know I'm no longer with ESP, right? I left, I'm back in LA."

She was talking fast and sounded afraid.

"Yeah, I just heard that. Hey, are you okay? What about Mark?"

"It's complicated," she said, haltingly. "He's still in. But I'm not calling about us, Catherine, I'm calling about India."

My heart skipped a beat, and I held my breath.

"Wh—what about India?"

"Catherine, I don't know if you know what's going on, but . . . you have to save her," Bonnie said. Her voice was trembling.

"You have to save India!"

PART 2

Saving India

8

AWAKENINGS

Save her?

"Bonnie, *what do you mean*?" I asked, still holding my breath. "Save India from *what*? From *whom*?!"

Bonnie took a deep breath.

"Catherine . . . India is a member of a secret slave-master group," she said, now speaking even more quickly—as if to get it all out before she was caught.

"She signed a lifetime vow of obedience and gave damaging collateral about herself and most likely you, too. Keith puts them on starvation diets and makes them sign away their possessions, their properties, their bank accounts, and even their future children. They get punished if they don't do as they're told. Each master has to recruit five or six slaves, and then the slaves become masters, too, and recruit slaves of their own. And . . ."

What the hell was she talking about? Slaves? Collateral? This was insane. India couldn't be part of anything as twisted as this.

"And Catherine," Bonnie whispered, "India isn't just a slave, she's a master, too."

I was too stunned to speak.

"There's so much more," Bonnie said, "but I need to tell you the rest in person. I'm scared to do this over the phone."

More? The idea of *more* filled me with dread. We made arrangements to meet the next day, and after we hung up, I called India's father, Bill.

"India's in jeopardy; she needs our help," I told him, repeating the bizarre details Bonnie had told me. "We need to take action. We need to get her home!"

Neither of us knew what to make of what Bonnie had said, but we knew we had to get her home as fast as possible to find out what was happening—and do so without tipping our hand. India's twenty-sixth birthday was seven weeks away, on June 7, so we came up with a plan to throw her a party and send her a plane ticket. If there was one thing I knew about my daughter, it was that she loved a good party. When she was four years old, she announced one day that her secret name was "Bunny Party Girl."

I texted her:

Your dad and I would love to fly you home for your birthday, darling, and we can throw a party and invite all your friends.

She replied, over-the-moon excited, saying she'd cried when she received my text. She could only get away for five days at the end of May, she said, because she had important classes during the week of her birthday. I was thankful for even that. I hated that they kept her on such a short leash, but at least she'd be home soon—and I planned to keep her here.

—

BY THE TIME I met Bonnie the next afternoon, I'd already booked India a one-way flight to LA. I was emotionally and physically incapable of booking the return for her—I told her that her father would do it.

Bonnie and I reunited at a dimly lit bar in Beverly Hills. It had been four years since I'd seen her, and she looked exactly the same except for one big difference: her ever-present cult smile had been replaced by a haunted look in her eyes.

We hugged, but she was so jittery, she could barely stand still for it. Before we sat down, she scanned the room to see if she'd been followed or if anyone was watching her.

For the next two hours, Bonnie unloaded a torrent of information nonstop, sometimes sounding discombobulated, as she zigzagged through the last two years. I took notes, barely saying a word, and tried to keep both of us calm.

Bonnie and India had become the best of friends around India's first V-week in 2012, she began explaining, but everything came crashing down once Allison Mack began mentoring India around the end of 2015 or early 2016.

"Allison derailed our friendship, as if she wanted to steal India away and wanted her for herself," she said. "She felt threatened by me. I was worried and tried to warn India about her; I'd seen some very, very bad results from Alli's mentoring."

When Allison lived with Bonnie and Mark, including during the time India and I were their houseguests, "she would flip out in the middle of the night, and I'd hear murderous screaming coming from her room. She would get up and walk around Clifton Park all night long."

Bonnie stopped to take a sip of water. Her hands were shaking.

Soon after Allison began mentoring India, she continued, India began to lose weight and act coldly toward Bonnie.

"Alli is obsessed with penance and weight," Bonnie said. "I found out that Keith kept all the women on diets of five hundred to eight hundred calories, and if they gained weight, he punished them. It was to build character, he told them, because women don't have any."

It was around that time she noticed the relationship between India and Keith ramping up.

"He'd had his eye on her for years," she said. "Then India told me last spring about a secret project she was working on with Keith and Allison. She called it 'the Project,' though I've since learned members use other code names for it, like 'the Vow' or 'the Agency' or 'DOS'—which is Latin for '*dominus obsequious sororium*' and means 'master over the slave women.'

"Someone else tipped me off about what the secret group was about. I can't say who—it would put us both in danger," she went on. "In this master-slave club, there's a lot of pressure for the women to sleep with Keith. Alli must have influenced India to get close to him because that's how Alli got his approval, by bringing him women."

Then came India's life-changing walk with Keith.

"One day, India announced that she'd been for a walk with Keith, and when she returned, her opinion of him had completely changed.

The way she talked about him was so different; she was flushed and almost giddy. I'm pretty sure Alli is having sex with Keith, and I think India is, too. He's having sex with at least twenty of them at the same time."

"Bonnie," I interrupted, for the first and only time during her monologue, "are you absolutely *sure* of this? Are you sure India is having sex with Keith?"

I couldn't bear to imagine this was true. I couldn't.

"No, I'm not sure. But it's very likely."

Bonnie explained that she'd been making plans to leave ESP well before she knew about DOS.

"I wasn't happy for a while," she said. "I was broke—we were all broke. The promise that once I reached proctor/orange sash I would finally be making money was a lie. Over time I started to notice major inconsistencies in the organization and blatant abuses."

When Bonnie started asking questions about what was going on, Allison had her kicked out of a Nxivm program for actors, called "the Source," and began ostracizing her and telling everyone else to shun her as well. Nancy accused Bonnie of being a narcissist and a "suppressive"—a term Keith had stolen from Scientology, no doubt.

"I began having panic attacks," she said. One day she left one of Keith's classes early because she wasn't feeling well. Afterward, he confronted her.

"He was furious. He said, 'You've committed an ethical breach you'll never be able to repair or heal in this lifetime, but you have to do everything you can to try!'

"Then a friend of mine, another coach, confided in me that she'd been removed from her position as head trainer because she'd committed an ethical breach against Keith by refusing to have his baby. In this secret society, all babies go to Keith—it's part of their vow of obedience. They have to sign a waiver that if they get pregnant with Keith's child—or anyone's, for that matter—they must give their babies to Keith."

As I took notes, each new piece of information was like a punch in the gut, but I wasn't about to allow myself to go down the emotional rabbit hole right there in public. This was a coping mechanism of mine in moments of emergencies and trauma: stay calm, carry on, take notes, digest everything. Later, I could scream and cry into my pillow.

During the last few months that Bonnie was still in Albany, Keith got even more psycho, she said.

Two longtime members of his harem—Pam and Mariana—lived with him, and Pam had taken ill with cancer. "She was basically dying in one room, while in the next room, he told everyone later, he was having sex with Mariana to conceive his baby—*with* Pam's blessing, as she was literally taking her last breath."

Keith had told a lot of his women that he'd father a child with them, that they were the chosen one, and that the baby would be an avatar who would change the world. Nine months later, the "Baby Avatar" was born.

But he was not Keith's first child. A decade earlier, one of Keith's girlfriends, Kristin Keeffe, gave birth to their son, Gaelen—and for years, Keith and the harem created a web of lies and mystery surrounding the child's origins. A story was concocted that Keith had adopted the boy, a foundling, after his mother had died in childbirth and no one knew who the father was. At the time, Keith was presenting himself as celibate—which was ironic, considering he had a full-time harem. Keith's foundling story, I thought, was the ultimate "Immaculate Deception."

"Pam died last November, and Keith kept the news from all of us for several weeks, until he suddenly announced there'd be a memorial. Soon after that, he started telling people that Pam had been poisoned. Another member of his harem, Barbara Jeske, had died from cancer just two years earlier, and he had also told the group she had been poisoned. (The following year, I would find out that Keith and Nancy had cornered Barb's sister right after Barb's death and asked to have her sister's body so they could freeze it. When the family refused, they requested the head only. The family didn't give them that, either.) He was convinced people were out to get him, and were poisoning those in his inner circle."

Multiple sources, including Pam's hairstylist, had heard Pam say that Keith was monitoring her cancer treatment and had administered a milky fluid for her to drink.

"But that's not even the worst of it," Bonnie said, stopping to catch her breath.

She leaned in closer.

"I was told by firsthand witnesses that Keith arranged to have Pam's body snuck out of the hospital before a death certificate could be issued and kept her body submerged in ice in one of his bathtubs at home. No one knows what happened to her body."

Bonnie paused for a moment, and we both let the horror of this sink in.

"Why would anyone do that?" I asked, appalled.

"Maybe so he could continue to use her credit cards? I don't know," she answered. "I couldn't stay any longer, Catherine. Mark begged me to, but I couldn't. A veil had been lifted, and I saw everything for what it really was: all lies."

Bonnie's whole body was shaking. She was fighting a decade of programming and indoctrination to talk this way about ESP and would now be considered a heretic because of it. I reached across the table and squeezed her hands, as if to still them.

"Thank you," I said, "for being brave enough to share this with me."

"I'm telling you these terrible things about your daughter," she stuttered, "but why is it *you're* the calm one and I'm shaking like a leaf!"

I smiled, somehow. "I'm a mother; I can handle a lot."

My mind was already working overtime thinking up ways to handle all the news she'd told me over the last twenty-four hours, and how to help India.

"You know, Bonnie, I always assumed India would wake up at some point and leave the group of her own accord."

"No, Catherine, listen to me. She won't. She went in too young, she was too impressionable. The only way to get her out now is to do an intervention."

I drove home along the Pacific Coast Highway, trying to absorb the evil I'd just heard.

In front of Bonnie, I had remained calm. And a big part of me was in shock. But inside, my heart and soul ripped apart at every word she uttered. Of all the many, many worries I harbored about India and ESP over the years, I never, ever, would have guessed anything like this was in the realm of possibility.

My India, starved, punished—a slave? How did this happen? Please, let my precious girl be safe!

She'd be arriving in six weeks, on May 25, and I was already planning to surprise her with her favorite things to do: massages, hikes, watsu, hot springs, road trips, *and lots of great restaurants,* I thought to myself, *to feed you.* At the same time, I was consumed with guilt. I'd never outright lied to India before, and here I was, setting her up to come for her birthday and then ambushing her. I fully intended to do what Bonnie urged: a full-out intervention, though I had no idea what it entailed yet.

As I drove by Zuma Beach, I slowed to catch a glimpse of a pod of dolphins breaching near the shore break. It reminded me of the time India was eleven, and we were driving along the coast not far from where I was now. She'd said a prayer then, and asked for dolphins to appear in the water to confirm that her prayer had been heard—and they did. She had a magical intuitive connection to nature, and I took the dolphins as a sign of hope.

When I got home, I sat on the couch and stared out the window for hours, not wanting to move or to believe anything I'd heard that day. I watched the sun slip into the Pacific. After the shock came rage, then indignation, then grief.

And finally, determination. As soon as the sun set, I sprang into action—there wasn't a minute to spare. Bonnie had already emailed me a list of books, films, articles, and cult experts: "Educate yourself," she said to me as we left the bar. "To help India, you've got to learn everything you can."

I put on *Holy Hell*, a recent documentary about another bizarre sex cult based in West LA, called Buddhafield, and attacked the list

Bonnie sent me, ordering books, reading articles, and making appointments, until it was morning.

—

THE FOLLOWING AFTERNOON, I was sitting in the office of Rachel Bernstein, a therapist, cult deprogrammer, and recovery specialist, strategizing on how to do an intervention for India.

Rachel came from a family of activists, like mine, and grew interested in this line of work after a family friend had been brainwashed by Scientology. She'd since helped hundreds of people recover from destructive cults and held support groups for former cult members. Some of her past patients had included "Expians," she told me— a moniker referring to defectors, or *ex*-Espians.

"They are a very dangerous, extreme cult," she said. "And they're known to be viciously litigious against defectors. But I've had success with several of them."

I asked her why India had been sucked into the group when we'd all taken the class and none of us had been?

"Anyone can be susceptible to cults and prone at different times in their lives," she said. "Cults often have a front organization that looks completely normal and legitimate offering practical tools— skills that one can use in the outside world.

"Keith is so ordinary as a cult leader, nothing original. He demands total belief in him and sacrifices such as proof of loyalty and devotion. You're asked to see the world in black and white and not question him. The mechanism of control is identical to most cult leaders. Fear induction is a potent behavior modification tool. Public shaming dissuades other members from challenging hierarchy."

My plan was to stage an intervention at the tail end of her visit; that way India could spend as much fun time with the family as possible first, before the axe dropped.

"That's not enough time," Rachel said. "It often takes months to put together a proper intervention."

"Rachel, there is no other time. It's nearly impossible to get her home. This is the only chance I have. Why does it take so long?"

"I usually educate the entire family. The way everyone communicates with the cult member is very different than usual; there are skills you all have to learn . . ."

I'd already checked with the girls, and they didn't feel comfortable getting involved. And Bill did not appear interested in meeting with any specialists.

"It's just me, Rachel. I'm it. I'm the entire family."

We talked about the possibility of my bringing India to Rachel's office when she came home for her birthday party. I had no idea if I'd be able to convince India to see her, so I wanted to be educated on what to say to her myself.

For the next few hours, Rachel coached me on how to talk to India during the intervention—what words to say and not say, how to pose questions to her, how to respond to her.

"A cult intervention bears no resemblance to an addiction intervention," she explained. "There is no confrontation, simply an invitation to have a conversation. The purpose is to ask questions to awaken her critical thinking. Cult members are handicapped when it comes to trusting their inner voice. She's been systematically taught to override that first impulse, so she's going to have to relearn how to listen to her inner guidance."

The most crucial instruction, she stressed, was to keep from being critical or judgmental of India during any of our communications with her.

"She's getting judged and controlled and criticized by the cult already, so you need to do the opposite: show her what unconditional love looks like, show her the difference. It's very important that people see her in a positive light and recognize her strengths. Saying anything negative about Keith or the cult will only make her defenses go up."

She described how cult members have two separate personalities. "The precult persona is the India you've always known. And the cult persona is the one that is distant, distracted, stressed, serious, dissociated, burdened, acting superior."

"Yep," I said, nodding. "I've seen that persona."

"Catherine, every opportunity you can find, engage her precult persona as much as possible. Remind her of her memories. The more you can get her to laugh, smile, and enjoy herself, the better. You want her to miss her time at home."

"The most important thing to remember in any interaction with her," she emphasized, "is to keep it light. This is not an ambush."

For the next hour, Rachel continued to drill me on questions, answers, phrasings, responses, good and bad words, and the do's and don'ts of an intervention. She also warned me how difficult it can be to get into and change a cult member's mind.

"Many defectors feel anxiety around freedom," she explained.

"They miss the appeal of the community, the 'high,' and the magic. They miss feeling specially chosen and following someone who seems to have all the answers. The ones who do not get deprogrammed often go cult shopping, leaving one cult for another. The loss of community is very real for them; it's very painful. So surround India with people who love her."

With what I'd learned in just one session, I was confident I'd be successful. Armed with my anti-cultspeak, I was sure I'd get through to India, and she wouldn't want to go back.

"Catherine, if India does go back to Albany this time, don't be disappointed and think the intervention failed," she said. "The goal is not to stop her from leaving. She may feel she has to go back because she is afraid of the repercussions, not because she wants to. Fear-induction techniques and planted phobias about betraying Keith and the doctrine are controlling her. Many times, people need to go back and figure it out for themselves and have their own awakening so that it can be their decision, not someone pushing them. But you will have planted the seeds of doubt.

"When cult members finally see the leader as a sociopath or narcissist, it's so freeing. But it may take time. We are dealing with an invisible art. There are no locks on the door, there is only a lock on your mind."

I thanked her, and left the office filled with hope—and in denial.

India, go back to that insanity? To me, that wasn't an option.

A few weeks later, I got another unexpected call: this time it was Mark, Bonnie's husband. He was with Bonnie in LA, and he'd just finished facilitating an intensive ESP class. It would be his last, he told me.

"Catherine, please keep this to yourself, but I'm defecting from the group, too," he told me. "No one knows yet except for Bonnie."

"Oh, Mark. Thank God."

This was big, big news. Not only would Mark's defection save his marriage, but also, as the first high-ranking man to leave the group, he would surely influence others to wake up and leave, too—maybe even India.

Like Rachel Bernstein had said, every cult member has to have his or her own awakening; his or her own way of connecting the dots. For Mark, it happened when he realized for the first time that Keith had told him a lie about something—just one small, little lie. When Mark confronted him about it, Keith lied a second time. And that's when something occurred to Mark for the first time like a bulb switching on in his brain:

Oh my God, what if he's lying about other things, too? What if he's been lying to me all along, about everything? What if all of this is a lie?

Hearing about DOS from Bonnie horrified him and hastened the departure he was already planning. His defection had been in the works for a while, but Bonnie couldn't tell me about it at our meeting because they feared for their lives. As soon as Mark announced his departure with an official resignation letter, and Keith and other cult members found out about it, he was certain he'd receive death threats, he said.

"I have so much shame, Catherine," he lamented. "I dedicated over twelve years of my life to this man and his mission, and then one day I realized the whole thing was an evil charade. To think I was a part of it, that I helped recruit thousands of people, the amount of destruction I unknowingly participated in—my guilt and shame are unbearable."

I could hear his muffled sobs before Bonnie took the phone.

"Catherine, Mark spoke to Sarah Edmondson this morning, and you need to hear what she had to say. She admitted to him that she's part of DOS and that she was branded on her body. Can we meet you somewhere to talk in person? We can't say any more over the phone."

Branded? I told her to meet me at my friend Greg's house that afternoon. He was someone we could trust who could give good advice and help them navigate their next steps, I told her.

We hung up, and for the second time in two weeks, the idea of hearing more from Bonnie filled me with dread.

—

GREG HANNLEY WAS a longtime neighbor and a successful entrepreneur, most notably the founder and CEO of the Soba Recovery Center rehabilitation facilities across the country. When Callum needed help with the alcohol problem that Nancy hadn't cured, and his insurance wouldn't cover another stint in rehab, Greg took care of him. (Callum had already done a gig at the Betty Ford Center in Rancho Mirage, California, and "escaped" three times, as he liked to tell it. The third time, he ran off into the desert until a Betty Ford worker pulled up in a mandatory white rehab van. "You know, you don't have to keep running away . . . and by the way, we have your wallet, your passport, and your phone," the employee said nicely. "We're not a prison. You can just leave." Callum always likes to remind everyone about the ungodly amount of Valium that the rehab center had administered to him, and blames this farcical escape story on the pill addiction he left Betty Ford with, which he didn't have going in.)

Greg was a no-bullshit, silver-haired, handsome guy, in that gangster-mensch sort of way. And he was connected. His latest rescue mission was saving young women from the sex-trafficking industry. As it turned out, Greg endured a year of hell in an abusive cult when he was a teenager.

He and a bunch of teens were prisoners of a man who controlled their every move and threatened their lives daily by putting a loaded gun to their heads. If you tried to escape, he ordered another cult member to drive you out to the desert and leave you there.

"How did you get out?" I asked him.

Bonnie's earlier words still echoed in my mind: that India wouldn't get out on her own because she went in too young and impressionable. But here was Greg, proof it was possible.

"The guy died," Greg said. He had advanced diabetes and one day just keeled over. "Had he not died, I don't know if I would have ever gotten out." It was not the answer I was hoping for.

A few hours after our phone call, Mark, Bonnie, and Mark's mother, Juliana—who'd been an accountant for ESP for more than a decade—met me and Greg at his house on Zuma Beach, a two-minute drive from mine.

After introductions, we sat down, and just as Bonnie had done weeks earlier, Mark began unloading information like a bursting dam.

"I don't know where to start. I talked to Sarah this morning," he said.

"I just found out from her that Keith is having women branded," he said. "She broke down crying on the phone and admitted that she was a member of this secret DOS group, and that she'd been branded. 'There are potentially dozens of other women who have been subjected to this as well,' she said.

"She says that when she was branded, a bunch of other women in her slave cell held her down on a table, naked, and they burned her in the pubic area with a searing hot cauterizing pen and no anesthetic. She witnessed the horror of seeing the others getting branded that day, too, and heard their screams."

Mark continued, "She was terrified to tell me about it, worried they'd release the collateral she'd given them if they found out she was speaking about it. 'Keith is involved with the group,' she said."

The first collateral the women in DOS usually gave were explicit, naked photos of themselves. After they joined and found out they had to give new, different collateral every month, they had to get creative. Future collateral could be about you or about members of your family, as long as each time it was something—a photo, information—that would be ruinous if revealed.

"Her most recent collateral, she told me, was something she'd made up. She'd run out of things to give, so Lauren told her to just make shit up."

Lauren, Nancy Salzman's daughter, was Sarah's best friend and had been maid of honor at her wedding to the actor Anthony ("Nippy") Ames, also a member of Nxivm (the coach who'd called me "Springsteen" in an early ESP class). She was also Sarah's master.

"Lauren videotaped her giving a false confession about her husband being an abusive father," Mark continued. "But she'd made it all up. She was crying, disgusted with herself that she'd done this and that Lauren would encourage her to do it. 'Women need to be humiliated in order to build character,' Lauren told her.

"She didn't even know what she'd been branded with. Lauren had told her it would be just a tiny tattoo, a symbol of female empowerment—not a two-inch-by-two-inch brand."

Mark and Sarah both figured out what the symbol was: a combination of Allison's and Keith's initials.

We were all silent for a moment, and I wished I could have stretched that moment into eternity. I didn't want to ask the next, inevitable question, but I had to.

"Does anyone know if India has been branded?"

Bonnie, sitting next to me, put her hand on my shoulder in support.

"From all indications," Mark said sadly, "the answer is yes."

If I'd thought my earlier conversation with Bonnie was a nightmare, now I felt like someone was pushing me through the gates of hell. I couldn't stop myself from imagining India's beautiful, ivory skin being burned and branded like an animal and feeling the searing pain on my own body. I felt helpless and hopeless, and worried now that I was too late to help her.

I looked over at Greg, who was so furious and repulsed by what he'd just heard, he was popping Nicorette gum like candy. Greg had a teenage daughter who'd been friends with Maya since kindergarten.

"If I was India's father," Greg said, "I would get on a plane and get over there, grab her, and tell her, 'That's enough, you're done and we're going home.' That's it. Case closed. Lucky for Keith she isn't my daughter, because he would be a dead man."

Lucky for Keith and unlucky for India, I thought. I wished one of India's fathers would do just as Greg described.

"Those ESP people, they're a nasty bunch," Juliana said in her thick South African brogue, shaking her head, "the whole lot of them."

"Bonnie, did they try to recruit you for DOS?" Greg asked.

"I think Keith tried to test me once for 'suggestibility' and 'subservience,' " she said. "He took me on a walk with him at three in the morning and told me to lick a puddle and then run into a tree. I did lick the puddle," she admits, "but refused the tree. So I guess I failed the test."

Lucky for Bonnie, I thought.

"He also tried to get me on an eight-hundred-calorie-a-day diet, and I basically said, fuck that. After that, there were no more walks at three a.m. Seems like he lost interest in me."

Even before Bonnie told him about DOS, Mark could see that something was off with some of the women around Keith. Several weeks earlier, in Albany, he'd confronted Keith about it.

"Whatever you're doing with these girls that's making them look like zombies and get so thin," he told Keith, "it's going to blow up in your face."

"I don't think so," Keith replied smugly. "Maybe other things, yes, but not that."

Mark had one more piece of important information from Sarah that might involve India.

"Sarah was supposed to fly back to Albany the first week of June to take part in a branding ceremony. But she broke down and said she couldn't do it; that the thought of subjecting others to the torture she'd endured was unbearable. She wants to get out and she needs help.

"I told her we'd help her, and the other girls," Mark said, looking at me.

I nodded.

"Of course we will," I answered. Then I realized with horror that India might indeed be involved with this upcoming branding. We'd booked her birthday trip a week ahead of time because she had important appointments in Albany that first week of June when her actual birthday was, she'd said.

Greg stood up and took the floor.

"Your job from now on, all of you," he said, "is to disrupt these people as much as you can. What you're describing here are crimes, for fuck's sake. Call the FBI! They can't just go around branding women on their crotches like that! It's not legal! Call the cops. You guys should be filming this, and you should go to the press! Expose these assholes! This is a criminal enterprise!" he said, pounding his hand on the tabletop.

"How do you know?" Mark asked. "How can you be sure of that?"

"It's obvious! Let me ask you a question, Bonnie: Did you ever get paid for all the work you did?"

"No. And I was on call twenty-four/seven, I worked nonstop."

"That's labor violations right there. Contact the Department of Labor, for starters. File a complaint! Your strategy from now on is to create as much disturbance as possible. Make it impossible for them to continue doing what they are doing. From the sound of it, these people are breaking the law all over the place. Don't stop until they are behind bars. You have to stop this!"

Bonnie had a thought. "Is it legal that he was using his girlfriend Pam's credit card after she died?"

"Using a dead person's Amex?" Greg asked. "That's a felony!"

"I had a feeling there was fishy business going on," said Juliana, putting her arm around her son, "but what could I do? Mark was never going to hear it from his mum—and where my boy went, I followed."

Greg listed all the potential crimes he thought ESP perpetrated just as standard operating procedure in Keith's totalitarian regime. Bonnie's and Mark's eyes popped out of their heads. They'd been living in Keith-land for so long and were so conditioned to normalize everything that they couldn't see all these crimes being committed. They also had no idea they'd been victims themselves—as I'd learned in Mexico, they'd been conditioned to think victims didn't exist.

"It's emotional terrorism, what Keith does," I said.

Greg scribbled down a name and number on a piece of paper and handed it to Mark.

"This is my contact at the FBI. Call him. Tell him everything you know. Ask for immunity for India—she's the victim here."

For the first time in two hours, Bonnie and Mark smiled.

Greg had given them—and me—hope that we were not powerless against the mighty cult intimidation machine and that we, in fact, had the upper hand. Mark and Bonnie talked about the shame they felt, that they'd been lured in—and for so long—by someone like Keith.

"No one signs up for a cult," Greg said. "No one knows it's a cult going in."

"I'm worried Keith will escape to Fiji," Mark said. "That's always been the official escape plan."

"Don't worry," Greg said, smiling. "You can get extradited from Fiji. No one's going to protect this creep from sex trafficking."

"Sex trafficking?" Mark asked.

"From what you've all described, I can almost guarantee you there's human trafficking going on," said Greg. "I can sniff it on Keith from miles away."

"How so?" I asked.

"Any time girls are transported across state lines—and, in this case, international borders—for the purposes of branding and/or sex, that's illegal."

We had our work cut out for us over the next two weeks: a birthday party, a branding ceremony, and a brainwashing intervention.

The way Greg talked, we were like the new Mod Squad about to infiltrate the criminal element in Albany, New York, by way of Malibu.

"All you guys together in this room is Keith's worst nightmare," Greg said, pointing at each of us one by one:

"The number two, the accountant, the mom, and the puddle licker. He won't know what hit him."

9

AN INTERVENTION PARTY

The days leading up to the intervention were nerve-racking.

Everybody who knew about it felt the pressure of the impending, pivotal moment to come. Even India, who didn't know about it, was plagued with crisis after crisis as we counted down the days before her arrival.

She texted from Albany asking me to set up a doctor's appointment for her for when she was in town so that she could get blood work done.

India: I haven't had a period in over a year. Do you think I need to go?

Me: Yes I do. I'll make an appt.

India: Mom could u also tell the doctor that i'm having a lot of hair loss.

On a different day, she texted to say she'd sprained her ankle and her car had been towed: "I feel like such a little kid right now. I've had a rough few days . . . I just feel like I want my mom. Haha."

Her last text to me was reminiscent of the precult India, allowing herself to be vulnerable and reach out to her mother in a time of need. That gave me much-needed hope, since most of the plans I'd put into place for the intervention party were collapsing one by one.

Relying on family, friends, and experts, I was trying to embed the intervention into her daylong birthday party so that, by the end of the day, she'd come to the painless realization that Keith was a sick phony. Then we'd all have cake and ice cream, and the nightmare would be over.

With that plan in mind, I'd arranged for Greg to attend so that he could ever so casually interrogate India about the cult over canapés and plant multiple seeds of doubt in her mind—sort of an "intervention-lite." Greg wasn't a close friend of India's and wouldn't have normally been on the invite list; I thought I was being clever by saying I wanted him to come over so that he and I could discuss his sex-trafficking efforts, but it totally backfired on me.

"Mom, that's not such a good fit: blending my birthday with a sex-trafficking theme!"

Bonnie and Mark were also supposed to attend and do some unobtrusive deprogramming on her during the party, until India bumped into them on the street the day before. She promptly notified the high-ranking grand pooh-bahs of Bonnie and Mark's whereabouts, which threw the two of them into a panic, and they canceled.

Mark had officially resigned from all his positions at Nxivm the week before—senior proctor, co-owner of the Vancouver and LA centers, founding member and high counsel of the Society of Protectors, and executive board member of ESP—and as far as we could tell, all hell broke loose at command central because of it.

He and Bonnie were in the process of moving into their new, secret "safe house" (I didn't even know where it was) and were doing everything possible to stay invisible and under ESP's radar. Because Mark was so high-ranking and knew so much, he and Bonnie were at risk of being followed, threatened, sued, and intimidated in any number of ways by Espians. It didn't occur to them that India, whom they considered a friend, would betray their location. Mark called to say that he and Bonnie wouldn't be attending the party.

With India unaware of the turmoil happening behind the scenes, she and the girls and I happily dove in to creating the birthday feast in the kitchen. India made a frittata, nut bread, roasted veggies, eggplant, insanely good meatballs, roasted corn soup, and berries with whipped cream. I made spinach ravioli with pesto and puttanesca sauces, chicken-avocado Caesar salad, and more.

The cooking was infused with a divine quality—all of us Oxenberg women together again, laughing and playing music in the kitchen as we chopped, baked, tasted, and sang. India introduced us to one of her favorite songs, "Crazy," by Cuban-American singer Kat Dahlia, and we danced around the kitchen to the beat.

It was a brief window of normalcy in a time that wasn't, so the happiness was tinged with sadness for me. I wished life could be only this: enjoying time with my girls and cooking with my darling India. But I was about to risk losing these moments forever with my impending agenda, and that reality hung over me. I had no idea what to expect after I, or any of us, confronted India about the cult. Would it change things between us? I cherished that morning, in case it would be the last one we'd all have like that.

But now three people who were to talk to India about the cult were not coming, and I agonized over whether I should say anything to her by myself or, as Rachel Bernstein suggested, wait until I had more time to prepare. I had my training from Rachel, but without Greg, Bonnie, or Mark there, I felt like I was flying by the seat of my pants. As it turned out, Mark drove over anyway to drop off some fried vegan pies for dessert and to confront India face-to-face.

"You endangered us!" he said to her out on the driveway.

They began arguing loudly, and it accelerated into a shouting match on the street before Mark drove off and India retreated to the garage for thirty minutes with her two phones in her trembling hands. Once again she called the Albany grand pooh-bahs with an updated report on the defectors.

Half the people in attendance—my friends; Bill; his other daughter, Carey—knew the purpose of the party and had been instructed to perform a variation on the intervention-lite theme: tell her how much you love and miss her, be curious about what she's doing, ask her a lot of questions (but nothing critical that would put her on the defensive), and remind her of happy times from before she joined ESP to elicit her precult self.

My friends who hadn't seen India in a while were slightly freaked out by how zealously gung-ho she was about the cult, and so was I. She'd invited several pretty, thin, young women who I didn't know—Emma and Ava, for example—and I wondered if they were involved. When I happened to go into my bedroom, just off the kitchen, to get something, I found India leaning onto my bed with one of the pretty partygoers I didn't know. She was typing on her laptop, filling out an enrollment form for the girl.

I froze, and my level of alarm hit a new all-time high. It was heartbreaking enough that India was a danger to herself. But recruiting innocent friends to be punished, tortured, and branded? She'd crossed a moral line. And because she was doing it in my home, I'd become unwittingly complicit.

My stomach turned, and as I walked back to the party, I made a decision: this couldn't wait six more months or one more month or even one more week. I had to take action *now*.

—

TWO DAYS LATER, after I'd wined, dined, watsu-ed, massaged, and filled India with the best chocolate we could find, I asked her to come to my bedroom for a talk.

Rachel had emphasized that the intervention had to be an elegant, subtle, and respectful process in which you challenge the cult member's declarative statements in a loving, kind, and curious way to engage their own critical thinking.

But that nonconfrontational approach went out the window the moment I saw India recruiting that girl. The sickening image of all her party guests being held down and branded by a madman made me *snap*.

I needed to be forthright with her, even if it meant I'd alienate her and she'd hate me for it.

We sat on the bed, and I cleared my throat:

"Darling, I know what's going on. You were recruiting slaves in my home. That's not okay with me."

India looked confused. She didn't even flinch when I used the word "slaves."

"What do you mean?" she asked. "I was only signing them up for V-week."

"Angel, even if you were, it's not okay with me that you sign anyone up for anything associated with Nxivm in my home."

I took a deep breath: "I know all about the master-slave group you're involved in, and the lifetime vow of obedience you've taken. I know about the starvation diet Keith put you on, and about the damaging collateral you give—and if you've given any about me, and that's what's keeping you there, I don't care about it.

"I know that Keith's having sex with all the women, and that you've drained your bank accounts.

"And . . . I know about the branding."

I couldn't bring myself to ask if she'd been branded, I just couldn't. But I was somehow able to ask about Keith.

"India, did you have sex with Keith? Are you having sex with him?"

"*No,* Mom."

I couldn't determine if she was telling me the truth or not. I continued:

"I have a moral obligation now to reach out to every person at your party and warn them what this is really about. I am going to have to expose you and the cult for what it is. I'm sorry, darling, but I can't let this go on any longer."

India looked hurt.

"Please don't do that, Mom. It will just make things worse for me."

I didn't realize then that if she didn't recruit her personal quota of slaves, she'd be severely punished. I kept going.

"Darling, you're brainwashed."

"I'm not brainwashed."

"Yes, you are."

"No! I'm not."

Surprisingly, we never raised our voices throughout the entire conversation.

"I don't believe in brainwashing, Mom."

"Well, don't take my word for it. Speak to a specialist. Will you?"

She shook her head. There went my idea to take her to Rachel, out the door.

"You're in a cult, India."

"No, I'm not. You may think that I am. But I'm not."

Even though every word we said to each other was saturated with love and tenderness, we were going in circles, getting no-where. As cult expert Rick Alan Ross would tell me soon after, I'd hit a brick wall, and there was no going through it or getting around it.

India looked sad, as if I were falsely accusing her of some heinous crime, and she couldn't understand why I was acting in this crazy way or why I'd want to hurt her.

"Darling, I'm doing this only because I love you, and I'm concerned for your safety."

My beautiful, gentle daughter looked at me with sympathy, sorry for my distress.

"I don't understand what you find so upsetting, Mom," she said.

We volleyed back and forth like this for an hour, until we both grew too tired and frustrated to talk anymore and went to bed, shaken up. I could only imagine how alone India must have felt that night, not understanding why her true champion, her mother, seemed so against her. Instead of sleeping in bed with one of her sisters—which is what she'd normally do—she curled up on the couch outside my bedroom door like a little kitten. A memory came to mind, one from when she was just four. The presidential election of 1996 was approaching and she asked me whom I planned to vote for.

"I haven't decided yet, Sweet Pea," I said.

"Mommy," she said, "vote for the one who freed the slaves!"

I went to bed with a glimmer of hope: maybe she hadn't been branded yet, since she didn't say she had been. And maybe because of our talk, she wouldn't get on the plane to Albany the next day. The alternatives kept me tossing and turning all night.

The next morning, before taking India to the doctor, I began frantically emailing and texting all the girls at the party and their mothers, if I knew them, to warn them.

Dear———,

I hope all is well with you. I wanted to reach out to you to warn

you about my beloved daughter India's involvement in a cult.

I was concerned that she might try to enroll your daughter.

I know that the two of them are close, and I would not want

to jeopardize that friendship. It breaks my heart to have to

intervene, but I feel that it is my moral responsibility as a

mother.

I am extremely concerned for her health and well-being.

If you would like more information, please feel free to reach

out to me. And if you feel your daughter could be at risk, I can

send you documentation of what the girls are actually being

recruited for.

Warmly,
Catherine Oxenberg

With Bonnie and Mark, I went over a list of who had been at
the party, and we tried to figure out if any of the girls were already
Nxivm members. One who fit the profile was Ava, a petite, slender
actress with pixie features and a sweet disposition, much like India.

Hi Ava,

this is Catherine India's mom. I'm asking u to please not fly to
Albany this week. U are participating in illegal activities that u

may not know about. The authorities are involved, and u would be at risk of being arrested—if u need more info please feel free to reach out to me and have your mom reach out to me as well. This is a dangerous cult.

An hour later, as we drove along the ocean's edge to India's doctor appointment, I couldn't face not knowing any longer.

It was a question I never imagined I would ask my daughter; a question no mother should ever have to ask. But I had no choice. Her life was in danger, and I needed to know.

"India . . . have you been *branded*?"

I clutched the steering wheel as I awaited her answer.

"Yes, Mom," she admitted hesitantly. "I've been branded. But why is that a problem? It was a good experience for me!"

My heart broke. I gripped the wheel tighter and forced my eyes to stay on the road.

"Darling," I said as calmly as I could, "if you can convince me how being branded can be a *good* experience, please, go ahead. I'm all ears."

India fell silent. She seemed confused again as she struggled to find an answer. Finally, she looked over at me with childlike sincerity through her weary eyes: "It's a good thing because . . . it's character building."

I wanted to scream. It was like someone had tampered with my child's brain or replaced her with an imposter. Her words and phrasing sounded preprogrammed, drilled into her head.

I answered slowly, reasonably.

"But India. The fact that you think mutilating your body permanently is character building is *proof* that you're brainwashed."

Again she looked bewildered and shook her head.

"India, do you even know what you have been branded with?"

"Yes, it's some Latin symbol."

"Are you trying to tell me that you mutilated your body, and you don't even know with what? They are the initials of Allison Mack and Keith Raniere! Angel, you're being manipulated by a psychopath."

"Mom, I'm not."

At the doctor's, I waited in a small examination room while my daughter underwent tests—a physical exam, bloodwork, and an ultrasound to address her amenorrhea.

I sat in that little room, crushed. Something occurred to me in that minute, as the doctor closed the door—something horrible that would fuel my fight to get India out of that cult no matter how difficult it would be or how long it would take.

What if that day in Albany, four years earlier, when I'd turned down Keith's request to do that roundtable together . . . what if that was the day, the moment, that the psychopath decided he was going to destroy my daughter and me? What if my refusing and humiliating him made him vow to steal her away and burn his initials onto her flawless body and mark her forever?

In other words, *What if this was my fault?*

I nearly fainted at the thought.

—

DRIVING AWAY FROM the doctor's, India was angry and dismissive. The doctor had done an ultrasound and told her that her uterine lining was as thin as a perimenopausal woman's and her ability to have children might be affected. After India had shared about her starvation diet, the doctor told her she needed serious psychiatric help.

India asked me to drop her off at a corner by her father's so she could get him to drive her to the airport that night for her flight to Albany.

I wanted to say something to scare her to her wits, to wake her up, to keep her from leaving the car, from getting on the plane.

"Darling, the authorities are going to move in to stop this organization any day now. What Keith and the others are doing is illegal. Please leave before it is too late!"

I didn't know this as a fact, but I said it anyway, hoping to get through to her. Mark had indeed contacted the FBI and begun a dialogue with them.

It didn't work, though. Nothing worked. The spell she was under was unbreakable. How could I rescue my daughter from hell if she didn't want to be rescued?

I'd lost her. I fucked up the intervention, and now I'd lost her. And I felt like I was losing my mind.

When India jumped out of my car that afternoon, it would be the last time I would see her lovely face for another nine months. What I suspected and worried would happen *did* happen: my haphazard intervention ripped open the gap between us even further. Now it was as wide as the Grand Canyon, and she and I were standing on opposite sides.

But in that devastating moment, there were two other truths I immediately knew as well.

First, I was going to do whatever it took to save my daughter from the clutches of this vicious cult and get her back.

Second, I was going to take down the cult.

I was not going to rest until I brought India home and put Keith Raniere behind bars.

10

EXPIANS AND EXODUS

Maybe India didn't want to be rescued from hell, but that didn't mean I'd stop trying.

When Hades, the god of the underworld, abducted the innocent Persephone and took her to hell, Persephone's mother, the Greek goddess Demeter, searched high and low for her. The mother's grief and despair were so profound that perpetual summer halted, winter was born, and all living things on earth began to die. But no matter what, Demeter refused to give up.

Hades never factored in the power of a mother's love. Well, neither did Keith Raniere.

I dropped off India at the corner and quickly drove off to my own secret sisterhood gathering. After the flurry of warning emails and texts I'd sent out that morning, Bonnie messaged me about meeting at a nearby café for an important, impromptu get-together. Our purpose: to prevent the next group of girls from being branded in Albany.

We rounded up Katie and two other Expian friends of ours: Sasha, who quit a year before me after a showdown with Gold Sash, and Heather, a recent defector who'd been Allison Mack's assistant. Heather is the person who had reached out to Bonnie and told her about DOS after she'd seen the starvation diet taped to Allison's fridge and caught sight of collateral and information on the Vow on Allison's computer. Bonnie hadn't mentioned her name as her source in our first face-to-face meeting in order to protect her identity.

What I didn't know until I arrived at the rendezvous was who else would be there, and that I'd essentially be leaving one intervention to participate in another.

Thirty minutes later, I was sitting across the table from two young women—Yasmine and Ava—who, until very recently, had been my daughter's "slaves." And for the umpteenth time during this strange and difficult journey, I felt like I was living in *The Twilight Zone*, with the chill factor escalating.

Yasmine was a striking, young Native American woman with an outspoken, ballsy, take-no-prisoners personality and the look of a rocker chick in her black leather jacket—not quite the type I'd expect to be taken captive by a cult at all. But I would soon find out that anyone was susceptible to the coercion of a cult, and the victims didn't fit the clichéd image of a gullible, naïve, pliable, weak-willed person—a common misperception. In fact, cults often "intentionally recruit 'valuable' people," says mental health counselor Steven Hassan, who has written several books on mind control. "They go after those who are intelligent, caring, and motivated. They want members who will work hard with little or no sleep."

"We were both told that DOS was a female empowerment group,"

Yasmine said. "It was pitched to us as an opportunity to be part of a women-only secret society, where we would receive free mentorship from a high-powered sisterhood [and it was free! An anomaly for anything Nxivm]. They said we'd be like ninja warrior women, but they wouldn't tell us any more about it until we gave them damaging collateral first—in order to protect the secrecy of the group."

It was yet *another* program pitched that would "change your life." How much life changing can one person endure?

Sitting next to Yasmine was Ava, whom I recognized as one of the pretty, slim guests at India's birthday party and one of the girls I'd texted that morning. She was a lovely blonde actress who'd recently moved from LA to Albany, at Keith's urging.

Yasmine, too, had left her career as a model-actress in LA and moved to Albany, she told us, after she'd taken one of those infamous walks with Keith and shared her dream of starting up an ethical T-shirt company.

"I already have equipment for that all set up," he told her as they strolled in the wee hours (*Doesn't Keith ever sleep?* I wondered), "and I've got the money for it. Let's do it together!" He touched her hands and talked to her a certain way, doing that deep-staring thing into the eyes that he does. (*Does he hypnotize them?* I asked myself.)

With one walk, he seemed to be able to steal away young girls' dreams.

India had career dreams of her own, too, when we started at ESP—it was the reason we had gone in the first place. She was going to have her own talk show or her own bakery company, and then suddenly she was running Keith's Rainbow school.

Bonnie had also put her acting career on hold and moved from

Hollywood to Albany. Even Pam, the heiress they put on ice, had aspirations until Keith convinced her she should be an Olympic runner, a friend of Pam's told me later. An Olympic runner? Pam had no running talent whatsoever, said the friend—she could barely jog a mile.

But he'd say and do anything to unplug you from the life you had and reattach you where it served his own needs, shaming you into thinking your own desires were superficial and that his mission was higher, more meaningful. Keith sucked the dreams out of people like a vampire. Everyone who walked in with one was talked out of it and rerouted to feed the bloodthirsty Vanguard machine.

Soon after Yasmine moved to Albany, she joined the sisterhood, with India as her "master." She endured seven months of disturbing rituals, which included "readiness drills," where you had to reply to your master's text within a minute or two or someone else in the group would get punished. These drills could go on all night, leading the women to get seriously sleep-deprived. They also had to give new collateral every month, and keep closely to their starvation diets.

As Yasmine spoke, I realized that this explained why India had always been glued to her phone during any time we spent together over the past year.

Yasmine had left DOS and ESP a few days ago after Allison— her "grandmaster"—had given her the assignment to seduce Keith. Allison took the job of pimping for Keith very seriously, and even gave herself appropriate titles for the position—"the Madam," "Madam Mack," or "Pimp Mack."

"This is a sexual, transactional, spiritual way of growing—not romantic," Allison explained to Yasmine. "Society doesn't understand.

He's helping you work on your body issues. There are certain things he can teach you only by being intimate with you. And, Yasmine, it will heal your sexual abuse. It's a privilege: you're the chosen one."

Allison knew very well that Keith was having sex with dozens of women on rotation, since she was often the one sending the women to him. As Bonnie said, it was one of the ways she earned Keith's approval. At the same time, I would hear from many slaves that Allison was also very territorial about Keith and felt threatened and jealous of each woman she sent to have sex with him—which resulted in her being very punitive and sadistic as a master.

Keith had Allison wrapped around his little finger. He'd approve of her, and then he'd shun her—for no reason. It was classic narcissistic behavior—sucker her in and then ignore her; give her love and then take it away.

One of the slaves told me later that when Keith was shunning Allison, she'd sit in a chair by the front window of her house all day, watching and waiting for Keith to walk by so she could catch a glimpse of him.

When Allison gave Yasmine the seduce-Keith assignment, she added two instructions:

"Make sure you let him take photos of you naked afterward, to prove you've completed this assignment, and send them to your master," she told her. And then she added, magnanimously, that she granted Yasmine permission to enjoy it.

We all retched at that last one. How kind of her to give this beautiful woman permission to enjoy sex with a disgusting old lecher.

As uncomfortable as it was for all of us, especially me, to hear this, it was even more trying for Yasmine to reveal it. She'd never admitted any of this to anyone, let alone to the mother of a girl who had enlisted her as a slave. She and I were beyond uneasy.

"I asked India if she was okay with this assignment," Yasmine continued, "and she said, 'Look, I freaked out when I got it, too. I thought, *Wow, is that what this is all about?* But I ended up finding it an important life lesson.'"

I shook my head, struggling to imagine these words coming out of India's mouth. Could this girl have misunderstood India? Could she have misheard her? Could Yasmine's memory be faulty? Had India lied to me when she said she hadn't had sex with Keith? Sadly, it seemed so.

I also wondered why these girls were able to wake up from Keith's spell, yet India was not. That's when I realized she'd been subjected to far more indoctrination than they had. These were fresh recruits from within the year, whereas my daughter had been under the cult's mind control for six years now! I learned later from a defector that India had been mind fucked and EM-ed more and worse than most of the others.

Keith was getting greedy and sloppy as his pathology advanced, I guessed. He was bringing girls into DOS before they were fully indoctrinated, so they were waking up faster. His carelessness and lust could lead to his undoing, I predicted.

Yasmine continued:

"I was afraid to say no because she had my collateral, but I told her I felt uncomfortable about the assignment. She told me I was freaking out because of my 'intimacy issues.'

"That's when I thought, *This is bullshit! This is not what I signed up for!* Plus, I was broke because I was still waiting for Keith to start the T-shirt business with me. I decided to bail. I mean, I love your daughter, Catherine, but . . . I'm just not into this stuff. It's too weird."

Again I shook my head. The India I knew wasn't into this stuff, either. *What have they done to her?*

Up until the day before, Ava had been Yasmine's slave—Yasmine had recruited her. But on a hike together that morning, Yasmine told Ava that she'd arranged with India that India would inherit her as her slave because Yasmine wasn't going back to Albany. She intended to "quietly get out and save myself" when my text popped up on Ava's phone as they were walking, and they read it together.

"It was too much of a coincidence," said Yasmine, "and I thought if Catherine could drop a bombshell like that, so could I—so *should* I. I told her, 'I want you to know what this is really about. This is about recruiting sex partners for Keith. I wasn't going to tell you this, but I felt I owed it to you as a friend.' "

Sitting next to Yasmine, Ava looked fragile and panic-stricken.

Keith had promised he'd start a new business with her, too. His "mentoring" so far had consisted of a lot of walks and crude sexual jokes that seemed aimed to groom her, she now sees. But so far, no business venture had panned out. Her next step, she was told, was to take part in the secret ceremony the following week.

She was scheduled to leave on the red-eye to Albany that night with India, and now she was quaking at the thought.

I checked the time on my phone: three o'clock. Time was ticking away on two critical matters: first, we had to prevent India, Ava, and that other slave who'd been at the birthday party, Emma, from getting on that flight.

Second, we had to try to stop the branding from happening.

I picked up the pace. Ava was already scared to death, but I was going to scare her more—whatever it took to stop this insanity. Saving a few girls from that barbaric ritual was a start.

"Are you aware, Ava, that if you go back there, you will be held down naked and burned, and even if you yell for it to stop, no one is going to listen?"

Ava looked like a rabbit caught in a car's headlights.

"I don't want to go, I don't want to be branded," she said, "but I'm terrified of what will happen if I don't. What if they punish India? I don't want to hurt or disappoint her!"

Punishment could be starvation, cold showers, running ten miles at three in the morning, getting whacked with a paddle, or being locked in a cage, I would find out later from other slaves.

"I don't know what to do. I don't know how to get out of it! What if they release my collateral? I'd be mortified! It would destroy my career!"

"So what?" I said to Ava. "You have to risk it. Listen to me! Staying for that reason is not worth it. You'll be giving away your entire self and your *life*!" I wanted to shake her. In a very real way, I was talking to India in that moment.

"Are you aware that Keith is the leader of DOS?" I asked.

They both shook their heads.

This information was only known by the top tier of DOS, because Keith was their master. Between seven and twelve DOS slaves directly reported to Keith, including Allison and Lauren.

"We were never told he was a part of it," Yasmine continued. "We don't even know who the other members of DOS are. You don't find that out until after you're branded and have that bond with your sister slaves."

Sister slaves. *This is a nightmare.* Just then, we were interrupted by a text from India. After Ava got my note that morning, she forwarded it to India in confusion and panic. I'm sure by now it had reached the cult's upper hierarchy, including Vanguard himself.

India: Please stop, you are scaring my friends.

Me: They don't want to come back with you, but they're afraid to tell you. Is that the kind of leadership you want to represent? One where people are afraid to tell you the truth and where you lie to them? Did you tell them the truth about DOS?

India: Mom, no one is being forced to do anything against their will.

But Ava was sitting in front of us, petrified and afraid to go back. The group looked at Ava, waiting to see what she'd do, hoping and willing her to do the right thing. Ava wasn't bold and ballsy like Yasmine, but I think the collective power of the women gathered around her that afternoon gave her the strength to find her voice. She was surrounded by women in their twenties, thirties, forties, and fifties—a multigenerational, communal force of female energy supporting her and encouraging her to speak up.

This was the true kind of sisterhood.

Ava took a deep breath, took out her iPhone, and began typing.

"I canceled my airline ticket," she said to us, a few minutes later, "and India's as well. We were on the same reservation because she asked me to book her ticket. Thank you, all of you, for keeping me from getting on that plane. Now I'll text India to tell her I'm not going with her."

India: Is my ticket canceled, too, or just yours?

Ava: Just mine.

Ava was afraid to tell her the whole truth. India didn't express any anger at Ava that we could see, even though she knew she'd just lost a slave and was probably now stranded. She was more likely focused on the fact that she was about to fail in two assignments: get back to Albany and bring her new recruit back with her. Showing anger toward others was rare for India. (The yelling match with Mark on her birthday was unprecedented.) Even her telling me to "please stop" was high voltage for my daughter, angerwise. Plus, she was probably in shock from what had transpired over the last twenty-four hours. She'd been living in a bubble, a weird, alternate reality, and both her doctor and I had just punctured it.

It would be a waiting game until the next morning before we knew. But even if she did return to Albany at least we'd stopped one woman from a horrible fate on the branding table.

Our next attempt was with Yasmine's best friend, Emma. Yasmine had tried to bring her to our clandestine meeting but she'd refused.

"I don't know what else to do to stop her from going," the young woman said sadly. "I told her about my assignment with Keith, and she knows Catherine's been warning everyone, but she made up her mind to go. She said she's trusting in her angels to lead her in the right direction."

At that, we were all silent for a moment.

"Maybe *we* can be her angels," I said.

Yasmine smiled and nodded, and then picked up her phone:

Yasmine: My intuition is going off, worried about u going to Albany. Are you sure you can trust your angels on this one?

Emma: Nothing can happen to me.

Yasmine: Okay, but let me know that you're OK, babe. Please call me or text me if you need anything. If you don't feel safe, let me know, and we can figure out how to get you somewhere safe. I love you very much, and I'm here for you. Please don't do anything you'll regret.

For the next few hours, we huddled on the terrace strategizing about how to stop the upcoming ceremonies and save more unsuspecting women. We discovered there were at least *two* ceremonies scheduled for the first week of June: the one that Sarah Edmondson was supposed to attend and the one for Ava's cell of slaves, of which India was master.

"The more information we can get," I told the team, "the more likely we can convince state police and the FBI to make a raid. Please, girls, if you have any more information . . ."

But the slaves were never given dates and locations in advance for secrecy purposes. "We were just given a deadline to be back in Albany by May 31," said Ava. "Tomorrow."

—

LITTLE DID WE know that as we plotted in our LA café, Sarah Edmondson was walking into an FBI office in Albany that day, about to pull down her trousers and show the agents the initials of Keith Raniere and Allison Mack burned on her body.

Sarah had recently been promoted to green sash and was one of the biggest recruiters in the company. When she first heard about DOS, she thought it sounded interesting, she told me a few days later on the phone. There was no mention of masters or slaves when she took her lifetime vow of obedience at the beginning. "The pitch was 'join a badass bitch boot camp!'" said Sarah. But the minute she gave Lauren her first collateral, she regretted it. And the deeper into it she got, the darker and more punitive it became—with girls beating subordinates when they failed to recruit new girls or when they gained five pounds or when they didn't answer their phone in sixty seconds.

Before she was branded that March, Sarah was told she'd be given a tiny tattoo: "a symbol of our sisterhood," she said.

She arrived at Lauren's house, was blindfolded and told to take her clothes off, and then was left to wait in the bedroom.

She was brought downstairs and told to sit down and take off her blindfold, whereupon she realized she was sitting in a semicircle in Lauren's living room with a group of women—all naked—who she knew from Nxivm. They were all part of Lauren's slave cell and were women Sarah had done business with, so the situation was more than a little awkward. Sarah noticed a camera mounted on the mantle piece: *Someone's filming this for kicks*, she thought.

They were all instructed to put their clothes back on, and, with their eyes covered, were driven to an unknown destination. But even with the blindfold on, Sarah could peek out the bottom and recognized Allison's rug from her townhouse once they got to the location.

"We were taken into a room with only a massage table and told to take off our clothes again and remove our blindfolds."

Of all the women who'd been held down and branded, Sarah might have been the only one who didn't scream.

"I disassociated," she recalled. "It was more painful than childbirth, but I didn't utter a single sound. I just wept quietly and thought of my baby boy the entire time."

Sarah's branding took over thirty-five minutes. Shortly after they were done with her, the putative branding doctor—Dr. Danielle Roberts, a doctor of osteopathy—moved her aside, and they hauled the next victim onto the table. Some of the women wore surgical masks to absorb the scent of burning flesh. For each branding, it took four women to hold down the burn victim. Because this was no tattoo—it was an angry, gaping two-inch-by-two-inch monstrosity.

As Sarah stood to the side, bleeding, Lauren shoved her iPhone into Sarah's hands.

"Film it," she ordered. Sarah held the phone with her shaking hands and did as her master said. That's when she saw a text come through on Lauren's phone from "KAR", asking, "How are the girls doing?" Later, she found out that Keith's initials were KAR: Keith Allen Raniere.

Like Yasmine and Ava, Sarah was a second-tier slave and had no idea up until that moment that Keith was behind DOS. Sometime after the ceremony, she confronted her best friend/maid of honor/master Lauren, who admitted that Keith was involved with DOS.

So much for a female empowerment group, Sarah thought. Then, when she discovered it was Keith's and Allison's initials on her crotch, she went ballistic. What the hell was she supposed to tell her husband? That she was now the property of another man? And woman?

But it wasn't until just a few days before speaking to me that Sarah's husband, Nippy, saw the brand.

She'd been avoiding him since the March ceremony, finding ways to create distance between them both physically and emotionally so that she wouldn't be naked in front of him—something I'm sure Keith relished. He liked to introduce obstacles between intimate partners so that their primary loyalty would always be to him. It gave him supreme power.

After Sarah finally showed Nippy the brand, she told him all about DOS—including that she'd made a false confession on film at Lauren's insistence, accusing him of being an abusive father.

Sarah already felt compromised and trapped because they had so much collateral on her, so she did it. She felt as if she were on a runaway train that kept picking up speed, and she didn't know how to get off.

"How could I have done that, Catherine?" she asked me. "And how could Lauren, someone I trusted and loved, direct me to do that?"

They'd flown into Albany separately. Unbeknownst to Nippy, Sarah's original mission in Albany was to attend a branding ceremony. But after she came clean with him, she and Nippy hatched a plan of defection. Sarah hopped on a train to Toronto, telling Lauren she had to visit an ailing relative in the hospital. Her husband, meanwhile, confronted Lauren in person at the office.

"You branded my wife's pussy? What the fuck is wrong with you?!!!"

Lauren tried to justify it and convince Nippy of the brand's importance, but Nippy wasn't having it.

"Don't you fucking try to EM your way out of this one!" he yelled at her. "You're fucking crazy!"

Before she left Albany, Sarah went to Victim Services and made that trip to the FBI office at Mark's prompting. He'd already called several branches of the FBI and state police investigators but was getting the runaround. He was told that Keith and his sordid cult had been under investigation over the years, but authorities hadn't been able to pin anything on them.

"Be careful who you tell you went to the authorities," one law enforcement official told Mark. "These are very dangerous people."

Sarah was convinced that once the agents saw her brand, they'd be outraged and galvanized into action. But the same door was slammed in her face, too.

"We'll look into it. But, lady, from what you're telling me, all the women involved are consenting adults," she was told, "So unless there are any underage girls involved, we can't do anything."

There *had* been valid accusations from several underage girls, but as I would find out later when I dove into a deep investigation of Keith and Nxivm, he was never held accountable.

—

THE NEXT MORNING, Bill called to say that India had gotten on the plane the night before and was probably landing in Albany at that very moment. My heart did more than sink—it plummeted. Somehow, she'd managed to finagle her way onto the plane.

After Bill's call came a text from Yasmine: "I sent a message to India last night officially quitting the Vow. I was strong and firm and expressed my disgust and desire to no longer be associated."

What happened next came from various sources.

Before Emma left town, she was confused and scared, but, "she was trying to prove something to herself for some reason," her ex-boyfriend told Yasmine. "She wanted to see for herself."

And did she ever. When she arrived in Albany that morning, Emma was picked up at the airport and brought to a cult member's home, where a bunch of high-ranking DOS and Espian women surrounded her for a cult pep talk. It was like a scene out of *Rosemary's Baby*.

"You must remain a woman of your word," they chanted, closing in on her. "You made a commitment to go through with the ritual, and you must keep your word. Or do you choose to be weak willed and back out? How could you let your master be punished for your own weakness?"

At some point, Emma was able to call her ex-boyfriend. She was crying and begging him to check up on her over the next few days—and if he didn't hear from her, to call 911.

Me: Yasmine, let Emma know we have Nippy standing by to help if she wants to escape.

Bonnie: Emma getting into a car and going to safe house now. She is figuring out a flight home. Apparently, she wanted to collect more data and investigate what is going on. But she's not safe until she is on a plane. Lauren could still do an EM on her and change her mind.

Me: Yes, that's because Lauren is a fricking sadist getting a lamb ready for slaughter.

Yasmine: I want to stop that from happening. She's not equipped to deal with the head fuck. Wow, people basically pay to get themselves brainwashed! I feel so silly thinking this was a women's empowerment group.

(Yasmine had since told us that before she left Albany, she'd found a way to copy all her slave cell's collateral to protect herself in case anyone threatened to release hers in the future.)

Next, I got a call from Sarah saying that she'd heard through the cult grapevine that because of all the shit-disturbance we'd caused, the branding session she was to attend had been canceled, as were the others.

I sent out a text to the team: "*Good News!!!* Apparently, all the ESP cronies found out about my intervention, and they got scared and stopped the ritual! So no more girls have been branded!! Yeah!!!!!"

It was good news, but I needed to make more happen, faster.

From the moment India had landed back in Albany, I'd gone into a crazed outreach frenzy, and called anyone and everyone under the sun who might be of help.

One man was Frank Parlato, Keith's former publicist from many years ago. In 2007, he'd been hired by political consultant Roger Stone—yes, *that* Roger Stone—to clean up Nxivm's image. (Stone had worked at Nxivm for a short stint. His advice to Keith? "If you don't want to come across as a cult, then don't act like one.") Today Parlato is a businessman, journalist, and creator of the *FrankReport*, a blog dedicated to exposing Keith Raniere and the criminal activities of the cult.

"If Clare Bronfman had never come after me with false, made-up charges, there wouldn't be a *FrankReport*," he would later tell me. "I will continue to do what Keith hired me to do as his publicist—tell the truth about Nxivm."

I pulled up his blog and began reading it voraciously, one post after the other.

I remember hearing his name whispered when I was taking ESP classes. The cult vilified Parlato as a purveyor of vile misinformation with a vendetta against Keith, and members were instructed not to read his blog. I could see why.

One post contained a video of Keith saying, "I've had people killed because of my beliefs, and for their beliefs, and because of things that I've said."

Another detailed allegation was that Keith had raped underage girls. Kristin Keeffe, one of Keith's ex-girlfriends, also revealed a kidnapping plot hatched by Keith and a high-ranking Espian in which they were going to lure Keith's ex-girlfriend Toni Natalie and three other defectors to Mexico for a phony anticult rally, and then have them kidnapped and thrown into a Mexican prison.

"Keith intended these women serious, serious emotional and

physical harm," said Kristin, in an email sent to Nxivm's executive board and lawyers.

But why was only the *FrankReport* writing about all this?

With just a little research, I found my answer online: Nxivm vigorously sued any and every publication that had written a negative word about it, so that by now, most investigative journalists were afraid to report on the group. They'd been silenced for fear of legal retribution.

Thanks to the limitless Bronfman billions, Nxivm had sued mainstream media publications such as *Vanity Fair* and had even gotten a respected reporter from the *Albany Times Union*, James Odato, put on leave—all because they dared to write the truth.

Almost everybody had been silenced. Except for Frank Parlato.

Oh, they'd gone after Frank, too—with accusations that led to two indictments and nineteen felony counts against him.

But Frank didn't let that stop him. He kept on writing.

The more I read about Nxivm on the *FrankReport*, the more shocked I was at what I read and how many famous names were linked to it—including Doug Rutnik, the father of New York senator Kirsten Gillibrand, as well as Sir Richard Branson and even the Dalai Lama.

I decided I was going to investigate all of it—the criminal stories, the celebrity links, the lawsuits—everything.

But first I wanted Frank's help.

I noticed he hadn't posted in a while, and I didn't see anything on his site about branding or DOS.

I cold-called him and got him on the phone. After introducing myself, I explained my background with the cult and about India.

"Mr. Parlato, are you aware that Nxivm has a secret master-slave sex society, and women are being tortured and branded?"

The pause was so long, I thought we'd been disconnected.

"No," he said carefully. "I wasn't aware of that."

Later, he told me that he thought I was one of two things: a crazy mom or a plant by the cult trying to feed him false evidence to open him up to more lawsuits. Understandably, he was suspicious and cautious, and asked me if anyone could corroborate what I was telling him. I told him I had a list of names, and he began his own investigation.

As soon as he realized that my claims were accurate, Frank went on a writing rampage about the cult that hasn't stopped churning out over a thousand blogs about the cult up to this day.

His first of many articles about DOS hit the internet on June 5, 2017, and it caused an uproar in Albany and in the ESP community:

PART 1: BRANDED SLAVES AND MASTER RANIERE;
SOURCES: HUMAN BRANDING PART OF RANIERE-
INSPIRED WOMEN'S GROUP

I wasn't sure if India saw it, but other cult members surely did. They began leaving Nxivm in droves that week, with hundreds of defections in the first few days after the article posted. So many fled, terrified, that the LA and Vancouver centers collapsed.

I saw it as a freeing of the slaves. An exodus.

Two days after the article posted was India's twenty-sixth birthday, on June 7. If she had any idea that I was partly behind the defections, she didn't let on yet:

Me: Darling I am wishing you a very happy birthday. I love you and miss you. ❤

India: Thank you. No call?

Me: Yes call—when are u free?

India: I'll let you know. 👍

Me: 👍

But she never did. After that last text, I wouldn't get another for months.

That night, I wrote an entry in my journal to the higher powers that might be. Like Demeter, I was preoccupied with my grief, but still refused to give up. In fact, I was planning on going deeper into hell to get her.

June 7

God, guide my pen—today is my daughter's birthday, and I am desolate.

I feel dissociative, I feel incapable of taking care of other tasks, I have so much fear, I am panic stricken, I can't take my mind off what is happening, I am consumed, I feel obsessive.

I know I need to let go, and I don't know how.

I need help, I feel like a zombie. I don't know what is proactive behavior, and what is codependent and intrusive, and meddling.

I don't want to be passive. Talking about the situation relieves my anxiety, but it is exhausting me. My head feels like it is spinning, I woke up in a full-blown anxiety attack, I am having a hard time breathing. I want guidance, but all the tension I feel might be preventing that guidance from filtering in. Please, help me take care of the other things in my life.

I see India burdened and alternatively focused, and right now I am infected by the same behavior. I am no better off.

There is a mass defection happening within the ranks at ESP.

All proctors have resigned except for one. There is dissention within the ranks. I've heard 100 defectors so far and more daily. The Vancouver center collapsed, LA too. ESP is shrinking. They want to pin it on a single troublemaker at a time, blaming Sarah, Mark, Bonnie, and me because they can't see that it is their behavior that is causing this to happen. In a way, it is a good thing that KR crossed the line & became reckless, as otherwise people might have been enslaved for life.

This branding may be what brings the whole organization down.

I ask for peace and faith today.

I am afraid for my child.

I have been able to successfully save other women from joining and getting mutilated, but I could not save my own child. That is the crux of my pain—my complete powerlessness over her and my inability to help her see the light.

And the fact that I was unable to protect her from harm.

And my naiveté at how easy it is to be brainwashed, the power of undue influence and mind control and coercion.

Never again will I be part of a large-group awareness training or anything that remotely resembles a cult. Nor will I expose my children to these organizations.

No more gurus, or anyone who poses as a godlike figure.

Forgive me, God, forgive me for being so blind. Forgive me for misplacing my devotion, forgive me for exposing my children to potential harm.

I am innocent, I am good, and I pray that any damage I have incurred can be reversed.

11

GANGSTA MOMS

I prayed and prayed, but still I spiraled into an abyss of despair.

Hundreds were leaving the cult, but not my India—and now she was refusing to talk to me, too. Once again I felt completely powerless to penetrate the cult's ironclad indoctrination of my daughter. All I could do was double my frenzied efforts to find help.

In addition to reaching out to Frank Parlato, I called the FBI again. They didn't return my calls.

I got in touch with a friend who owned a private plane and asked if we could whisk India away to a deserted island with no cell phone reception and have her forcibly deprogrammed. "Isn't that illegal?" my friend asked.

I checked with two top security firms to ask if they could kidnap India and bring her home. The days of forced cult extractions and interventions were over, I was told. A cult member had recently sued his parents for $4 million for kidnapping him from a cult—and won.

The only people I didn't try were the US Special Forces and the

Mafia, but, believe me, I asked everyone I knew if they had a Guido in their back pocket just in case.

My powerlessness was made all the worse by the guilt and unanswered questions that began haunting me at night when I desperately needed sleep to keep sane and remain a functioning mom to Grace, Maya, and Celeste through this nightmare.

Why had this happened to India? I wanted to know.

Had she inherited a gene that predisposed her to brainwashing? Did this happen because I took her to Deepak Chopra's ashram when she was a baby? Should I not have told her about the self-help adventures of my past? Was her entrapment my fault because of what I did to Keith or because I took her to ESP in the first place? Why, why, why?

I spent days and nights pondering and agonizing over those questions and blaming myself.

Then I remembered someone who might have the answers.

Ranking right up there with Frank was one other man just as vilified by Keith Raniere and considered an archenemy by all Espians: Rick Alan Ross.

Rick has been called a "cult deprogrammer" or cult intervention specialist—some say he is a "cult buster." He is the founder of the nonprofit Cult Education Institute and online educational database. In the 1980s, he deprogrammed two former members of the Branch Davidians religious cult, long before the 1993 siege in Waco, Texas. More recently, he'd had success deprogramming Espians. As with Frank, the Espians had all been ordered not to pay attention to anything Rick said—which was one big reason why I knew I had to call him. If Keith said someone was lying, you could be sure he or she was a truth teller.

Keith, backed by the Nxivm clan, tried for fourteen years in federal court to sue Rick into oblivion. He claimed Rick had defamed the cult by posting online the reports by a psychologist and a psychiatrist who were critical of Nxivm's programs and practices. The lawsuit also claimed that the doctors' reports somehow violated copyright and trade secret laws because they were largely based on the study notes of an ESP defector (whom the cult also sued).

Like Frank, Rick never gave up and wouldn't be silenced. The lawsuit against Ross was finally dismissed in January 2017.

I tracked Rick down—he was based in New Jersey—and called him. He gave me the assurances, information, and wake-up call I needed.

"Catherine, it's meaningless to investigate why certain people are suggestible; in fact, it is a form of victim shaming," he explained. "Anyone and everyone can potentially be susceptible. It is a fallacy to believe that you can't fall prey to this. There are successful, extremely well-educated, sophisticated people in this cult. We need to stop talking about who does and doesn't get brainwashed, and focus on what the groups did to ensnare them.

"Cult leaders and the people that run the cult use deception and misrepresent their motivation and goals. Through confession, they extract secrets about you, they expose your vulnerabilities, and everyone has them. Their ulterior goal is to exploit you."

"But . . . do you think I created a susceptibility in India," I asked him, "because I exposed her to ashrams and gurus since she was little? We have alcoholics in my family. I was bulimic. Could there be a genetic link—"

Rick cut me off. "Stop right there," he said sharply. "Stop blaming yourself. Destructive cults are well-oiled machines. Your daughter never stood a chance. It doesn't mean she's weak, defective, malleable, or stupid. The only common denominator so far seems to be people who are 'in transition' in their lives."

I thought about India's bakery and TV job that fell through a week before our first class began, and her having left school a few months before that.

"Everything that cults do is calculated," he said. "It's all a trap."

When I described my intervention attempt, Rick wasn't surprised it nose-dived.

"Members of Nxivm are some of the hardest cult members to deprogram because of all the implanted phobias."

"Rick, India doesn't believe she's brainwashed."

"No one who's brainwashed thinks they are," he said. "The term 'brainwashing' is really describing a synthesis of coercive persuasion and influence techniques used to gain undue influence over people. The way you recognize undue influence is you will see people acting against their own best interest but consistently acting in the best interest of a person who has undue influence over them."

"That's exactly what I see happening with my daughter. Nothing she's made to do is in her best interest, only Keith's." I hung up, feeling mortified that I had blundered the intervention so badly, but also relieved because this expert was confident that India was indeed a victim of brainwashing, and that her susceptibility wasn't my fault. I would turn to Rick countless times over the next months whenever I needed an expert's advice and opinion, or to try to understand my daughter's thoughts, feelings, and challenges.

I was still at a loss, though, over what to try next to help her.

In late June, I went to Greg's to tell him about the hundreds of defections from the cult and that India was still digging in her heels.

"I pray she won't be the last woman standing," I told him.

I also updated him that Mark and Sarah had filed a report with the senior investigator at the NY State Police and that Sarah and several victims had filed complaints with the Department of Health.

Greg, in turn, gave me some updates of his own.

He described more details about his sex-trafficking work and the neglected young women he'd seen on the street. He wanted to dedicate his life to helping these victims because no one else did.

One woman Greg had recently rescued was Stella, a former straight-A student and cheerleader who'd been kidnapped by a sex-trafficking ring, chained to a bed, shot up with speedballs and heroin for weeks, and then sent out on the streets to hook.

The ringleader was nicknamed "the Murderer."

"How could this be happening in our own backyard?" I asked, but we both knew the answer to that. It happened the same way a sex-slave cult happened in our own backyard: we had a broken system that protected the perpetrators and neglected the victims.

"How did you even find these girls, Greg?"

"Their mothers reached out to me."

Never underestimate the power of a mother's love, I thought. Perhaps it was the pain of being powerless to help my own daughter. Or maybe it was because these girls actually *wanted* to be rescued, unlike India.

Whatever it was, I knew I needed to help someone, somewhere, and that helping these girls might be the very balm my broken heart needed.

"Do you need help?" I asked.

I hadn't even been clear on the definition of "sex trafficking" when Greg mentioned it at our meeting weeks earlier with Mark and Bonnie. But soon after, I'd looked it up on the website of the US Department of Homeland Security to clarify the official description: "Human trafficking," it read, "is modern-day slavery and involves the use of force, fraud, or coercion to obtain some type of labor or commercial sex act."

Greg was certain that Keith's master-slave operation amounted to sex trafficking—which was all the more reason why I wanted to help with his work.

My nonprofit foundation had just become an active 501(c)(3), I told Greg, and I would now expand my mission from research to actively protecting women from various forms of subjugation, exploitation, and abuse—including victims of sex trafficking.

Within days, inspired by Greg's mission, I'd conceived of another project that would expose this alarming crisis—a docuseries about domestic sex trafficking—*Gangsta Moms*—that followed mothers who rescued their daughters off the street.

"Gangsta Moms?!" Celeste asked quizzically over breakfast one morning.

"Mom, you seriously can't call it that," Maya said. "That title is *super lame!*"

"I promise, it's just a working title," I said.

"Good. Because this is the first thing you've done that I'm really proud of," she said. "That *Sexology* stuff was embarrassing!"

Callum came on board as director and cowriter after Greg got a call about another young woman who needed to be rescued, and we got to work.

Twenty-three-year-old Nina had become entangled in a dark, seedy, drug-infested, sex-trafficking underworld in Myrtle Beach, South Carolina. Nina was a witness in a lawsuit against a bunch of corrupt policemen who'd been feeding her heroin in exchange for sexual favors. Her boyfriend, a criminal wanted by the law, had been holding her hostage in a hotel room and her mother feared he might be pimping her out. Meanwhile, the corrupt cops were searching for her—they'd have liked nothing more than for Nina to "accidentally" overdose before the day she was supposed to testify.

As I waited anxiously in LA, our undercover team in Myrtle Beach—which included an ex-marine-turned-private eye—rescued Nina and put her on a plane to San Antonio, Texas. Over the phone, I coordinated for her to be picked up and taken to Greg's Soba rehab facility to receive treatment for her drug addiction.

When Nina was pulled from her abusers and landed safely in Texas, I felt like we'd just freed India from the clutches of Nxivm.

Every daughter we helped was like helping my own.

—

WORKING ON THE series threw me into the world of drug dealers, vice squads, drug cartels, bail bondsmen, Russian and Albanian mobsters, and sex workers. I spent the summer of 2017 alternating between two dark worlds: the gangster-street-sex-trafficking world and Keith's deviant cult. The scary thing was, they weren't so different.

At home, my living room became like a war room.

I'd vowed to investigate everything I could about Nxivm, and that's what I began to do. I researched early in the morning before the kids woke up and late into the night after they'd gone to bed: reading, writing, and organizing the information into hundreds of color-coded, cross-referenced folders.

During the day, I was the go-to place for new cult defectors, foundation donors, and *Gangsta Mom* meetings, with a phone that didn't stop ringing.

The *FrankReport* and Rick Alan Ross's Cult Education Institute were treasure troves of information, as I dug up past news articles and testimonies about Keith from five, ten, twenty years earlier.

I started with the basics: What the heck was "Nxivm"? Just a bit of research brought up the word "nexum"—an ancient Roman contract that meant "debt bondage" or "debt control"—in which a debtor pledged themselves as collateral if they defaulted on a loan. If they defaulted, the person would effectively act as a "slave" to the person they owed until they paid off their debt. Keith had picked the name Nxivm back in 2003. I wondered, did this mean that this had been his plan all along?

I moved on to Keith Raniere's bio. It didn't take long to pretty much debunk everything he'd ever said about himself regarding his IQ; his education; his childhood talents in piano, reading, math, and judo, and that he was speaking in full sentences by the age of one; his listing in *The Guinness Book of World Records*; his "original" business ideas—the list went on. Most of his claims, I found, were either baseless, greatly exaggerated, or bald-faced lies.

For example, his genius IQ we were told about at the pitch for ESP was the result of an unmonitored, untimed, obscure take-home

IQ test from 1988 called the Mega Test—administered by a society that he himself would later control. Members of his harem have since admitted to writing the test for him and called it "The Project."

No records or proof seems to exist for his claims that he was an East Coast judo champion at age eleven or had tied the record for New York's fastest one-hundred-yard dash as a teen—insofar as Frank had thoroughly checked judo champ records for those years.

Many of the patents Keith claimed were pending were actually rejected. One he did get patented was "how to rehabilitate a Luciferian." I looked it up, and apparently a Luciferian was a kind of sociopath, a person who commits destructive acts and who looks to be sane on the outside but isn't. Was this some desperate plea for help?

In February 2015, Keith filed a lawsuit against Microsoft and AT&T for patent infringement, claiming the tech giants were using a teleconferencing invention he owned and patented. Two years later, the US Patent and Trademark Office's Trial and Appeal Board determined that the patents were not his at all, and belonged to a company that had dissolved more than a dozen years earlier.

Judge Barbara M. G. Lynn said that Keith's "conduct throughout this litigation, culminating in his untruthful testimony . . . demonstrates a pattern of obfuscation and bad faith . . . (and) an abuse of the judicial process."

The deeper I dug, the sleazier it got.

Keith's past business history, I discovered, was, to put it charitably, checkered.

His first company, Consumers Buyline, went bust when multiple states sued him for allegedly operating an illegal, multimillion-dollar pyramid scheme.

Then came the women—or should I say, mostly girls.

I read about a twelve-year-old girl, Rhiannon, who first met Keith when harem member Pam Cafritz hired the girl to walk her dog twice a day. Rhiannon's mother worked with Keith at Consumers Buyline. Keith offered to tutor Rhiannon for free, which led to sexual encounters in which they had sex in elevators, offices, and broom closets, she had said. The relationship lasted several months, included at least sixty sexual encounters, and prompted Rhiannon to skip school and leave home. Two years after it ended, she went to the police but ended up not pressing charges.

Another girl, Gina Melita, bravely went public in 2012, giving an interview to the *Albany Times Union*. Keith had been her Latin and algebra tutor when she was fifteen and he was twenty-four, and then he became her molester—taking her virginity and having sex with her even though she told him it was painful. Together, they spent time at video arcades playing Pac-Man and a game called: Vanguard, in which destroying enemies increased the fuel in a player's tank. During their relationship, he pestered her to lose weight and warned her to keep their time together a secret from her mother.

Before Gina Melita escaped Keith's clutches, she introduced him to a fifteen-year-old friend, Gina Hutchinson. whom he also went on to rape repeatedly. Keith convinced Gina H. to drop out of high school so he could tutor her as well. When Gina's older sister discovered they were having sex, Keith told her "your sister's soul is much older than her biological age" and that she was a "Buddhist goddess meant to be with him." Years later, Gina would go to a monastery and shoot herself.

I read about the disappearance of Kristin Snyder, who became unhinged after taking two sixteen-day Nxivm seminars and allowing Keith to conduct experiments on her—trying to convert her from being gay. She told friends that Keith had made her pregnant, then she disappeared. Her death was ruled a suicide, even though many believed foul play was involved. Her body was never found.

Why, I wondered, had Keith never been charged with anything—especially since at least one of the girls—twelve-year-old Rhiannon—made a report with the police?

The answer was: They were all too afraid of him to press charges. One of them was asked by police to wear a wire in order to catch him in the act, but she was too scared to even be in the same room again with him.

Then I discovered that Nxivm had spent more than $50 million against their critics and initiated more than fifty lawsuits many of which the Bronfmans had either participated in or backed, targeting anyone who wrote or spoke negatively about the cult: former members, journalists, ex-girlfriends—anybody.

In 2013, *Times Union* reporter James Odato—who wrote the scathing four-part series on the cult, "Secrets of Nxivm"—was sued by the organization, which claimed that he had used unauthorized passwords to get on its website and gain information. Odato was put on leave of absence and saw his career at the newspaper end. (He later landed on his feet, becoming a reporter for the Reuters news service, which helped bolster his reputation for being ethical and respected.)

Citing the same reason, Nxivm also filed lawsuits against blogger John J. Tighe and *Vanity Fair* contributing editor Suzanna Andrews (who'd written the feature story, "The Heiresses and the Cult," that I asked Esther, the green-sashed enforcer, about).

Keith's ex-girlfriend Toni Natalie has been in court for twenty years because of him. He was still suing her today in two bogus lawsuits—just because she had the audacity to leave him.

He had her followed and hounded, ordered her dog poisoned, had his lawyers urge law enforcement to bring false criminal charges against her, got the Bureau of Criminal Investigation to ransack her home, sued her until she and her mother went bankrupt, and Toni believes to this day that Keith had a hand in her brother's suicide.

In 2003, one judge wrote: "This matter smacks of a jilted fellow's attempt at revenge or retaliation against his former girlfriend, with many attempts at tripping her up along the way."

Another unwitting victim, Barbara Bouchey (who became the Bronfmans' financial planner), lent Keith her life savings, and he lost it all on the commodities market. After she left him, she demanded her money back.

Keith, backed by Bronfman money, went after her and eight other defectors, falsely accusing them of extortion and racketeering. The cases were dismissed, but not before most of the falsely accused suffered financial ruin. They were henceforth known as the "Infamous Nxivm Nine."

Like Toni, Barbara did nothing wrong except leave Keith Raniere. But a man who makes women sign a lifetime vow to him and brands his initials on their bodies has serious abandonment issues. When one follower in her early twenties developed romantic feelings for a man other than Keith and refused to join his harem, he confined her to her bedroom for eighteen months. She abided by his orders because she was in the country illegally and worried he'd report her if she didn't. When the woman finally did leave the room, the defendant, as he had threatened, had her driven to the Mexican border and ordered to walk across, without money or identification papers.

Keith and his cronies didn't care so much if they won their cases—in fact, they often lost. Their goal wasn't to win but to harass, intimidate, bankrupt, and keep their enemies chained in the legal system until they were ruined every which way. And it worked.

"They used and abused the legal system as an ongoing stalking device," Toni Natalie said to me when I finally met her. "It's called 'vexatious litigation.'"

The more I researched, the more complicated and corrupt the stories became. I read and heard rumors about bribery, blackmail, financial contributions, and kickbacks involving DAs, special prosecutors, state police, Nxivm lawyers, PI firms, and politicians. Court records from 2015 show that the Bronfmans hired a Canadian investigative firm, Canaprobe, to access bank records of judges involved in Nxivm cases—and of other officials, including one of the state's two US senators, Chuck Schumer—so they would have "leverage" over them.

What was going on here? It sounded like a fictionalized thriller written by a novelist like John Grisham, not real life. My delving into the web of corruption was only beginning, and there was no end in sight. It was like taking on a ten-headed Gorgon beast, and everywhere I looked, there was a new head.

—

BY JULY, I had put out an SOS through all channels imploring defectors to please call me in my war room. It had now been more than a month since I'd spoken to India, and I was desperate for any kind of info about her that would help me get her out.

Lisa, a new defector, heard my distress signal through the grapevine and came out of hiding in mid-July to call me.

Like the others, Lisa was lured into DOS by the "secret sisterhood for independent women" pitch, and the deal was sealed after several flattery-filled walks with Keith. Lisa gave some insight into the hypnotizing mind games Keith conducted during these strolls:

"If I pulled away from him, he would ask me why I was choosing to be violent toward him in my mind. 'Why are you making me bad in your head?' he'd ask me. 'You're being destructive.' He didn't force himself on me, he baited me."

Keith broke DOS protocol by telling Lisa directly that "I am the mastermind behind DOS," information she would not normally be privy to because of her second-tier status in the DOS pyramid.

Throughout Lisa's involvement, Keith constantly asked about her weight, she said.

"I went from a hundred thirty-two pounds to a hundred two pounds in quite a short time span," she recounted, "and I had fainting spells. I'm five foot four. Keith would tell me to eat no more than two hundred calories a meal, followed by forty-five minutes of vigorous exercise."

Why did Keith groom all his girls to be so thin? The mystery might be solved by what he'd told one slave I spoke to: "An ounce of fat on a woman turns me off so much, I can't get an erection because of it." So, basically, Rubenesque women need not apply to DOS.

Lisa had no idea she was about to be branded when her master, Joan, told her excitedly that she was going to take part in a special ceremony in early June—scheduled the same week as the branding ceremonies that Ava, Yasmine, and Sarah skipped out on.

"All I was told was that I'd be on lockdown for a few days," she said.

(Joan, by the way, had been one of the multicultural diversity specialists at Keith's Rainbow Cultural Garden school and had been assigned the children of A-list actors. I wonder if these parents had any idea the nanny-slash-unaccredited-teacher taking care of their children was a branded slave.)

Lisa never made it to that special ceremony.

"You created such a fiasco," she told me, "sending texts that the FBI was going to raid us, that they got scared and postponed the ritual."

She found out days later, after reading the contraband *Frank-Report*, that she'd had a near miss with the branding iron.

"I don't have a brand of *KR* on my body," she said. "I'm so grateful. I have you to thank for that."

Lisa confronted Keith about the branding, and he admitted to knowing all about it, calling it "a form of tribute to me. If it was Abe Lincoln's or Bill Gate's initials, no one would care," he said dismissively, stressing that his importance to the world was just as great, because "if DOS didn't continue, it would be one of the biggest tragedies of the world."

A few weeks later, Lisa finally had her connect-the-dots epiphany that the entire Nxivm setup was a scam.

"It was thanks to India that I woke up," she said. "It was something she said to me—and *didn't* say. I asked her if DOS was 'honorable,' and she paused. Her pause was so long, and what she said after made me think. I don't even remember *what* she said, but I remember *how* she said it—like she was regurgitating someone else's words by rote. I suddenly saw that she was being used, and, consequently, so were all of us. Everything started to make sense—or rather, make *no* sense. I woke up."

I smiled at the bittersweetness of that. Without even knowing it, India had helped this woman regain her wits and leave. But she couldn't do the same thing for herself.

Lisa also recalled something from the last time she was with India. My daughter, giggling, showed her a text she'd sent Keith:

"If all goes south, there's always Fiji."

Fiji? That was the second time I'd heard talk about the isolated South Pacific island; the first was when Mark mentioned it as Keith's official escape destination.

And there was something Keith told Lisa that I hadn't heard before from any other defector:

"He said, 'There are things I'm going to ask the women to do soon that I don't have the strength to yet.'"

She didn't know what that meant, and it would take me a little time to find out—but I would.

After her awakening, Lisa called her parents, and they planned an escape: Lisa's mother arrived to help her pack her belongings, while her father, Jim—a highly trained US government secret agent, who'd been captured, imprisoned, and survived time in a desolate

Eastern Bloc detention camp—had a federal marshal on standby in the neighborhood, ready to step in if anyone tried to get in their way.

She was relieved to get out of the cult, but like so many defectors, Lisa was afraid.

She was scared to share what she'd just told me, petrified of being persecuted by the cult for the rest of her life, and worried that her collateral would be released.

It almost didn't even matter that these women were officially and physically out of the cult's grasp and perhaps thousands of miles away. Their minds were still enslaved—it was a psychological slavery.

A lot of defectors went off the grid and into hiding once they got out. They'd been brutalized and beaten down—mentally, spiritually, and emotionally—and were paranoid they were being watched and that punishment was imminent.

Which they were. And which it was.

The paranoia was real, and everyone's fears would skyrocket once the flying monkeys came swooping down.

12

CUE THE FLYING MONKEYS

Lisa was afraid, but there was a reason she was brave enough to escape when she did.

Frank started posting on his blog that no collateral had been released to date, and this was a huge revelation to the young women still trapped in DOS. Many of them were desperate to escape but remained for fear that Keith and his goons would release their damaging photos and videos to the world. Hearing that none had been released so far gave more slave sisters the confidence to defect.

There were other kinds of retaliation in store for defectors, though. And as the summer progressed, Keith's flying monkeys were dispatched to deliver them.

"Flying monkeys" is a phrase in pop psychology to describe the henchmen surrounding a narcissist or psychopath who dole out the leader's abuse by proxy. The phrase was inspired by the film *The Wizard of Oz*, and the Wicked Witch of the West's army of flying monkeys who scared the crap out of every kid who watched it. ("Take your army to the haunted forest and bring me that girl and her dog! Now, fly! Fly!")

As the defections continued, Vanguard's flying monkeys—the Bronfman sisters, Emiliano Salinas, Alex Betancourt (co-owner of Nxivm Mexico with Emiliano), Nancy and Lauren Salzman, Allison Mack, and a host of others—were ordered to carry out frenzied attacks on the defectors in the form of spying, intimidating letters, legal accusations, computer hacking, and more.

Keith loved to pit friends or family against each other—it was one of his favorite cruel strategies. So my intimidation began immediately by someone who called himself a friend. My intervention attempt and interference with the branding ceremony had solidly plopped me on the Nxivm archenemy list, alongside Frank and Rick, and I received the first of many emails in June by Manuel, one of the organization's "Ethics Police," and someone I'd met in Albany in 2012.

He started off kindly: asking if I wanted to talk to him as a friend of the family "about the weird stuff going on." I didn't answer the first email, or the second, or even the third, but they kept coming every few weeks, each escalating in tone and desperation until I finally replied. By mid-July 2017, Manuel was hysterically accusing me of mudslinging and promoting lies.

> Me: Manuel—I am sure u have gotten this feedback before, but your behavior feels like bullying to me. I'm withdrawing from this conversation. Sending love

Manuel's emails were only the beginning for me.

At the end of July, when I was out of town, India showed up at the house unannounced and ransacked the war room—rifling through all my notes and folders and taking photos of everything. She picked a folder labeled "Sex Trafficking Girls" and thought they were notes about Nxivm, when, in fact, she was looking at Callum's notes for *Gangsta Moms*.

"Mom is very confused," she told her younger sisters as they watched silently from the sidelines. "Mom is acting in a really, really weird way."

Even family members, it seemed, could be flying monkeys.

Soon after that, the threatening legal letters began arriving. Sarah, Lisa, Yasmine, me, and others received registered letters from lawyers working for Nxivm Mexico, charging us with various crimes, including extortion.

Meanwhile, Clare Bronfman went to the Vancouver Police Department and accused Sarah Edmondson of "theft, fraud, and mischief," urging them to open a criminal investigation against Sarah, which they did. The motion alleged that more than 125 students in Vancouver left ESP because of Sarah's "mischievous and fraudulent" activities.

In Mexico, former ESP coach Antonio Zarattini sounded the alarm to the local Espian community about DOS and Keith's sexcapades, prompting an uproar among the coaches, proctors, and students. The uproar was quickly silenced when Emiliano Salinas and Nxivm Mexico stepped in and attacked Zarattini for his whistle-blowing, filing trumped-up extortion charges against him and trying to get him arrested—adding him to the defunct and previously dismissed Nxivm Nine lawsuit, none of whom he'd ever met.

The court finally threw out the case, a process which cost Zarattini upwards of half a million dollars. No one dared defect after that because they were terrified of being targeted and having their lives ruined or worse, being killed.

As the flying monkeys did Keith's bidding, the fear grew.

Every week, Keith and his henchmen had a new enemy du jour to vanquish. In a conversation I had with Lisa's father, he called Keith's tactics "an act of terrorism."

I got a call from Sasha asking me not to post any photos of us together on social media.

"My company is based in Mexico," she said, "and I don't want to be killed. You don't know how dangerous Carlos Salinas is. I can't be seen with you, Catherine. It's too risky."

I'd had enough of Keith's terrorism. He thought it would shut me up? He didn't know me so well. Instead of keeping me quiet, it only made me want to fight louder and harder.

Keith had his flying monkeys, but I had access to a powerful army, too, and an American institution at that: the free press.

If they were against you, they could annihilate you, but if they were on your side, you could move mountains and make miracles happen.

I'd failed at the intervention. My hope that the defections of friends India knew and trusted, starting with Bonnie and Mark, would trigger her own defection was dashed. We'd banged on the doors of law enforcement for months only to have them slammed in our faces. Mark had just gotten word from the senior investigator with the NY State Police that he'd closed his investigation on the cult: "There is no case," he told Mark. Over the next many months, we'd learn more about this so-called investigation—and this is where things get more nefarious.

This senior investigator on the case, we'd later discover, was the direct supervisor of another investigator who'd been working closely with Nxivm to condemn the defectors. Was it a coincidence that every defector who gave this supervisor confidential testimony—and later spoke to the press off the record—received threatening letters from Nxivm attorneys when their identities had been so carefully hidden? We don't think so. Was there a corrupt reason why the supervisor closed the case on Nxivm amid so much damning evidence? We think so. Sarah and the other defectors got a response from the Health Department stating they'd found no wrongdoing regarding the medical conduct of the doctors in the cult.

When I told Rick that law enforcement barely blinked an eye at Sarah's brand, he suggested she was too fresh from the cult to be able to relate the details of her experience to them properly.

"She needs time to organize her thinking and unpack what has happened to her first—she was too discombobulated to go to law enforcement so soon. Same with the others," Rick said.

Frank's series of articles instigated an uproar and exodus of Espians in three countries, but still India didn't budge. I didn't have money to match the Bronfmans' billions to try to fight Nxivm in the legal arena. I'd exhausted every other option. And yet, I knew in my gut and with every fiber of my being that even though law enforcement was shrugging it off, what was happening at Nxivm could not be legal.

Aside from sex trafficking laws, there's the Thirteenth Amendment, which prohibits slavery. Adding to that, "there's an important body of law that declares it illegal to consent to certain types of physical harm, whether it's sexual or not," says Wendy Murphy, a professor of sexual violence law at New England Law. "You can't consent to torture."

My only recourse now was to find a way to generate public outrage that would put pressure on law enforcement to reconsider and take action. The power of the press was my last hope.

It was also a horrendously painful option, going to the media and exposing my daughter's private journey publicly for the world to see.

It was a decision that came with many, many risks. First, I risked alienating my daughter for a long time—maybe even forever. How would India ever forgive me?

"Your love for her is bigger than that," a friend assured me. "And you love her more than needing her to like you right now."

Second, would going public stigmatize India for the rest of her life, and make it impossible for her to move forward if and when she left the cult? I didn't know.

If I could, I would try to expose Nxivm and leave her out of it or conceal her identity in some way. If there was a way for me to talk about the horrors and not mention I had a daughter involved, that's what I'd do.

Finally, there was the risk of incurring the wrath of Vanguard and all the damage his network of intimidation and flying monkeys could inflict: physical harm, financial ruin, emotional trauma, imprisonment, and more.

But it was either take those risks or leave my daughter shackled for the rest of her nonlife as a brainwashed member of a madman's harem.

So, really, there was no other choice for this mother to make. India's safety came first, even if it was at the cost of our relationship.

—

THROUGH A FRIEND, I got in touch with a top editor at *People*, and Mark Vicente put me in touch with Oscar-nominated documentary filmmaker Karim Amer, who connected me to Barry Meier, a Pulitzer Prize–winning journalist for the *New York Times*.

Over the phone, I broke down in tears and told Barry everything about my ordeal with India and the cult. I told him about the brainwashing, the diet, the collateral, the branding, the slave pods, the coercion, and the horror of it all. I unburdened myself.

Barry got to work investigating and they slotted the story to run at the end of August.

I asked him if there was any way to expose the cult without naming India outright. At the same time, I understood he had to write the story in a way that would elicit maximum impact. Even if India were to get angry that I gave the interview, I truly believed she would read the article and have her come-to-Jesus moment, as would others in ESP. From what the defectors had told me, many on-the-fence Espians were simply waiting for another mainstream, "credible" news outlet to report on the cult's wrongdoings, and then they'd believe it and leave. They were instructed to disregard the *FrankReport* as the workings of an irate, disgruntled maniac, hell-bent on discrediting their precious Vanguard.

But surely they, and India, would not dispute the credibility of a Pulitzer-winning reporter and the *New York Times*?

With my new connection to filmmaker Karim, another project was born to help expose the cult.

Mark had opened up to his longtime friend Karim about his harrowing experience with the cult and, in the process, began sobbing. Karim instinctively picked up his camera and began filming. Mark talked, and talked, and fell apart on camera the same way I fell apart on the phone with Barry. Mark told him to keep recording, so he could have his side of the story on tape for his own protection.

Karim was so troubled and moved by Mark's testimony, he asked if he could interview me as well. And what began as one interview became an ongoing documentation of my fight for India's freedom.

Greg's directive was disrupt, disrupt, disrupt and *expose, expose, expose*. And do it in a way that will reach as many people as possible as loudly as possible—and that's what I was doing.

Karim had now joined my army—along with Greg, Callum, Barry, Mark, Bonnie, Frank, my mother, Sarah, Nippy, and the other defectors—to help us use the media in every which way that we could to take this nightmare out of the shadows and into the light.

—

BY MID-AUGUST, AN estimated four hundred people had left ESP, and a third center, in San Francisco, had closed. More than half of the cult had defected, from what I could gather. The *FrankReport* kept pumping out damning blog posts about the cult that revealed more sordid details, including a comprehensive list of fifty branded slaves. India was on the list. I felt nauseated and grief-stricken.

I received another call from Sasha, who'd gotten a call from someone linked to DOS.

I heard that "ESP has hired a team of lawyers and they're going to sue you for slander and put you in jail. Apparently everyone is packed for Fiji, ready to go."

It was now the third time I'd heard about Fiji, and I was freaking out.

I shifted into overdrive—a near-perpetual state for me now—and began investigating what link ESP had with Fiji and what the remote island nation's extradition laws were. Even worse than India being at command central in Albany was India being under Keith's spell on a private island in Fiji, where I'd probably lose her for good.

It took one Google search to find out that a year earlier, Clare Bronfman had bought 80 percent of Wakaya, a five-square-mile private island in Fiji (population, three hundred to six hundred). With a little more digging, I discovered that she'd bought her house from someone I knew: John, a British American business exec who'd courted me before I met Casper and once owned the movie equipment company Panavision (and offered to name a camera lens after me at the time). Also, the man from whom Clare purchased her stake in the island had been one of my father's best friends.

Bonnie was shocked at how well connected I was.

"Well, when you've been around for as long as I have, you tend to know everyone," I said, and I put out calls to both. I relished the moment when Keith's army would find out that I already had eyes and ears on his damn island.

My biggest fear now—and every week I had a new, more troubling one—was that India was also packed and ready to go off to the South Pacific. I lay in bed at night trying to figure out if it was possible to get Special Ops to take a boat from the main island, Viti Levu, and rescue India off Wakaya in the middle of the night—if she were to go.

John returned my call, and I explained the situation and peppered him with questions:

"How close is Wakaya to the main island? What's the access? Would I be able to locate India if she was there and pluck her off the island?"

I relaxed after he checked with sources to find there were no impending arrivals due on the island.

A week before the *New York Times* article was slated to run, I met up with Sarah and Nippy in LA at Karim's house, and for the first time ever, I saw the brand up close and in the flesh, as it were.

Sarah stood up, unzipped her pants, and pulled down the fabric covering her left hip. And there it was. My stomach lurched.

K-R A-M.

It was ugly. I tried not to imagine it on India's body, but that was impossible. All three of us cried, and I hugged Sarah for being so brave to expose this ugliness to me and to the world.

—

VANGUARD WEEK WAS fast approaching, so we set out to cause a commotion.

From the moment Greg gave me the marching orders to "create a disturbance," this shit-disturber looked for every opportunity to do so.

"How can we mess up V-week?" I asked. "How can we stop it from happening at all?"

V-week was Clare's baby; she organized it every year. We wrote letters to the Silver Bay YMCA Conference and Family Retreat Center—on the shore of pristine Lake George, an hour-plus drive north of Albany—alerting management that they would be housing a branding sex cult in its rambling 115-year-old facility, in hopes that enough complaints might get them to cancel the event. A few days later, while Callum and I were in Vegas doing research for *Gangsta Moms*, I got him to rewrite my letter on hotel stationery in his handwriting and mail it himself (in case anyone dusted for fingerprints) from the hotel, so it couldn't be traced to me. Which was a fine plan, until we posted a photo of ourselves in front of our hotel on the Vegas strip on Instagram and completely foiled my attempt at subterfuge.

Ironically, while we were planning how to disrupt V-week, the green sashes were holed up in a war room of their own, planning the demise of the whistle-blowers.

Although we weren't successful in getting V-week canceled, spies at the YMCA helped us cause a major shit storm.

Frank got some YMCA employees to surreptitiously take candid photos and notes of the goings-on, and Frank posted them on the *FrankReport* all week like a kid gleefully sending his parents snapshots and letters from summer camp. The Espians went wild, trying to figure out who in their group was the disloyal mole feeding the *FR*. The green-sashed ones had even disabled the resort's internet and activated their own server to try to control information leaks.

Contrary to the ESP propaganda machine, we heard that attendance was low and that it had cost Nxivm more than $500,000 to pull off the celebration. And the higher ranks barely made appearances—Keith attended only one forum, with Baby Avatar and Mariana in tow. Whether or not Baby Avatar's presence was a deterrent from his usual naked romps in the woods, we weren't sure.

I searched India's Instagram page for photos of her at V-week, grateful she hadn't blocked me, as the majority of Espians had been directed to do. I may have been shunned, but I hadn't been blocked—and that was a victory in my eyes. I was surprised to see that instead of V-week, she'd gone to a friend's wedding here in California, in Napa Valley, and had posted a photo. She looked beautiful! The photo made me miss her so. I clicked the heart emoticon underneath it.

In the three months since I'd last seen her, India hadn't returned any of my texts, calls, or emails, so I'd been relying on updates about her from her sisters and my mother, with whom she kept in touch. And I "loved" her from afar by clicking the heart under every photo of herself that she posted.

"The last thing you want her to feel is isolated in the cult," Rick Alan Ross had advised me. "She has to know there is an avenue of communication with the family and know she has a place to go, because they try to convince her that she doesn't."

Despite the network of intimidation, this Gangsta Mom refused to be silenced. Seeing Sarah's brand in person that August only made me want to create a bigger disturbance. I was buoyed further by a birthday text from India on September 22—my very first birthday wish that day, and the first communication she'd sent me in four months.

It was a little tradition of ours that she had stubbornly held on to ever since she was a little girl: she had to be the *first* one to wish me happy birthday and happy Mother's Day. I was wondering if she'd keep tradition this year, and then at seven in the morning, I heard the *ping!*:

Happy Birthday, Mom.

That was it, but it was enough to tell me that her noncult persona was safe somewhere in the recesses of her heart and mind, alive and well, and reaching out to tell me she loved me.

The *New York Times* article was supposed to be published already, causing a major uproar, but it had been delayed.

"One more month," Barry said, "be patient."

But I wasn't patient. My child was getting mind fucked every day she stayed under the influence of those lunatics.

I had to think of something else to do to disrupt and expose while I was waiting, and came up with an idea.

Everyone knew there was strength in numbers, right? Maybe it was time to organize as many defectors as possible and get them on board for a civil case against Nxivm to demand retribution. We needed to mobilize! There were hundreds of Expians—plenty to form another small, strong army to vanquish Vanguard.

Through a friend, I found an attorney, Anne Champion—a partner at Gibson, Dunn & Crutcher's Manhattan office—who specialized in class action lawsuits. I sent her the highlights of the research I'd done over the summer to prep her for our first phone call.

My first question to Anne wasn't about the civil case I envisioned per se, it was about law enforcement in Albany and the bleak stories of collusion, negligence, and injustice I'd read about in the *FrankReport*.

"I came across so much of what looked like cover-ups of Nxivm's criminal activities," I began. "If these stories are accurate, this organization has been blatantly breaking the law for years, decades, and no one in law enforcement has done anything about it and gone after them. I read about officials and politicians being paid off or compromised in some way. Is it possible, Anne, that what I read was really true, or is it too far-fetched?"

Anne chuckled.

"Oh, Albany is famously corrupt!" she said matter-of-factly—almost surprised that I wouldn't know that.

"We didn't get anywhere with law enforcement there when I told them about the branding and the sex slaves," I told her. "All I heard was that everyone was a consenting adult. That can't be right!"

"It's not. It's a violation of anti-slavery laws. Catherine, listen. I understand you're interested in a civil case. But after doing some research of my own, I see clear evidence of RICO here."

"RICO?"

"The Racketeer Influenced and Corrupt Organizations Act. It's when racketeering activity—like extortion, money laundering, loan-sharking, obstruction of justice, and bribery—is performed as part of an ongoing criminal enterprise."

This is what Greg predicted months ago! And something else dawned on me as Anne continued to explain it. By now, I'd reviewed so many lawsuits filed by Nxivm during my research, I realized that this was the crime they often accused and charged their enemies of! And now we were going to use their own ammo against them.

"You should go after them with a criminal case first," she continued, "and once you have arrests, then you have the basis for a civil case."

"Really?"

"Yes. Sex crimes are harder to prove. Go after them for the financial crimes and the racketeering. That's how they got Al Capone, you know. On tax evasion."

Al Capone! When we hung up, I was charged up.

I started making calls to round up the troops and put together the fight plan. We were going to go after Keith the same way that Eliot Ness, a famed US Prohibition agent during the Roaring Twenties and the Great Depression, went after the ruthless Chicago mobster Capone.

That was the new strategy: we were going to *Al Capone* Keith Raniere.

13

THE RING OF FIRE

What happened next was a divine concurrence.

My struggle to free my daughter and the other enslaved women in the cult intersected with another fight against oppression, abuse, and exploitive men: the momentous "Me Too" movement of 2017. The voices and energy of that crusade would give my battle wings, lifting it out of obscurity and onto the front pages of newspapers around the world.

By early October, the *New York Times* feature was two months behind its originally scheduled pub date, and I was in agony because of it. Everything hinged on the publication of this story—I couldn't talk to any other media until it ran because I'd given the *Times* first rights, and *People* was holding their story until after the *Times* published theirs. And nothing would happen with law enforcement until the story appeared. That was the whole point of doing the story: to spur them into action. Law enforcement agents paid attention to only a few select journalists, I was told, and Barry was one of the few who carried that clout.

The story had already been vetted by the paper's ultracautious legal department and met its exacting standards, which was our first difficult hurdle. This meant the editors had confidence in the veracity of our claims and had the guts to move forward with it. The *Times* was not intimidated by the litigious Bronfman-Raniere monster.

But apparently the story was considered what they call in the newsroom an "evergreen": one without a specific news peg that could run anytime. So we kept getting bumped for others that had to run right away. And bumped again.

Then Barry said the editors were waiting for enough space to place such a large story as ours. Then the story wasn't "relevant" enough. To whom, I wasn't sure. When the Harvey Weinstein sex abuse scandal hit the news on October 10, I thought our moment had finally come.

"Are we relevant *now?*" I asked Barry.

Yeah, we were relevant. But now we were too *similar* to the Weinstein story: women being taken advantage of by an asshole guy. Plus, our asshole wasn't as famous as the other asshole and didn't bring the same kind of A-list talent with him. Weinstein's story had Uma Thurman, Daryl Hannah, Salma Hayek, Ashley Judd, Gwyneth Paltrow, and Kate Beckinsale, to name just a few. The most famous Hollywood celebrity DOS could boast was Allison Mack, whose stardom had gone from *Smallville* to Smalbany.

I was starting to get paranoid. I'd read that Mexican business magnate Carlos Slim—recently ranked by *Forbes* magazine as the richest man in the world three years in a row—owned a 17 percent share in the *New York Times*. Could he have killed the cult story as a favor to his buddy Carlos Salinas, the former Mexican president and father of Emiliano? Good God, I was becoming a full-blown conspiracy theorist.

I was in an anxious holding pattern. It was like being in labor experiencing excruciating contractions, but the stern nurse yells at you not to push because you're not dilated enough. In that moment, you actually pray for "the ring of fire" to happen: the moment when the baby's head crowns, and you're finally allowed to push. Even though it's *the* most painful moment during labor, it means the wait is over—and the wait is harder to bear than the pain.

I desperately wanted to *push*.

Meanwhile, Vanguard and his flying monkeys had gotten wind of the impending *Times* story because Barry had reached out to get a comment. They doubled their scare tactics to muzzle the whistle-blowers, sending out threatening letters to Barry and to everyone else who'd given interviews for his story.

Or, at least, that's what we *thought* had happened. The truth was more devious, which we would find out later.

That October, I received threatening letters from a Nxivm lawyer and a state attorney general in Mexico, accusing me of numerous felonies, including fraud and extortion. Somehow, they had resurrected one of their old, phony lawsuits originally filed against the legendary Nxivm Nine and roped me into it. It was a bizarre strategy, especially because the case had been dismissed six years earlier, and I hadn't met a single one of the nine.

My failure to stop engaging in said criminal activities, the lawyer wrote, could lead "up to an arrest for 36 hours alongside criminal responsibilities that shall arise." However, in noting that his "services have been engaged by Nxiv*n* Mexico," he couldn't even spell the name of his client correctly!

The letter was signed with the word *Bufete* in front of the attorney's name. What the hell was *Bufete*? "Buffoon" in Spanish? I looked it up; it meant from "law firm of." Okay, fine.

I looked closely at the letter again: my listed accusers and witnesses were the same cast of characters on the numerous Nxivm lawsuits I'd researched from the last decade, including one filed against Kirsten Gillibrand's father, Doug Rutnik. It was the same old Nxivm posse dispatched once again; they were a traveling roadkill show that went from town to town and person to person, ready to pitch their tent and perform litigation theater at a venue near you.

I forwarded the letter to Anne Champion, who laughed when she read it, dismissing it as ludicrous and baseless.

"No US lawyer would have ever sent this," she said. We deduced that they must have exhausted all efforts trying to find anyone in the States who'd passed the bar exam to send a letter like this, before resorting to a corrupt Mexican lawyer and attorney general to do their flying monkey work.

I then forwarded the letter to India, hoping it would have an effect:

Darling India,

Are you aware that Nxivm has sent me this letter?
*   It is a little concerning bc it says that I am criminally*
involved in an extortion case against Nxivm Mexico that goes

back to 2009. This is strange for a humanitarian, ethics-based company.

In case you would like to read the letter, there is an English translation below. I guess no more trips to Mexico unless I want to vacation in jail!

Too bad bc i loved spending time with you in Tulum.

And if you would like to know more or you have more information about this, call me.

I love you
Mom

I didn't receive a reply. I was still getting radio silence penance.

The next day, Frank Parlato called to say that Clare Bronfman had gone to the assistant US district attorney in New York State's Western District, Elizabeth Moellering, and accused him of stalking her and victimizing her and all Nxivm members.

It was an accusation we both found especially comical, since the Nxivm mission statement (which I'd heard read aloud at least fifty times) stated clearly, "There are no ultimate victims." And as I'd learned in Mexico, they believed that the so-called victim was the abuser—an underhanded conditioning that made it difficult for defectors to admit later on that they were, indeed, victims.

Frank hadn't anticipated that Clare would play the victim card, and it caught him off guard. She was using it to demand that the judge throw him in jail indefinitely until his trial, which had no set date, and shut down the *FrankReport* for bogus reasons.

He was due in court a few days later, he said.

There was *no way* we could afford to lose Frank and his blog; his voice was the only one in the media still brave enough (pending the *People* and the *New York Times* stories) to speak the truth about Raniere and his cronies. Parlato's blogs had indisputably convinced many Espians to defect and saved numerous women the horror of being branded with Keith's and Allison's initials.

If we lost *People* and the *New York Times* and Frank was silenced, too, we were screwed.

Parlato asked if I'd be willing to write a letter to the judge, appealing to him to refrain from gagging the *FrankReport* and explaining why it was valuable. And while I was at it, he added, I should demand that the judge open a criminal investigation into Nxivm!

I got on it, writing an impassioned missive about how the cult's practices rose "to a level that is more than just extortion. It has now become sex trafficking.

"Some people such as my daughter will argue that this is all voluntary, that there is no crime . . . that is not accurate because every step of the way there were inducements that were fraudulent, involving consistent undue influence and persuasive control without her informed consent. These impressionable young women have been defrauded every step of the way, and with each successive step, it becomes harder and harder to escape."

After I finished, I initiated a full-scale offensive to rally hundreds of other defectors to write letters as well to the same judge.

"Some of you may have your issues with the *FrankReport*," I wrote to them. "It was horrendous for me to see my daughter proclaimed as a branded sex slave on the blog," I admitted. "But our resources as far as spearheading a criminal investigation are limited right now, and this is our first—and maybe only—opportunity to access government officials with our words! Our letters could be a tipping point to get their attention!"

Dozens of current and longtime defectors, family members, other victims, and even one of Keith's underage rape victims wrote powerful testimonies. As I read through them, I was moved by their tragic stories of families torn asunder and lives left in ruins. The cult's wake of destruction spanned decades.

The same day as Frank's call, Anne emailed a long list of legal strategies on how to "extract" India out of the cult, and we got on the phone to discuss them. At the top of the list was the shocking suggestion to prove India mentally incapacitated to make her own decisions.

"Hold it right there," I said to Anne. "I can't . . . I can't even . . ."

I never thought I'd reach the point where one of my last options to save India included taking away her rights as an adult. Even though an aggressive move like that would make getting her out easier and quicker, I couldn't imagine anything more devastating for a parent to do to her grown child. She and our family would never recover.

"That's a bridge I'm not willing to cross," I said firmly. Especially after glancing at the part about how she'd be "involuntarily committed to a mental institution for a period of time." I'd been through that before, when I had to admit my father to a psychiatric hospital against his will. It was one of the most traumatic moments in our relationship.

Just . . . no. Besides, India was not crazy—she was brainwashed.

To spur a criminal investigation, Anne said, I'd need to gather as much proof of criminal activity as I could and put together what's called an evidence packet. Her firm charged a $50,000 fee for that task, but I could do it more cost effectively by using a company like Kroll International—a private investigation and security company—which would do the scouring and digging for me.

The other alternative, Anne said, was to wait until the *New York Times* article came out, and the story would cause such an uproar that the government would be pressured to take action immediately. And as far as the civil class action suit, "you'll have lawyers lining up around the block to represent you pro bono."

I emailed Barry Meier:

Dear Barry,

I hope all is well on your end.

Waiting for this article is like watching a pot boil! I'm trying to be patient (failing) but Sept has come and gone. And, of course, I keep indulging in catastrophic thinking, jumping to the worst case scenario—that the story may never run and that India may slip between my fingers and escape to Fiji in the clutches of a madman. Exacerbating my fears was recent news that she is dangerously thin.

If you have the chance, please let me know when you get word about the status—either way.

Warmly,
Catherine

Four days later, on October 17, merciful fate intervened.

Mark, Bonnie, me, and the rest of our core team on the West Coast set our phone volumes to high as we waited on pins and needles at five in the morning to hear the outcome of Frank's court appearance that morning in Buffalo.

Would he be taken away in shackles? Would we lose the *Frank-Report?*

The first good news of the day came at 5:10 a.m. PST with Frank's relieved voice on my phone.

The hearing had lasted only ten minutes, he said. Assistant DA Moellering was there as well as another assistant DA from the Western District, Clare's lawyer, three FBI agents, and a criminal agent from the Internal Revenue Service.

"They made a motion before the judge to revoke my release and remand me into custody until trial," said Frank. "That means, keep me in jail."

They presented his blog as evidence, saying it was a threat and danger to the victims—Clare and all members of ESP. They also accused Frank of witness intimidation and claimed that the blog showed that Frank had been snooping around Clifton Park, stalking Clare.

The judge looked dubious and asked Frank, "Were you in Clifton Park?"

No, he answered.

"Your Honor," the prosecutor piped up, "we want to protect the victims from Mr. Parlato."

"What evidence do you have that anyone is a victim?" the judge asked.

"We don't have any," Moellering admitted.

"There is no basis for this," said the judge. "Overruled! Mr. Parlato, I will take your word for it. Deny the motion." He banged the gavel, and Frank rushed outside to call and give us the good news.

"I just got out of the courtroom," Frank said, adding, "I don't think Moellering is in Bronfman's pocket; I think she was just misled. She looked like she was going through the motions and that Clare was putting the pressure on her."

Frank's win was a victory for us all at a time when we really, really needed some good news.

And then came more.

—

THE ME TOO movement had begun quietly two days earlier but ignited overnight. By that afternoon, it had spread across the internet—and the world—like a California wildfire.

I watched in awe after I hung up with Frank as, one by one, hundreds of thousands of women stood up and found their voices— speaking out for the first time about horrendous abuse, past and present. They were shouting out loud about the same crimes I was; the misuse of power, manipulation, and the silencing of victims— though the cult took those horrors a step further and brainwashed women to turn on one another, their own sisters.

The tidal wave of reckoning created an energy, a zeitgeist, and put a wind in the sails of our story to take it airborne.

The editors at the *New York Times* felt it, too.

Then, Frank tipped off Barry that the *Albany Times Union* was about to break their own feature about DOS.

Five minutes later, Barry called to say our story was going online that night, and when I hung up the phone, my hands were shaking.

I saw it before I went to bed, and I was in such shock that it had finally happened that I could barely sleep. Everything I'd been gearing up for over the past few months culminated in this moment when the story would hit, and I was primed with every sinew of my body to launch an attack first thing in the morning. I wanted Anne to brandish the article in the faces of government officials and tell them "Wake up! Do your job!"

But I was also anxious and worried about India. *What will she think? Will she respond? Will she hate me?*

My internal struggle was constant. I could tap into the pain and betrayal I knew India would feel once she saw the story. If I let this cult take her life away, that would be the ultimate betrayal.

What I was doing was dreadfully hard for both of us, but to stand by and do nothing was worse.

The next morning, my phone buzzed nonstop, the first call coming from Bonnie and Mark.

"Did you see it? Oh my God, Catherine. The story is on the front page—*above* the fold!"

I jumped out of bed, picked up as many copies as I could from the nearest grocery store, and met them at Bill's house—along with Karim and the crew—so we could all read the story together for the cameras.

Photos of India at varying ages hung on the walls around us as

Bonnie slowly unfolded the newspaper on Bill's living room coffee table. The first thing we all saw was Sarah's pelvis and that red, angry brand burned into her skin.

Reading the piece in print made the horror even more concrete. In fact, as I read Barry's story I discovered new horrors I hadn't known before.

For the first time, I read about Dr. Brandon Porter's unauthorized experiments at something called the Ethical Science Foundation, fronted by Clare Bronfman, in which the internist hooked women up to electroencephalogram (EEG) machines to measure brain wave activity and forced them to watch snuff films of women being decapitated and dismembered by machetes; an African American male being savagely kicked by a Nazi; a man forced to eat part of his own brain matter; and a vicious gang rape. I would later find out that at least one hundred subjects were exposed to these "fright studies."

Oh God, what incomprehensible depravity. Has India been subjected to this? The thought of it nearly sent me over the edge. It reminded me of terrorist training: the women watching these videos were being desensitized, radicalized, and weaponized to tolerate violence against other women—and against themselves. No wonder they didn't flinch at the idea of branding. The extreme pain of branding, too, causes severe dissociation—which, in turn, makes the women more suggestible and easier to mind control. (DOS slaves are told the ritual is to experience the body separate from pain as a way to build character: "You are more than your body," the masters tell their slaves.)

"I know where some of those images come from," Mark said, mortified. "When I was filming the documentary about the kidnapping and ransom epidemic in Mexico, I was shown film clips from cartel executions. I told Keith about them, and he asked me to send them to him. He must have given them to Brandon." Mark shook his head.

"This is an act of torture," he said. "If Keith is another Hitler, then Brandon is stepping in as his Dr. Mengele. *Dr. Death.*"

Following the publication of the *Times* story, ESP was quick to put up a word salad statement on its website, ostensibly writing off the newspaper as fake news: that dismissive label currently favored by extremists. That phrase wasn't used in the statement, but through the cult grapevine, I heard that's what they were saying.

They might as well have called Barry and his colleagues *Lügenpresse*: the Nazi term for "lying press."

"This story might be a criminal product of criminal minds who, in the end, are also hurting the victims of the story," said the cult's official statement, which also noted, "We will explore any and all legal remedies to correct these lies."

Great. I could only imagine what remedies they had in store for me.

As the day progressed, my phone continued to buzz like one long, uninterrupted *bzzzzzzzzzz*.

I got a call from my sister Ashley, who'd read the story and apologized for not reaching out earlier.

"Honestly, Catherine, I didn't take what I'd read seriously. I thought: *India? Impossible!* She's the last person in the world I would ever imagine getting involved in a cult. She was always so level-headed!"

But the certain relief I'd expected to feel with the story's publication never came. I knew I'd now crossed the line of no return in so many ways, most of all with India. I'd reached the ring of fire. And now I had to face the grim repercussions of that. Part of me half expected, and certainly hoped, that one of the calls today would be from my daughter and that, after reading the article, she'd realize the truth about Keith and his ilk and say, "Mom, come and get me. I want to come home."

But no such call came.

That night, I hopped the red-eye and landed the next morning in Washington, DC.

I was there to attend a conference on the barbaric practice of female genital mutilation and meet the keynote speaker, Dr. Pierre Foldès, a French Hungarian doctor who'd pioneered the clitoral restoration surgery that repaired the damage caused by female genital mutilation.

I'd been eager to track him down and invite him to join the advisory board for my foundation, and after we had dinner together in DC, he graciously accepted. I had planned to stay in the city another day or so and take part in more conference activities, including an anti-FGM march, but once again my phone was buzzing nonstop.

Apparently, the *New York Times* had published an explosive follow-up the day after breaking our story, announcing that Governor Andrew Cuomo of New York was opening an investigation with the Health Department to look into the activities of the branding doctor, Danielle Roberts, and the physician conducting those "fright studies," Brandon Porter, who was named in the story.

A modeling shot taken in Monte Carlo for the skincare line Zepter in 1996.

Another shoot for Zepter in 1997. India came on location with me for work all over the world: "My mommy works in a trailer," she told a reporter when she was two.

June 7, 1991:
Three hours after
India's birth,
we're home from
the hospital.
Photo taken by
my father.

Playing peekaboo
under India's tutu
at home in Beverly
Hills—a present
from Uncle Stanley
circa 1996.

With Mommy at work at a modeling shoot in Milan, 1997. At six, India was already wise beyond her years.

India at thirteen as we taped *I Married a Princess* at home in Malibu. Her sense of humor popped on-screen.

Between takes shooting *Sexology*, a comforting hug from India a few days after my separation from Casper. This was the last time I truly felt her; the cult pulled her away soon after.

Courtesy of the author

Courtesy of the author

India loves animals; here she is as a teen petting a pygmy goat in our backyard in Malibu at one of the kids' birthday parties.

India, thirteen, taking a break from *I Married a Princess* as the family sailed the Gulf of Mexico. Casper and I renewed our wedding vows in this episode, and India and her sisters were our bridesmaids.

In South Africa while Casper filmed *Starship Troopers 3: Marauder*, India embraced tribal face paint and made exotic animal friends at a nearby reserve.

India's first modeling headshot at age thirteen.
She was a natural in front of the camera.

On safari in Capetown in 2007—
that's an elephant, her favorite animal, behind India.

India at the rocky Cape of Good Hope in South Africa
in 2007 while vacationing with the family.

Our first trip to Tulum, Mexico, in September 2015.
Casper had just filed for divorce and Keith had just
come up with the idea for DOS. A few months later,
India would be lured in.

Graduating from Malibu
High in 2009!

Taken at my fifty-fifth
birthday party in Malibu,
September 2016. India
had just given away her
possessions and moved to
Albany at this point.

Paris, November 2008, as India makes her debut at the annual Le
Bal des Débutantes at the Hôtel de Crillon with her proud mom
and grandmother, Princess Elizabeth of Yugoslavia.

Back in Tulum in April
2017, but this time India
is preoccupied with her
phones and constant
"readiness drills" and I'm
concerned. My mother
took the photo.

The beautiful Toni Natalie with Keith when they were dating. He had a Vanguard video game in the basement and put her through decades of litigation hell after they split.

Sex with Keith was the "only way to true enlightenment," said one coach.

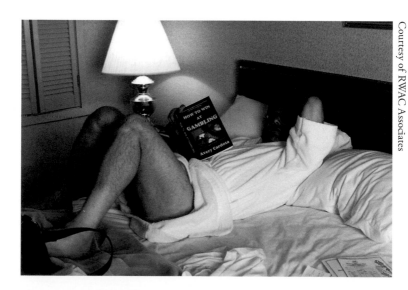

The gambling book didn't help; Keith lost $65 million of the Bronfman sisters' billions on the stock market.

The original harem (from left): Dawn Morrison, Barb Jeske, Karen Unterreiner, and Pam Cafritz.

ABOVE: Cult central: the Nxivm headquarters near Albany, New York.

LEFT: Nancy Salzman, aka "Gold Sash" at V-week—without her usual pasted-on cult grin.

LEFT: India's "master," *Smallville* actress Allison Mack, aka "Pimp Mack," who procured women for Keith and told the slaves to "feel the pain" as they were being branded.

BELOW: Sarah Edmondson and India on the beach in Santa Monica during an ESP "Humanties Event." Sarah's is the first brand I ever saw.

ABOVE: Emiliano Salinas, son of the former president of Mexico, Carlos Salinas de Gortari, and former co-owner of Nxivm Mexico. His lawyers accused me of fraud and extortion.

A selfie with my bestie Callum Blue, shortly after we
tried to sabotage V-week 2017.

The Dalai Lama demotes Keith to white-sash
status in 2009, then challenges the media to
investigate the psychopathic cult leader.

ABOVE: Clare Bronfman—heiress to the Seagram's fortune and Keith's top flying monkey.

BELOW: *Battlestar Galactica* actress Nicki Clyne—I heard through the cult grapevine that India attended the wedding ceremony for Nicki and Allison Mack in 2017.

Sara Bronfman, sister of Clare—her romance with the Dalai Lama's Buddhist monk "gatekeeper" caused heads to roll.

RIGHT: Checking out Keith's new digs, the Metropolitan Detention Center in Brooklyn, the day before his court appearance on Friday, April 13, 2018.

BELOW: Friday the 13—our lucky day; celebrating with Toni Natalie in Brooklyn Heights after staring Keith down in court. Our next stop: the chocolate shop!

The 2" by 2" brand with Keith's and Allison's initials; it takes thirty minutes using a hot cauterizing iron. Slaves wore surgical masks to lessen the stench of burning flesh.

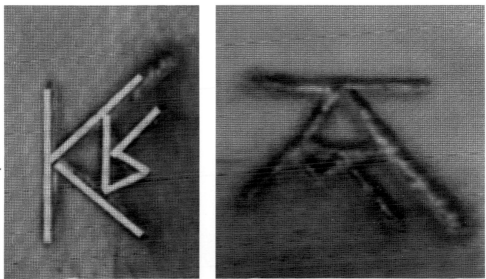

Courtesy of AP Images

Courtesy of Getty Images

ABOVE: Keith in court in April, surrounded by his three stooges; he was the same smug, arrogant Vanguard as always.

LEFT: Allison Mack arriving in court in Brooklyn in early May 2018. She was released on $5 million bail and is now serving home detention until the trial.

I could barely believe it. Only twenty-four hours after our story hit the stands, and already the reaction was so swift and immediate. It was what we'd been hoping and praying for.

Barry had skillfully skewed the article specifically to spur authorities to open an investigation. He pointed out the repeated lapses by law enforcement every time complaints had been issued and yet victims were turned away by various government agencies.

I was able to indulge in a few hours of relief and gratitude that night. Not only would our story have legs and not be leaving the news cycle anytime soon, but it was already opening doors with law enforcement. The relief lasted until I saw India's early morning Facebook post in support of the cult. She'd shared ESP's official statement in a public post that anyone could see and comment on, and added one of her own:

For anyone who's read the recent articles in the *New York Times*, this may help answer some questions and alleviate any confusion. Thank you for your care and concern; it's been an incredibly sad situation and I've been anticipating this article.

I'm absolutely fine, great actually. I would never put myself or the people I love into any danger.

These are my friends and colleagues. I've never seen anything but good come out of this work.

Her page went nuts after that. Hundreds of concerned Facebookers reached out to India and commented on her public post with a mixture of concern and, sometimes, humor:

This is a cult and you are brainwashed.

I pray that you are saved before it's too late.

You are in denial, you are defending that man and his craziness, don't worry about him. Worry about you cause you are #1 not him.

Keith is about power, control, sex, money, and evil!!!! Pure Evil!!!

Well the first problem is you have to move to *Albany*.

Get out before you die!! Please listen to your mother . . . the only one that *really* cares about *you*!!!!!!

India, *no one* who truly *cares* about you would want to brand you like cattle. India run don't walk to the nearest door and run to the people who love you. Truly love you.

I think you're beautiful and too good to be anyone's puppet.

If I couldn't get through to her, maybe a stranger could. Maybe, out of the litany of voices, one would resonate and pierce that protective cult armor.

Of the hundreds of comments, only one or two were trolls saying hurtful, cruel things that were painful to read. Another few were cult members trying to start a #ProudlyESP hashtag that didn't pick up any traction and fizzled out fast.

It was mostly an outpouring of kindness and concern from strangers, which gave me hope, as did the fact that India didn't erase them. While other cult members were quick to delete any anticult posts as fast as people posted them, my daughter did not. I was afraid to read too much into it, but I wondered if it meant that at some level she was open to other points of view. It wasn't just her mother talking now—it was people from all walks of life, from all over the world, giving her their unbiased opinions and advice: *"India, go home!"*

Another part of me worried that she'd been ordered to keep up the posts as penance, because I had caused destruction—"an ethical breach"—against Keith and the cult. Now she had to pay for what I'd done and stand in front of the crowds as they threw stones at her, or hang on the cross as they jeered at her—she had to sacrifice herself and do penance for my sins.

I hoped that was not the case. I hoped their words made her think.

But even if the *New York Times* or hundreds of strangers didn't get through to India, I had to keep the faith that I was doing the right thing and keep going.

Throughout this battle, I'd been continually humbled and re-minded that every time I had an expectation about India and a be-lief that something I did would sway her thought process, I'd been proven wrong. So the challenge for me now was to let go of those disappointments whenever they cropped up, refocus, and then direct my energies where I did have control: calling attention to the horrors perpetrated by this organization and exposing its abuse.

Because although my efforts weren't moving my own daughter, they were moving mountains elsewhere.

The day after India's FB post, I got a call from Lisa's father, Jim.

"Catherine! The chief investigator in New York Attorney General Eric Schneiderman's office wants to speak with you! Can you call him?"

"What? Of course I can! This is what I've been waiting for! But Jim, how did you pull this off?"

"I've been pressuring Senator Chuck Schumer for months," he said. "He must have pulled some strings."

"Oh my God, Jim. Who should I get in touch with? Who?"

"His name is Antoine Karam. And he's expecting your call."

14

BATTLE CRY

A few days later, I spoke to Deputy Chief Karam and breathlessly sputtered bits and pieces of information at him over the phone: "sex slaves," "trapped," "my daughter," "evil people," "women in cages," "need your help." I probably sounded hysterical.

I probably *was* hysterical.

"I must see you face-to-face," I implored. "The situation is too dire and too important to explain properly over the phone."

As it turned out, his office was in Albany—cult command central. *Ugh.* I never thought I'd return to the belly of the beast, but I made an appointment to meet the deputy chief in twelve days, on November 6.

I got busy putting together the evidence packet Anne had described, sending out emails to anyone I could think of who could provide proof of Nxivm's criminality. So far, I had the defectors' letters from Frank's court appearance, pertinent information downloaded from Rick Alan Ross's Cult Education Institute website, copies of some slave-master texts, and evidence of identity theft. I needed more. So much more.

"In my opinion, Keith's a psychopath," Rick told me over the phone, "but he's a very *methodical* psychopath. I've been studying him for years. If you're going to take him down, you have to match him. You have to be just as methodical as he is. Don't be impetuous. If you make one careless mistake, one slip, he will take you down. That's what happened to the others, like James Odato."

Five days before the meeting with Antoine, I was on my way to New York to appear on *Megyn Kelly Today*. The *New York Times* article had been quickly followed by a three-page feature in *People* magazine, and, on the heels of both, I was inundated with TV interview requests. Everything began moving at warp speed. The day before, I had given my first interview, to a Mexican TV station, Televisa, in hopes that it would spread the story there. I wasn't surprised anymore when every step of the way, I met with people's fears. As the interviewer left my home, he asked me not to mention his name or that I'd done the interview until it aired—"or I'll be killed," he said. He wasn't joking.

Not only was he referencing the cult's potential power in Mexico, because it was populated with so many of the country's rich, famous, and most elite citizens, but he was also acknowledging the danger that one of those citizens was Emiliano Salinas. His father, Carlos, the most feared man in the country, would do anything for his son.

Carlos's violent upbringing began at age four, when he and his older brother, Raul, five, and an eight-year-old friend "accidentally" executed the family's twelve-year-old maid. A reporter who brought up the incident when Carlos was running for election ended up in prison, a not-surprising turn of events.

During the five-hour plane ride to New York, I jotted down notes on what I'd say to Megyn Kelly. Sarah Edmondson was to appear with me but canceled at the last minute: her publicists worried Megyn might not be a "friendly" interviewer. But how could anyone not be sympathetic to this story? It never occurred to me that she'd be anything but fair. I'd met Megyn almost a decade before when we were both ambassadors for Childhelp USA, a charity that protects children from abuse and neglect, and I liked and trusted her. A few days before I boarded the flight, she'd left me a compassionate voice mail that reassured me.

Sarah also wasn't comfortable because the show was live, and that made me nervous, too. There'd be no chance for a "take two" or for editing or retracting. One slip of the tongue could put me in litigation hell with the Nxivm mob for the rest of my life. But, heck, I'd already called Keith a "dangerous psychopath" in the British tabloid the *Daily Mail* twelve days earlier—I couldn't be much more offensive than that.

Either way, canceling wasn't an option for me.

Besides being afraid to speak out about the cult, defectors who'd been emotionally damaged by Keith's reign of terror and lost years of their lives wanted to move on and never look back—it was the constant refrain I heard from them. But I still had a trapped child in jeopardy in that cult, and there'd be no moving on for me until I got her out.

The NBC hallway and dressing room in Rockefeller Center looked eerily familiar, and then I found out why: it was the original *Saturday Night Live* studio. The décor was like a shrine to the eighties, with not one detail changed. I'd been there more than thirty years earlier, in 1986, when I cohosted the show, with Paul Simon and the South African group Ladysmith Black Mambazo as musical guests. Same nerves; different platform. Thirty years ago, I made the audience laugh; this time my monologue would possibly induce tears and outrage.

Karim and crew crammed into the tiny dressing room with me as I studied and memorized a list of phrases to preface my statements with and supposedly protect myself from slander: "It appears," "It seems," "I believe," "I was told," "I heard," "According to sources," "Allegedly," "I strongly suspect," "I learned," "I wonder," "Apparently," "My impression is," "There are allegations of," "I view this as," "In my opinion" . . .

I smiled at the irony. The first time I learned how to avoid slander or libel was in that first ESP course I took with India six and a half years earlier, never imagining that one day I'd be using what they taught me against them, to expose them. The preferred nonlibelous phrase of ESP was "In my opinion"; I made a mental note to include that one in my interview as an F-U to them.

As I stepped in front of the cameras, I worried my mind would go blank or that I'd get carried away with my emotions and go off on a tirade, but, thankfully, that didn't happen. My interview with Megyn ended up being the strongest, clearest interview I'd ever done in my life—the power and conviction of my words stunned even me. "To me, brainwashing is not consent," I told Megyn. "Extortion is not consent. Blackmail is not consent . . . I'm only doing this to bring awareness because without awareness, there can be no outrage. And unless there's outrage, authorities are not going to step in and do what they should do, which is shut this down and stop this from happening." As I left the stage, Megyn continued talking about the

Me Too movement, and Matt Lauer, who'd interviewed me several times over the years, was standing on the sidelines waiting to say hello to me. Less than a month later, he, too, would be outed by the Me Too movement and terminated from his job because of previous sexual misconduct.

In the dressing room, I collapsed into a chair and dissolved into tears.

"Home run," Karim said, giving me a hug. Maybe so. But to me, I'd reached my breaking point. I was done giving interviews. The anguish of exposing India on camera was unbearable.

—

BACK AT MY Lower East Side hotel that afternoon, I combined back-to-back meetings.

The first to arrive was an old family friend, Stanley Zareff, who'd been one of my first acting coaches (after Richard Burton) and who used to accompany me to auditions in the early 1980s, rubbing my back to calm my nerves. Stanley is a flamboyant Texan with an outlandish Auntie Mame optimism who can always make me laugh. He was the perfect antidote to my high-stress, high-stakes morning. Funnily enough, Stanley had been in the audience with my mother when I'd hosted *SNL* back in '86.

When I saw him now, I hugged him like a drowning woman clings to a life jacket. Stanley had stayed in touch with India and my mom over the years, taking them to the theater whenever they passed through the city. I asked him to text India, to see if we'd get a response. I'd sent her a note that I'd be in New York but hadn't heard back.

After Stanley, Karim, and his crew arrived, a few minutes later, so did cult buster Rick Alan Ross. It was my first time meeting Rick after having spoken to him for months on the phone about all things cultish. He'd driven up from Trenton, New Jersey, so we could meet and shoot some footage with Karim.

We were all crammed in my hotel room, I was still a bit emotional from the interview that morning. I was telling Stanley that India had told her fathers and sisters that I was "victim shaming" her with what I'd been saying in my interviews, and even by giving interviews at all. (But if the cult didn't believe in victims, how could I be victim shaming her?)

"Catherine, I read your print interviews and watched your Megyn Kelly interview this morning," Rick said, "and not one thing you said about India was derogatory or critical or shamed her. You attacked Keith and Nxivm. But all you showed for India was love and concern and fear about what she's involved in. What you are doing is *not* shaming."

"But she can't separate herself from Keith; that's the problem."

"That's the indoctrination," explained Rick. "She feels one and the same with him, so she has to defend him."

It was pretty helpful to have a cult expert on hand, especially because, a minute later, India started texting me—and about the very topic we'd just been discussing.

Mom, I love you. But I don't agree with your approach, publicly shaming me and people I care for. That's hard for me to see as loving for me. That's not very considerate of our private relationship. I'm sorry if you're afraid, that's very sad for me to hear especially when there's no reason for you to be. I've been cautious about our communication and don't think the people you're working with have your or my best interest.

It was obvious she was being scripted by someone else—the wording wasn't her style at all—and after a few back-and-forths, there were long pauses in between her texts. Since I had a cult expert by my side, I made good use of him.

"How should I answer her, Rick?" He began coaching me, too. I wrote:

You have every right to be angry with me. In spite of that, I hope u can understand that I am coming from love. No one is telling me to do this, no one is using me for their agenda. My agenda is to make sure that u are safe, and I have concerns for your well-being. I am a mother afraid for her daughter. I respect your right to make choices, and I hope that you can do the same for me. I look forward to seeing u soon.

India: What do you think is happening? Safe from what? What is the danger that you see that I'm in? There's many people I speak to on a regular basis who do not see this. So it's strange to me since no one else seems to see that there's anything happening that's bad or dangerous.

So she was being coached on her end, and I was being coached on my end. What happened next bordered on farce. I got a text from one of my neighborhood watches in Albany, who'd just seen India walk past her window . . . with Nancy Salzman and Keith! So now I had a good idea of who might be writing those texts: the Beast himself and Gold Sash!

With Rick coaching me what to write in Manhattan, and Keith likely dictating to India what to write in Albany, the conversation essentially became a psychological sparring between Keith the Cult Leader and Rick the Cult Buster. Had the circumstances not been so serious, I would have been laughing my ass off.

Our texting session finally ended with me telling India I'd like to visit her in Albany, and her saying she'd be out of town.

———

I SPENT THE next two days in Manhattan fielding calls from lawyers. Anne Champion had been right: they were lining up to work pro bono after the *Times* article came out.

I decided on two incredible law firms whose attorneys graciously stepped up to the plate to champion the cause: Art Middlemiss and Anthony Capozzolo at Lewis Baach Kaufmann Middlemiss, PLLC, and Neil Glazer at Kohn, Swift & Graf, P.C.

I was so moved by these solid, decent men who wanted to help India and me and the other victims. Art volunteered to make the long drive from Manhattan to Albany to be with me during my meeting with Deputy Chief Antoine Karam of the New York State Attorney General's Office.

Art, Anthony, and Neil were three more angels I added to my army. All along, one of the main advantages Raniere had over his victims was Clare Bronfman's endless billions at his disposal for lawyers and litigation costs. Now I had the unlimited support of three of the finest and fiercest attorneys on the East Coast. So I was about to give Keith the old one-two punch, with the law and the press behind me.

At least, that's what I hoped. Four days before my meeting with Antoine, Karim attended a cocktail party on November 2 where he chatted with then–Attorney General of New York Eric Schneiderman's girlfriend, Tanya Selvaratnam. Karim was talking about what he was working on and told her about Keith and the cult.

"I wouldn't count on too much help from Eric," she said to Karim, obliquely. "He has too many similarities [to Keith]."

The day after Tanya gave the cryptic message to Karim, she moved out of Schneiderman's apartment.

Karim and I didn't understand Tanya's comment until six months later, when four women, including Tanya, asserted in a *New Yorker* article that Schneiderman used his stature to threaten them physically and emotionally.

He would insist Tanya call him "Master" while he called her his "brown slave" and his "property," Tanya told the magazine.

Another ex-girlfriend claimed Schneiderman controlled what she ate and enforced such a strict diet that she lost thirty pounds and her hair began falling out. Two of the women interviewed claimed he threatened to kill them if they left him.

Three hours after the *New Yorker* feature hit the news cycle, Schneiderman resigned.

—

THE CLOCK WAS ticking. I now had forty-eight hours until my meeting with Antoine, and I still needed to get my hands on some hard evidence. I'd been making frantic calls, but people were afraid. Everyone was always afraid.

I boarded a flight to Buffalo. Only one man now could help me, and he wasn't afraid.

Frank Parlato had aggregated piles of evidence over the years after countless victims had reached out to him. But would he give it to me? I wasn't sure. He was like a fire-breathing dragon sitting on his mountain of loot. But I was also a fierce mother lioness, and I intended to go into that meeting with enough ammo to take down Keith, and I intended on making Frank my secret weapon.

Frank had needed my help before, and now I needed his.

I was both excited and apprehensive about our first meeting. He's the kind of man who could elicit both those feelings from you simultaneously.

We'd already had some drama in the days leading up to our meeting. First, Frank had been sparring with one of my new lawyers. Second, I was bringing Karim and the crew with me, and Frank made it very clear that he didn't want to be on camera. Then he canceled our meeting twice.

The latest word was that the meeting was on, but I wasn't sure about anything else.

When we arrived at his home in the afternoon of November 4, there was no sign of Frank. We were greeted by Chitra and Debbie, two friends of his who had offered to help us with the paperwork ahead, they said, which was a good sign.

Twenty minutes later, Frank arrived, flanked by a Felliniesque posse. On his right stood a giant biker wearing ginger chops, Hells Angels gear, and a belly like a battering ram. He was also sporting a huge hunting knife, very visibly. To Frank's left was a very elderly gentleman sporting a chic beret and mumbling through his thick white mustache. He took copious notes on a giant legal pad the entire time he was there and then left with them.

Frank himself looked like a cross between Sherlock Holmes and a crime reporter plucked out of a 1970s newsroom. He was in his sixties, of medium height and build, wore a tweed jacket, and slicked his hair to the side. He delivered hilarious zingers, but his face remained deadpan—was he smiling or sneering? You never knew.

Frank circled us, eyeing the camera suspiciously.

"No cameras. I told you I want to focus on the work," he said. "We have to get this done, and I don't want any interruptions. Everyone has to be in the same headspace, or it will interfere with my concentration."

I tried to convince him, but one look at Karim's talent release form, and Frank announced there was no way he could agree to the terms. He wanted 100 percent control of his likeness. Then Karim put down his foot: no way could he allow that, as it would prevent him from selling the project.

I suggested we just start working with no filming, and once we got into a rhythm, we could reassess. Putting together the evidence packet was number one on the agenda. But that didn't work, either.

"Karim's moping about," said Frank. "I can feel it."

Now I put down *my* foot. The sun was going down, and we hadn't gotten any work done yet. Frank was also frustrated. He suggested the camera crew go check into their hotel, and then he banished his two assistants.

Now the house was empty—it was just Frank and me—and I had a blinding headache. Was he going to help me, or was I stuck with this uncompromising man in his *Addams Family* house with his colorful cast of characters, never to be heard from again?

Frank suggested we move from the dining room into the living room, farther from the hope of work, where he offered to work on my back and neck to get rid of my building migraine. He started digging his thumbs into the pressure points in my neck.

"Have you ever had your palms read?" he asked.

He transitioned instantly from shiatsu practitioner to palm reader, grabbing one of my hands and inspecting my palm.

"You have a very well developed Mount of Venus. Did you know that?"

Where was he going with this?

He took my hands into his and started pressing into my Mounts of Venus, the fleshy areas at the base of the thumbs.

"You are a very evolved person," he said, looking at the lines in my hand. "And you are strong energetically . . . Your health is good."

Good health, that was nice to hear. Because I felt like I was falling apart. Then Frank started to wax lyrically about how he could help me with India on an energetic level by "mixing *prana*"—Sanskrit for "life force." He moved his hands together as if they were blending. Apparently Frank was a Renaissance man who wore many hats.

Before I had a chance to ask what "prana mixing" entailed, Frank jumped up and announced it was time for the crew to return so we could all go sightseeing.

To Niagara Falls. At ten o'clock on a cold, drizzling night. The crew returned, and we all climbed into Frank's silver Lexus to trudge to the Falls. It was only a thirty-minute drive, and as we got closer, we could hear the water's roar. We parked and got out to walk a short distance to the Falls—just as the drizzle turned into a monsoon. By the time we got to the lookout point, we were drenched. Sensing that a *moment* was to come, Karim turned on his camera.

"You know, I used to catch rattlesnakes when I was a kid," Frank yelled over the rumbling water. "At first, the bite was excruciating. But eventually I got used to it."

Karim and the others looked both stunned and enthralled.

"Um, Frank!" I shouted. "How many times did you have to get bitten before you developed a tolerance for it?"

He shrugged. "A lot."

And standing there by the thundering waterfalls, soaking wet, I started to laugh.

Was it any wonder why Frank wasn't afraid of Keith and his minions? He had inoculated himself against rattlesnake venom; he was like a snake medicine man! He'd harnessed nature's poison, and it had given him a superpower to fight the Beast! Right there in that moment, I decided I liked Frank—very much. A snake master like him was exactly what I needed to help me fight this unusual battle between good and evil.

"Hey, Frank!" I yelled again. "Why were you catching the snakes in the first place, especially after they kept biting you? What kid in his right mind would do such a thing?"

Frank looked at me as if what he'd done was the most normal thing in the world for a kid to do.

"Why, to eat them, of course."

Yes, sir. Frank was the man for this job.

—

THE NEXT DAY, Frank's living room turned into a war room like mine back home.

Whatever had happened to Frank in Niagara Falls the night before—some sort of alchemic baptizing from the water from the sky mixed with the water from the Falls—had turned him into a powerhouse.

I stayed in his guest room that night, and when I walked into the war room the next morning, he was working at his computer—right where we'd left him the night before, in his damp, dark, rumpled clothes—typing up the comprehensive memo that was to go with the evidence packet. It would outline and explain every possible state or federal crime committed and law broken by Raniere and his group, and would include instructions on navigating the packet section by section, complete with ID codes and numbers.

Like magic, all sorts of other evidence began pouring in that morning from the people I'd reached out to the week before, and from Frank, who'd opened his coffers.

I was printing, Frank was printing, Chitra and Debbie were printing. The whirring of the printers and crunching of the hole punchers and staplers were nonstop.

Chitra and Debbie stacked hundreds of pages of evidence and sorted them into five giant folders lined up on a long table like an assembly line.

In the middle of our busy activity I got a tip that the so-called branding doctor, Danielle Roberts, was going to be speaking about "wellness" at the Naval Expo in New York City and Long Island over the next two days and that a bunch of women from the cult, including India, would be accompanying her. They were probably going to use the expo as a recruiting venue!

I immediately alerted the producers at *20/20*, who were working on a story about the cult to air in December, so they could send a reporter with a camera to confront the doctor.

Then, I got one of the expo organizers on the phone and tried to get her to cancel Danielle's talk, explaining that her idea of wellness was branding other women.

"It's all over the news!" I told her.

"Well, you can't believe everything you read," the organizer said.

"Well, she branded my daughter!" I said, exasperated.

The organizer hung up on me.

Right around then, Frank's biker friend—whom I'd nicknamed "Chops"—arrived. He wanted to help, too, and became our newest towering crusader.

"I'll call them, too, Catherine," said Chops. "I'll lodge a complaint. You need backup!" (*20/20* did show up and caused quite a stir, scaring off DOS attendees and potential recruits.)

In the afternoon, Toni Natalie, Keith's former girlfriend, arrived from Rochester to meet me. She was a beautiful, elegant woman, and even though she'd been through hell at the hands of this madman and suffered debilitating PTSD, she looked radiant and was warm and loving.

"The last thing Keith ever said to me," Toni told me, "was: 'I'll see you dead or in jail.' "

She was the first one brave enough to come out against Keith publicly, and he used her as an example to keep others from doing the same.

"But Keith underestimated three things," she said: "the internet, the *FrankReport*, and the power of a mother's love.

"Catherine," she said to me, "all this time I was waiting for a Prince Charming to rescue me from this nightmare. And it turned out to be you, a princess, who would do it."

I did want to rescue Toni, and all of them, along with my daughter. Toni helped with the last of the paperwork, and by the time we finished, it was ten thirty at night. Each evidence packet was more than three hundred pages thick.

Before we left Frank's, he gave me a final coaching session in the kitchen, the same way that a trainer preps a boxer before he heads toward the ring.

"When you get in the meeting room, place the evidence packet right in the middle of the table," he instructed. "Watch if they lean in and pull it toward them. If they do, that's a good sign. Sit like this and put your hands like this," he said, placing his fingers together like a steeple. "It looks authoritative. And drink some pineapple juice before you go."

With that, he handed me a bottle of juice, I hugged Chops, and Toni gave me a tight hug.

"We are bookends, you and I," she said. "I started this. Now you go and finish it."

—

WE DROVE AT breakneck speed through the inky blackness and arrived in Albany at three in the morning. While still at Frank's, I'd texted India again, asking if we could meet up. I also told her I'd like to get together with Keith, with Nancy, with all of them. I didn't hear back.

In Albany, I was back in enemy territory, but this time I was there to declare war, and I had my comrades with me.

Frank was still furiously working on the memo when I went to sleep and I prayed he'd email it to me in the morning and that I'd be of sane mind—compos mentis—for the meeting a few hours later.

After four hours of fitful sleep, I got up to meditate, pray, fling myself in the shower, and obediently drink my mandated pineapple juice.

When I met Art in the hotel lobby, I was still texting Frank: "Where's the memo?! We're leaving!"

Minutes before our departure, Frank's email finally arrived. The front desk hurriedly printed all twenty-six pages before I dashed into the car with them. Then it was an ordeal leaving the hotel. The front driveway was filled with chanting picketers and union reps handing out flyers and urging guests to boycott the hotel.

Somehow we got out of the driveway. But then we couldn't locate Antoine's office. Karim and the crew were with us, and he drove around in circles until we had to make a few phone calls for help in order to find our destination: a building in a sea of identical, unmarked black towering monoliths. It looked like something out of Stanley Kubrick's film *2001: A Space Odyssey*.

Inside, Antoine ushered Art and me into a large conference room, and before we started, I quickly signed retainer papers with Art to be protected by client-attorney privilege. As I wrote my name, I had a sudden moment of paranoia.

What if this is a trap? What if I am going to be dragged away in handcuffs, framed for something dastardly? It wouldn't be the first time an enemy of the cult had become the target.

As I was thinking this, six burly men in suits filed into the conference room from various departments of law enforcement. They all handed me their cards: NY State Police, Special Crimes Investigations, Financial Crimes Unit. It was too late to make a run for it. I prayed none of them had been bought off by Bronfman money.

Antoine, a clean-cut, nice-looking man who looked to be in his early forties, sat at the head of the table. I handed the memo to one of the men, who made multiple copies for everyone. Then I did as Frank instructed: I plunked the book of evidence in the center of the table with a loud thud. That thing was *heavy*.

They all leaned in.

I had dressed conservatively for the meeting: navy-blue skirt, gray Armani sweater, a dignified scarf around my neck. But my boots! They were gray suede and thigh high. To paraphrase Nancy Sinatra, those boots were made for ass-kickin'! They meant business.

I opened the cover of the packet to reveal the first page to them all: a giant color photograph of the jagged red brand of Keith's and Allison's initials on a slave's pubic region.

Then, with my kick-ass boots, I pushed myself back from the table on my castor-wheeled chair so they could all see my body, and I pointed to my crotch:

"It's here, *right here*," I said to them, making eye contact with each man in that room. "And it's happening in your own backyard."

Silence.

I may have overdone the dramatics.

Art took over then and gave them an outline of what was in the packet. Then he handed the floor back to me.

"This is clear evidence of RICO, gentlemen," I said with conviction. Never mind that two months earlier, I had no idea what RICO was.

I opened the packet and began to flip through pages and point to my layperson conclusions that I hoped would finally prompt an investigation, including money laundering, human trafficking, unlicensed school, unpaid taxes, branding, bribery, forgery, and fraud.

I went on and on, offering a smorgasbord of crimes for them to pick from. When I was done, I asked one of the men which crime they might be interested in.

"Everything," he said, very seriously. "All of them."

That's when I gave Art the nod, and I stood up. I was a trained actress, I knew when and how to exit a scene.

"Gentlemen," I said, "I think we all know we are dealing with criminals here. Let's find the most expedient way to bring them to justice, shall we?"

They all nodded in agreement, and I strode out of the room with those boots that meant business.

—

AFTER THE MEETING, Karim, the crew, and I drove to meet my number-one Clifton Park spy, Lori Christina, who'd been my greatest source of information about the minute-to-minute movements of every cult member. We were also going to meet Chris Burbs, who had briefly dated a DOS slave (until she tried to recruit him into ESP).

Lori lived in Keith's neighborhood and saw all the comings and goings of the cult peeps—she was my very own neighborhood watchdog. She wasn't an Espian, but she had lived long enough in the neighborhood to know all their names, where they lived, and the Nxivm weekly schedules. I found her through Frank, and then after the media blitz, I gathered a few more volunteers who lived in Clifton Park and Halfmoon, where the slaves and high-ranking cult members resided. Keith's neighbors hated him, so they were happy to feed me information. Even before all the press hit, no one liked the creepy guy who walked around at all hours of the night with a different skinny girl each time.

"He devalues the neighborhood!" one spy complained to me.

Another, responding to the *New York Times* story, emailed:

This creep Keith lives in my condo development. He walks around our neighborhood 15 miles per day . . . usually with a different girl. I never knew who he was until recently but always felt he was totally whacked. My neighbor sprayed him with her hose the other day. He is so gross, and I don't understand how he has manipulated all these women. 2 of those crazy doctors have been fired from a local Albany hospital.

I hope they bring criminal charges against this freak and get him the fuck out of my neighborhood.

As we sat in the restaurant, we got an urgent text from Chris Burb with a tip that a DOS master was at a café a few blocks away, aggressively trying to convince another DOS member not to defect. We zipped over, and Karim outfitted Chris with a hidden camera.

The plan was for us to wait in the parking lot while Chris went inside and got close enough to record what was happening. Karim had failed to instruct Chris to act like a secret agent and be inconspicuous, figuring the phrase "hidden camera" was self-explanatory.

Chris, who looked like a cross between the Marlboro Man and a bearded Tom Brady, walked right up to the female recruiter and the near defector, also a woman, and, in front of the entire restaurant, yelled:

"Give my friend her collateral back!"

The Espian freaked out and called for SOP backup. Chris pointed out the window at our car in the lot, and shouted again in a booming voice:

"India Oxenberg's mom, Catherine, is in the parking lot! What do you have to say to her?!"

Some big guy showed up just then—from the SOP, I assumed—to usher the two women out of danger.

My cover was officially blown, and now I was vaguely worried that some psycho Espian would be dispatched by the flying monkeys to find me and hunt me down.

We piled into the car and fled, and my spy took us on a scenic tour of all things cult. She knew where they all lived and hung out. Everything and everybody was a ten-minute drive away from one another; they were all embedded in normal, middle-to-upper-class suburban communities.

She drove us past their run-down clubhouse, formerly a restaurant, called Apropos; the gym where Keith played volleyball each week;

and the condo Keith reserved for various intimate encounters . . . he called it "the Library." We drove by the houses of Nxivm top brass—one house owned by a reject from Keith's harem whom I called "Rapunzel," had windows blocked by white paper and tape. For years, Keith didn't let her cut her hair because of a breach she'd committed; it grew so long that it dragged on the ground.

It was like a Beverly Hills tour of movie stars' homes, but not.

I wondered if India was really out of town, or if we'd get a sighting of her. That's what I was hoping for. I wanted to scoop her up and take her away. As it got dark, we turned a corner, and Lori Christina pointed out 21 Oregon Trail: the spacious five-bedroom house where Keith lived with his harem. Certainly not the lifestyle of a renunciant.

As we drove by slowly, we saw three silhouettes walking on the road: a short male wearing droopy gray sweats flanked by two women, both brunettes.

"Oh my God!" I shrieked. "It's *Keith*!"

By the time we caught up to the trio, Keith had scuttled away, disappearing into the house. Seconds later, we saw someone peer out from behind the curtains. Was that Keith hiding? Karim got out of the car as I hid under the dashboard. I wasn't about to give them any excuse to accuse me of gnome-stalking as Clare had done to Frank. Karim rang the bell, but no one answered. And I didn't have any time to wait around.

We had to drive back to New York City that night because I had more meetings there in the morning.

When I woke up the next day, I was a bit shell-shocked from my trip—the long-awaited meeting with Antoine and spotting Keith had both incited and drained me.

The cult leader was a deranged criminal roaming the streets for all to see. And those burly men at the AG office with their business cards were only a thirty-minute drive away. They had the three-hundred-page evidence packet. Were they going to do anything about this?

On the way to the airport the following day, I got my answer when Art and Anthony called.

"We wanted to let you know that the AUSA of the Eastern District has moved in aggressively and has enlisted the FBI," Art said. You don't have to carry this burden on your shoulders alone anymore. You have help. They are taking this very seriously."

I burst into tears in the back of the taxi. I had never anticipated the Eastern District.

"I didn't think they had jurisdiction!" I said. The Eastern District's jurisdiction covered Brooklyn, Staten Island, and all of Long Island—all of them about 160 miles from Albany.

"They're looking at ports of entry," Anthony explained.

I immediately understood the implication: the airports the women flew in and out of. They were going for trafficking! This was huge!

"Assistant US Attorney Moira Kim Penza was particularly moved by your story," Art added.

I held the phone still but couldn't speak.

It had taken a woman and a mother to understand.

It had taken a woman to respond to my call for help. And it was going to take a group of women to take down Keith Raniere.

And when it was all over, I knew that's what would infuriate him the most.

15

D-DAY OR DOOMSDAY

The FBI was on the case, and I was right there with them.

After I left the attorney general's office in Albany, I'd sent dozens of witnesses and defectors to their point people to provide testimony and evidence, overwhelming them and jamming their phone lines. But within twenty-four hours of the FBI's involvement, I'd rerouted and funneled everyone to the bureau. In the meantime, Neil's law firm agreed to represent the DOS victims pro bono.

For a moment, I allowed myself some hope. How could I not? I envisioned the FBI slapping handcuffs on Keith Raniere, ransacking cult headquarters, and India free at last.

But even though the investigation was now in good, official hands, my anxiety continued to grow over the next few months as I waited for the Feds to complete their probe and take action. When would they storm the ESP offices in Albany and handcuff Keith and his cronies? My biggest worry now was not just that they wouldn't capture Keith but that they wouldn't capture him *in time*.

Would they get to him before India was pulled in so deep she wouldn't be able to get out? For the first time since Bonnie's urgent phone call six months earlier, I was realizing that not only was I being called to save her from the cult, but also I was in a race against time to save her *life*.

And not only hers.

Under the new pressure stirred up by the media exposure and the FBI hunt, what if Keith went berserk and, in a bold, deranged statement, ordered his flock to take part in a glorified doomsday pact together? It was possible. Rick Alan Ross had been worried about the same scenario.

"I feared we'd end up dealing with a mass suicide situation," he told me later, "but I didn't tell you at the time because I didn't want to scare you."

Well, I was scared with or without him telling me. And there was more to be scared about: like Keith's grandiose scheme to take over the world and achieve global domination.

Keith had been playing and positioning his devoted follower Emiliano Salinas as his pawn for years while Emi's family groomed him to follow in his father's political footsteps. From what I heard from high-ranking defectors, the supposed plan was to get Emi into office in Mexico's next presidential election in the summer of 2018 so that a top-ranking Espian and Nxivm devotee would have power on the world's political stage. His father, Carlos, would use his Machiavellian methods to ensure his son's election win, and then Keith would use Emi as his puppet and rule Mexico.

And that wasn't all. According to Bonnie, Sara Bronfman's husband, Libyan businessman Basit Igtet, had taken Nxivm classes for several months. Igtet was a Libyan national and supporter of the Libyan revolution. Could Keith have been mentoring Igtet, as he had with Salinas, in the hope of expanding Nxivm's tentacles to positions of power around the world?

It hadn't worked—yet. Once it did, Nxivm would be planted in Libya as well.

But Libya and Mexico were just warm-ups for Keith's ultimate target: the superpower of America.

Keith told Lisa the year before that he was planning to give his slaves orders that he didn't have the strength to give yet. After my talks with Frank, Rick, and many defectors, we decided that Keith's warning meant that he was going to ask his DOS slaves to sacrifice their lives for the cause somehow; we just weren't sure how.

Either way, their sacrifices would be so that Keith could attain more power to influence and take over the world.

I know, I know: it sounds like a fictional plot for a political or sci-fi thriller. But this was no Hollywood movie. Keith was a real-life Dr. Evil.

Think about it: he was training young children in his school to be his mindless drones, a little army of Rainbow Culture Children, and ten to fifteen years down the road they'd be of fighting age and under his power—his own Aryan Nation.

He'd already trained his slaves to have sex on command and take postcoital proof photos. According to one of his harem members, when he was confronted with legal troubles in Albany, he'd ordered his harem to strategically seduce and photograph certain law enforcement officials in flagrante, including cops and district attorneys, to blackmail them for his legal advantage.

Taking it one step further, his ninja concubines had then been desensitized and trained using violent films and branding to give them the ability to tolerate, endure, and inflict unbearable pain. So now he had a small army of loyal, brainwashed, fearless, desensitized women ready to go undercover at his beck and call and do whatever it took to please their master.

After all that, my final worry—and I don't even know how to rank which one of these was "worst"—was that Keith and his flying monkeys would set up the DOS slaves, or maybe just India, to take the fall.

A few days after that phone call from my lawyer, I got another big call—from Assistant US Attorney Moira Kim Penza, FBI special agent Mike W., and one of my lawyers. They called to apologize for the Albany office's lack of a quicker, better response over the summer.

"I want to offer my most sincere apology," Mike W. said. "I can imagine how hard this is for you."

Moira asked if I'd be willing to fly to New York to testify in front of a grand jury.

"Of course," I said. "Whatever it takes. Whenever you need me."

"One more thing," Mike said on the phone. "You did the right thing, Ms. Oxenberg. You shone the light where it needed to be. So now, uh, you can stop investigating and let us do our job, okay?"

I laughed, relieved to hand over the baton to them. But as I've said, my relief was always short-lived. On the tail end of my Albany trip, I found out that India had flown to Los Angeles to escape the media attention and, possibly, to avoid seeing me—which was heartbreaking. But, I reasoned, at least it got her away from the cult epicenter, and that was good. And then I'd heard she planned to stay in LA for good and that she'd been staying with Casper, but neither Casper nor Bill had let me know.

"I thought I could count on solidarity from you!" I said to Bill on the phone.

"Don't expect it," he said. "Look, India's fine. In fact, she's better than ever."

I wanted to say to him: "Bill, you are in denial along with her. At some point you will have to deal with reality!" Instead, I hung up, stunned and exasperated. India didn't want to see me, and that was to be expected. But I couldn't understand how the entire world was outraged after hearing defectors describe publicly how they were coerced, extorted, blackmailed, abused, and tortured— and yet her father thought India was "fine" and in no danger.

Assuming he'd read the *New York Times* article, why was he not disturbed by it when the FBI was *so* disturbed, they were charging in?

Unfortunately, Bill was buying into India's narrative hook, line, and sinker, and it seemed like Casper was, too. She was trying to convince everyone that I was exaggerating and what they'd read in the news was made up. When I needed her fathers the most to stand by me in order to help her, all I felt was their resistance.

Once again I went to Rick Alan Ross for help to understand it all.

"You know, it's not such a bad setup," he observed. "Let the dads be the 'good cops,' and you can be the 'bad cop' and play that game even if it hurts your feelings. The dynamic can work for you behind the scenes to your advantage."

He stressed again how important it was for India to keep a link, a lifeline, to the family and to have some members she felt she could trust. This way the cult wouldn't take over her life entirely.

"She needs a safe harbor, so let her feel she has it with her dads," said Rick. "Swallow your pride. They can't *really* think she's okay."

When I picked up the girls from Casper's after my return from Albany, they piled into the car upset and angry. They'd just spent a week with India and she'd gotten them all riled up.

"What you've done to India is terrible!" Celeste and Maya said in unison.

"She can't walk outside without the press chasing her. You ruined her life, Mom! She says she's stigmatized."

I stayed calm and talked them through it as we drove home.

"Girls, you know if I could have done anything else, I would have . . . and that I tried everything, right?"

They nodded.

"This was my last resort. If you needed saving, wouldn't you want me to do everything I could to save you?"

They nodded again.

When we got home, I was drained. I had plenty of support from friends and now, finally, law enforcement, but very little from my own family. I'd reached an emotional threshold I didn't think I could bear on my own. Feeling utterly alone, I called my mother in Belgrade.

"Shall I come to LA, darling?"

"Yes, please," I said, bursting into tears. Mom immediately booked a flight to arrive a few days later. She didn't quite understand the depth of danger India was in, and she came from a generation that didn't put credence in the concept of brainwashing. ("This sounds like nonsense," she said when I tried to explain what was going on.) But my mother understood enough to know that her family needed her, and she got on that plane as fast as she could to help and show solidarity.

—

EVEN THOUSANDS OF miles away, the Albany contingency had its hooks into India deeper than ever. She was on her cell phones even more than before, her sisters reported. And a call from Bonnie confirmed my suspicions that she wasn't in LA only to skip seeing me in Albany.

She was also here on orders.

"I think the DOS girls have been sent out on missions," Bonnie said. "It's what they've been trained for."

Lisa agreed, telling me: "All DOS girls are trained to fight for Keith and fight for the cause."

But what had they been sent out to do?

When I began speaking to defectors in the summer, some speculated that if Keith got in trouble and needed a diversion, he'd push a loyal DOS slave to commit an "honor" suicide.

And then I remembered something. I called Bonnie and asked her about the early modules India and I had done during our first classes at ESP—the ones India later repeated hundreds of times in Ethos. Sure enough, my memory was correct. On day five, one of the modules under the "Good and Bad" theme posed the question: "When is suicide honorable?"

The coaches built up to the question like a logical, mathematical equation: Survival and values were "good" while the destruction of values and counter-survival was "bad." But could these concepts ever overlap or intermingle? The groups in class were asked:

Can you think of anything that is counter-survival and/or destroys value that is good?

Can you think of anything that is pro-survival and builds value that is bad?

When is suicide good?

"Right from the start," Bonnie said, "we talked about cases when suicide would be considered good." I remembered during the Characterization class Casper and I took—our final class before we left ESP for good—the coach talked about the Vietnamese Mahayana Buddhist monk Thích Quảng Đức, who set himself on fire in 1963 in the middle of a busy intersection in Saigon. He was an example of tremendous character, said the coach, because he felt joy as his body burned and he died for his beliefs, becoming a martyr for the good of the cause.

Keith talked about that monk all the time, and other examples like Nelson Mandela and Gandhi, who sacrificed for their beliefs. The thing about Keith, though, was that he enjoyed watching *others* do the sacrificing. Being the malignant, narcissistic, punitive, and vindictive psychopath that he was, I could see Keith ordering his slaves to drink the cyanide-laced Kool-Aid while he ended up sipping piña coladas in a thatched hut in Fiji.

Was this the fate of the DOS women? The murky details of their mission would become clearer over the next few weeks as I continued to try convincing my daughter via text to get out.

Me: Sweetheart—I know u think u are part of something good, but please research the law to understand the seriousness. I don't want u to get into trouble.

India: I have, mom. Plenty, actually tons. The people that you're working with are actually accused criminals. Frank your expert has only ever written slander and has been paid money to do so. It's devastating for me to see you being this convinced to the point of destroying my image and publicly painting me as a victim and a violator of woman. The accusations you've made against me are outstandingly false and traumatic. I'm now dealing with them constantly, and the effects have put a huge weight and disturbance to my life that I don't even think you can image. I have had zero issues spending time with family and friends here in LA or elsewhere. I've actively decided to not speak with you out of principle because I think what you're doing is so damaging to me and my friends and family. So for you to say I'm trapped or blocking you is not true. I've actually only said kind things about you in your defense and tried to understand your perspective. At this point, my conversations with you seem futile since your absolutely convinced that I'm brainwashed or crazy, and I don't see the point in trying to convince or prove otherwise to you. If that's what you believe, I can't change your mind about me. your just the only one who seems to see me unwell. That's all I have to say at this point. I'm interested in seeing Elizabeth tomorrow if she would like.

I could see that this text was definitely not written by India; I wondered which cult handler helped her with this one. You would think by now I would have learned not to use the "B" word, but no . . .

Me: You are brainwashed. Many people have left ESP and there are some very disturbing stories. As a mother, it is normal that I would be concerned. Frank is not my expert—I'm not sure where u got that from—I am working with Rachel Bernstein. As a mother, I would hope that you would see your daughter and not just believe hearsay or other people's opinions.

I have asked to see u—and am available any time.

India: I have also offered to see you but not under your current perspective, it's somewhat futile if your just convinced that I'm brainwashed but with a neutral mediator. I'll see Elizabeth separately.

Me: Then see me with a neutral arbitrator. When u are ready.

India: I would like to see my grandma if she wants to tomorrow.

Me: She would love to—and she will be there.

My heart broke again (how many times can a heart actually break and still stay intact?) when I read India's last bit about seeing her grandma. I could hear the little girl in her wanting nurturing and love, and I wished I could be the one she was running to. I was grateful that my mother could be a safe harbor for her until I would be a possibility again.

But for now, I was the enemy.

"She looks through a specific lens that redefines good and evil," Diane Benscoter, one of my cult-expert friends, told me, "and she has redefined you as evil."

Diane is a former Moonie and wrote the book *Shoes of a Servant: My Unconditional Devotion to a Lie.*

Even though India was redefining me as the enemy, "she has to know you wouldn't risk losing her just for publicity or fame or money. You've already had all those things."

Mom arrived in LA, and before her meeting with India the next day, I briefed her on what to ask and how to respond. The following day, I dropped her off in Santa Monica, at the same corner where I'd dropped off India six months earlier. As I pulled to the curb, I looked up—and there was beautiful India, walking toward us a short distance away. I stuck my arm out of my car and waved, and then blew her a kiss. She smiled and waved back.

It was the first time in six months I'd seen her lovely face. And even though it was brief and from afar, my heart leapt.

When I picked up Mom two hours later, India had already left, and Mom began telling me details as soon as she got in the car.

"She was sweet and so loving, Catherine," my mother told me, "and very happy to see me."

She relayed the conversation as we drove:

"What do you want me to tell you, Grandma?"

"I'd like you to tell me all about what goes on in Albany. There are about thirty defectors who I hear were good friends of yours. Would you like to talk to them?"

"I would," she said to my mother. But I knew it was only lip service—she'd shunned every defector.

"Do you have to ask for permission before you do anything?"

"No."

I knew that DOS slaves did have to ask permission for pretty much everything from their masters.

"They've lost a lot of business because of all the press," said India, quickly changing the subject.

"But India . . . all these girls have been harassed and abused."

"It's not true, Grandma. I haven't heard any of that or seen any abuse!"

"If that was true, would you leave? It's very possible that some things have happened that you don't know about. I'm concerned—there is a legal aspect here. These young girls are coming over the border from Mexico . . . to . . . it looks like slavery and prostitution. I guess they all ended up in bed with Keith."

"Of course not."

"Well, when you need a lawyer, your mother has one for you. This branding . . . it's not like a tattoo," my mother said. "It is a sexual area, and it's his initials."

"They are not his initials, and it is not sexual. I love my mom, and I miss her. This is not going to go on forever between me and my mom . . . but she has not put my interest first by doing all this publicity."

"She didn't have a choice. It was the only way to get this thing moving if it is indeed a sinister cult."

"Yes, she did. She could have come up to Albany and talked to me. She didn't have to use me. I want to leave and get away from all the press and go as far away as possible. Maybe I can go to Tasmania."

"In the end, all press is good press. You can bloody well use all this attention to build a fantastic career."

"You are right. But I don't like living in LA. I don't like the movie world."

"That's BS, India. You were about to do that TV show, but it didn't work out. I hear you've been given a company, Delegates, by Keith?"

"No. That's not true. Keith is a very nice man, Grandma." Mom tried not to show her distaste at this comment. "My life is ESP," India continued. I knew what that meant: She was completely aligned with her cult persona; she was mainlining the Kool-Aid. "I know Mom thinks I'm crazy, but I'm seeing a doctor and doing tests to prove I'm not crazy. I'm on my way to Long Beach after this to do a written test to show I'm not crazy or brainwashed . . ."

I'd never in my life called her crazy; I had never used that word in conversation with her. And I was bewildered that she couldn't recall—or didn't think I would—the chat we had a year before when she excitedly told me that Keith was creating Delegates—the TaskRabbit copycat company—just for her. Either what she told my mother was a bald-faced lie, or she'd been conditioned to believe a new reality—an "alternate fact," as they say today.

I didn't understand what she meant about doctors and tests until I saw Keith's second official statement on the ESP website a week or two later. Not only did he distance himself from DOS and any criminal activity yet again, but he also announced that a team of experts had tested the women in DOS and said they were "thriving, healthy, better off, and haven't been coerced."

I heard from Barry at the *New York Times* right away, asking me if India was part of these so-called "investigations" that Raniere had announced.

I didn't know yet. It would be a few more days before I'd hear from this mysterious doctor that India had mentioned to my mother and that Keith had mentioned in the statement.

—

UNTIL THEN, I focused on another task in mid-November: getting the celebrities who'd been linked to the cult to denounce it publicly.

Disruption, disruption—I was always thinking of new ways to cause it.

My first letter was to British business magnate and billionaire Sir Richard Branson, who'd been photographed with Sara Bronfman on his private island in the British Virgin Islands, Necker Island, for a Nxivm retreat. He'd also been quoted giving an endorsement for the World Ethical Foundations Consortium, founded by Keith and the Bronfman sisters.

Sir Richard Branson
Founder, Virgin Group

The tools you have for compassionately dealing with complex ethical and global issues are not only unique, but also extremely valuable. This, along with a program of coordinated, organized resources, makes for an innovative approach to transforming our society. I think your founding event will be extraordinary and potentially world changing!

A friend of mine who knew Branson forwarded a letter from me. He responded to her the next day.

Dear ———,

I don't believe I know anything about this organisation. If I've been linked to it in the press, can somebody let me know in what context?
    So sorry to hear what your friend is going through.

X Richard

My head was reeling: Did everyone linked to Nxivm catch automatic amnesia?

My next letter was to the Dalai Lama. Mom had gotten the email address of his personal assistant through her royal connections. In 2009, His Holiness the Dalai Lama had been invited to speak at one of the foundation's functions but then publicly canceled after negative media attention about the cult hit the papers.

According to multiple high-level defectors, the Bronfman brats, Nancy, and Keith apparently flew to India to beg him in person to reconsider, which he did. According to a high-ranking defector, they doubled their initial offer of a $1 million "donation." A few days later, the Dalai Lama Trust magically became active in New York State with over $2 million in its account.

His Holiness had given a talk in Albany on May 6, sponsored by the WEFC, and Keith and cronies heralded that as a victory—especially the symbolic moment when Keith went onstage, and His Holiness placed a traditional white ceremonial Tibetan scarf, a *khata*, around his neck. In one fell swoop, the Dalai Lama had demoted Keith to novice, white-sash level.

They never mention that their victory backfired when the Dalai Lama was asked during a Q&A session why he'd previously canceled his visit.

He cited the negative press and then said to Keith, "If you have done something wrong, you must accept, you must admit, change, make correction. If you have not done [anything wrong], make clear all these allegations [are untrue], truthfully, honestly, openly, transparently." Then he asked the media to investigate Raniere and report truthfully what they found. (Which, as we've seen, didn't work out so well for the journalists who did follow up on his request.)

Despite the Dalai Lama's directive, his visit was spun by Keith and Nxivm cronies as an endorsement, and Keith milked it for years—riding on the Dalai Lama's coattails as if he himself were a philosophical leader in his own right on the global stage. I emailed the Dalai Lama in mid-November:

"I urge you to make a public statement distancing yourself from this dangerous cult," I wrote, "by stressing that your appearance was in no way an endorsement of this group."

That very day, scandal erupted on the Dalai Lama front when

it hit the news that his emissary to the United States, Lama Tenzin Dhonden—also known as "the Dalai Lama's gatekeeper"—had been involved in an affair with Sara Bronfman and had accepted millions in exchange for access to the Dalai Lama. Witnesses shared that they were spotted canoodling in a hot tub. Dhonden, who was a Buddhist monk and had taken a vow of chastity, was suspended from his post immediately, right around the time their office was reading my note.

There was an ensuing investigation into allegations by a prominent Washington businessman that Dhonden had abused his role and extorted money in return for ensuring the spiritual leader's appearance at a major Washington state event.

I never heard back from the Dalai Lama, but his office did issue an official statement saying that it never received money from Nxivm.

I did hear from Elizabeth Smart, the young woman who'd gained national attention at age fourteen after being abducted in Salt Lake City in 2002 and held captive for nine months by husband-and-wife cult members.

Today she's a mother and works as a child safety activist and contributor for ABC News. After reading the *Times* and *People* magazine stories, she kindly reached out, asking if she could be of help.

We made a plan for her to send an email to India asking if she needed support, explaining that she, too, had been a victim of media exposure and had experienced many emotions that India might be going through. Elizabeth wrote a wonderful, heartfelt letter. But India never responded.

During this same week in November, the *New York Post* linked New York senator Kirsten Gillibrand to the cult via her father, Doug

Rutnik, who worked as a lobbyist for Nxivm in 2004. (Why does a cult need a lobbyist?) After he sniffed that something smelled rotten in the state of Denmark—er, the city of Albany—he left the job after four months, and the litigious flying monkeys got to work in retaliation. Nancy Salzman went after him with her Nxivm posse. The settlement was sealed. Nancy got back all the consulting fees they'd paid Rutnik *and* got him to sign a confidentiality agreement not to talk about it.

Like Branson, Gillibrand refused to talk when asked about her father's link to the cult.

"Senator Gillibrand had never heard of this group until she recently read about them in the newspaper," said her spokesman.

It was frightening how far-reaching this group's tentacles were and how many varied people it had reached. Even more frightening was how or why so many remained silent about it.

—

ON THANKSGIVING I got the news that Vanguard, the coward, had fled town.

Except for his jaunt to Dharamsala to grovel at the Dalai Lama's feet and a foray to Fiji, this guy *never* left Albany. But somewhere in those two and a half weeks since I saw him prowling the streets of Clifton Park, he likely boarded a private plane and flew to Mexico with Clare Bronfman, Mariana Fernandez, and the Baby Avatar.

Keith always promised his flock that he'd never, ever abandon them, but now he told them he'd been forced to because his life had been threatened. By whom? I wondered. Maybe it was simply the sight of this angry mother on his doorstep with a camera crew a few weeks earlier that had scared him away.

How could the FBI let him escape like that? Did this mean they'd dropped the ball? I was totally confused, and worried that out of the country he'd go off the grid and never be captured. I tried to have faith that the FBI knew what they were doing. Maybe they were even more methodical than Keith?

By the time December rolled around the following week, India's own missions were becoming clearer—and so were the cult's devious and obvious attempts to use her.

We found out that the "doctor" she'd mentioned to my mother was Dr. Park Dietz MD, MPH, PhD, a well-known forensic psychiatrist who'd made a name for himself profiling sociopaths such as Richard Kuklinski, the prolific Mafia hit man known as the Iceman; Unabomber Ted Kaczynski; Jeffrey Dahmer; and other notable serial killers and cannibals. He'd testified as an expert witness at the murder trials of Dahmer, John Hinckley Jr., Betty Broderick, and Joel Rifkin.

Basically, he's the guy you call when you want to prove competency in even the most heinous criminals. Prosecutors call him when they want to prevent an insanity plea.

Dr. Dietz sent me a letter explaining he'd been retained on behalf of Nxivm "to conduct a psychiatric evaluation of your daughter India's competence to participate in Nxivm and ESP programs and her current mental state," he wrote. (Like the attorney in Mexico, Dr. Dietz would also spell the name Nxivm wrong. Maybe he got the spelling from *Bufete*?)

"I've already examined and tested India, and as part of my evaluation of her would like to interview you." His request struck me as odd, and Rachel Bernstein agreed—"it's highly irregular" that he should need me to complete the evaluation.

So, either India had been lying that she had found this doctor herself and that he'd been her choice, or she was now part of a hive mentality and could not separate herself from the cult—as if they were both one, which was alarming.

India texted, asking me to take the meeting with Dietz and her. And while my heart leapt at the thought of seeing her, the whole thing felt like a monumental trap for both of us.

Of course Keith would hire this guy. How transparent! He hired someone who he expected would prove competence—100 percent guaranteed, foolproof. He was willing to overpay this star forensic psychiatrist to show that India was not brainwashed; that way the cult could point out that anything she did—even if it was following orders—was done of her own free will.

I sent Dietz's letter to Frank, Barry, Rick, Rachel, and another cult expert, Rosanne Henry.

My lawyers' advice was not to respond to the letter until they'd spoken to the FBI about it.

Rick Alan Ross told me, "Dietz has probably been paid a very substantial amount of money supplied by the Bronfmans. His professional history did not seem to qualify him as an expert on cults, the coercive persuasion methods used by cults or specifically evaluating cult members. He's known for his examination and evaluations of psychopaths, murderers, and deeply disturbed individuals with narcissistic disorders. He profiled David Koresh. He would be highly qualified to evaluate and profile Keith Raniere, but not necessarily a cult victim."

Both Rick and Rachel thought the meeting was a setup to get me to say something that could be used against me or used to incriminate India in the future.

"Keith is setting up India to take the fall!" Barry emailed.

I didn't know what move to make, and I could feel the eyes of Keith on me, barreling toward destruction.

The FBI said to speak with Dietz, but not in person . . . and they suggested I tape record the conversation. And so, a few days later, I embarked on my first secret assignment for the FBI—without any preparation from them, I might add.

I was dealing with the world's foremost forensic psychiatrist at the behest of one of the world's most devious psychopaths, and all I was instructed to do was "get information." No list of questions, no other guidance, nothing. It's not like I was a trained expert at waterboarding or information extraction.

But I prepared like hell, putting together a list of dozens of questions. And when I got Dr. Dietz on the phone, I barraged him unrelentingly, rattling off my questions like gunfire. So much so that he suspiciously asked me: "Who are you on a fishing expedition for?"

In the process, I obtained some good intel and derailed the so-called "experiment" that could have proven disastrous for India.

First, Dr. Dietz confirmed to me that India was the only cult member he was examining, suggesting only India was being targeted versus the whole bunch of them, as per Keith's statement on the Nxivm website.

Second, he had been misinformed by the cult and India as to why he'd been hired. He thought he'd been hired to evaluate and prove the competency of a student of ESP and Nxivm; he hadn't been told anything about DOS. Keith's statement had said their testing was to show that the DOS women were "flourishing."

Third, I confirmed that Nxivm had hired him and that it intended to publish the results of the evaluation online and give it to the media. Well, there was no way I could let his evaluation be made public.

"Dr. Dietz, what if I told you that India was examined by a medical doctor a few months ago? And that there was physical evidence that this group was endangering her health. And that she was also told to seek psychological help, too."

He was silent.

"Are you aware that in this group, my daughter is a 'slave,' and she has a 'master'?"

"*Who* is a slave?" he asked. He sounded nervous now. It turned out that Dr. Dietz was being used as well.

A combination of our talk and Barry's story in the *Times* put the final kibosh on Keith's plan—Dr. Dietz's evaluation never saw the light of day, and Nxivm's plan to throw my daughter under the bus had failed. I was under strict instructions not to go to the media, but my mother's instinct overruled that, and I told him everything. I got my hands slapped by my lawyers, but it was the right choice. Dietz spoke to Barry for the article, saying that India appeared "happy" and that he found no evidence of "brainwashing"; she just seemed troubled by the negative media reports about the group, he said. Barry ended the article on a more truthful, tragic note, quoting Antonio Zarattini in Mexico—the former coach who'd been targeted by the cult.

His friends still in the cult, he told Barry, "are in some ways kidnapped; their minds, their emotions have been taken for ransom."

Dietz never ended up doing any finalized testing or giving any conclusive, official results to Nxivm after that.

Once it dawned on me that the evaluation was counting on my participation, I held the trump card because there was no way I was going to comply. Keith's dastardly plan to set me up fizzled like a wet petard. I got my hands slapped for a second time when I let it slip that Mark and Bonnie were in the room with me, filming my entire conversation with Dietz.

"What?" Anthony asked over the phone. "You did what?"

Art and Anthony gave me a good talking to after that. If I were to spy for the FBI, apparently I shouldn't do it with other witnesses for the investigation in the room, watching.

"Oopsy daisy," I said with a smile. "Sorry, I didn't know!"

———

INDIA WAS NOT happy, and she texted my mother about it. It was so hard being hated by her. If there was ever a definition of tough love from a mother, this was it. But she didn't get the result she wanted from her grandmother, either:

India: Mom is still actively working against me not with me, and her approach is pushing me farther away from her no one else, so it's very sad for me to see her unwillingness to even speak under my terms. She's not respecting what I want at all but insisting that I lie and I won't lie. I'm sorry, but I don't see it as loving, it's not the truth, and I can't pretend to agree with tactics like this. I'm sorry that you're in a challenging position. The loving thing would be to believe her own daughter and not other people who have motives of their own. I'm just telling you the truth. Whether you want to accept it or not, I hope you can see how from my perspective it's not loving. It's loving her mission to destroy my friends and our relationship in my opinion that's more important to her right now.

Elizabeth: Darling, I know this man Dietz may seem like a dear old dicky bird, but he has been paid a huge sum of money by Nxivm to report to them what they want to hear, so how can he be a mediator??

You were always exceptionally bright, so there is no excuse to suddenly lose all perspective and pretend not to understand . . . please get a grip on reality.

I love you, darling, but this situation is too stupid and is taking too long . . .

May the sun in 2018 shine some light and help you to wake up.

with deepest love g xoxox

In early December, I got word that while it might look like the FBI had dropped the ball on the case when Keith fled, and nothing was happening, quite the contrary was true: the investigation had gained momentum.

From what I could glean, they were now focusing on the sex crimes instead of going the Al Capone financial route, which Anne had said would be easier.

I was blown away. This was incredibly ballsy of them! The sex crimes would mean a much more complex argument than the cut-and-dried he-didn't-pay-his-taxes one. What this meant to me was that they must have undeniable proof. But my fear now was that they might see India as a perpetrator, not a victim.

And now, a moral dilemma haunted me. All these DOS women were ultimately victims at the hands of the mastermind, Keith Raniere. But as far as the law was concerned, where would they draw the line between victim and perpetrator, especially when many of the victims had been *turned into* perpetrators via coercion?

I was anxious for the FBI to get India in for questioning. Many of the other women had already been interviewed. Until then, she was at risk to be further exploited by the cult, which would actively use her to her detriment to exonerate itself.

—

BY MID-DECEMBER, INDIA'S second mission surfaced.

She wanted to sign up for a vegan culinary school in New York or LA called Plantlab and asked both my mother and me if we could foot the bill for the $7,000 tuition. This put us in a conundrum. There was nothing we wanted more than for her to get away from Albany and move on with her life separate from the cult, but, as with the Dietz invitation, I didn't trust it.

I was hearing rumors from *insiders* that the cult planned to re-brand itself in Brooklyn and funnel recruitment through "the Source" (a very expensive program Allison Mack had already begun, targeted toward the acting community). I'd also heard it planned to open a restaurant in Brooklyn as a front for recruiting.

Who better to run it than India, a born entrepreneur who, as a kid, was obsessed with the Food Network? And in her other life, once upon a time, she'd dreamed of success in the food industry! Those guys were clever. Now the missionary work Bonnie had mentioned made sense: India was being sent out into the world like an apostle to spread the good news and gather new followers.

She began her petitioning to get the tuition money from us, and I was yearning to say to her, "Keith already took all your inheritance. Why don't you get *him* to pay for it?"

I again discussed the situation with Rick, who said, "Don't you dare pay for this! They want to use your money to increase India's value in the cult!"

Mom and I told India we'd gladly help with tuition—*if* she ended her relationship with ESP. A week or two of tense emails between India and me, and India and my mother, ensued, until India finally gave up on us, saying she would not leave the cult.

Bill, meanwhile, didn't understand why I wouldn't give her the money without conditions, but my mother, thank God, stood by me and saw it was the right thing. She wrote to India, "My heart wants to support you unconditionally, but my logic dictates that I should help you once you are free from ESP and have decided to move on with your life and in a new direction."

India spent Christmas with her fathers and refused to see me, though I sent lovely presents for her with her sisters as go-betweens, including a backpack that her sisters told me that she loved and began using right away.

A few days later, India announced to Bill that she was going back to Albany in early January to attend an ESP coach summit. She had bought a one-way ticket. She cited me as the main reason she was going back.

She wrote to Bill, and he forwarded me her text, where she blamed me for making it impossible for her to get a job and move forward in life.

I freaked out. Reading between the lines, I saw something more than just a daughter angry at her mother because she didn't get what she asked for. She'd failed at her assignments that month: getting me to see Dr. Dietz and getting the tuition for school. She was batting zero, and now she had to go back to cult command central and face the consequences.

But what would they be? What would they make her do as penance? Why did she have only a one-way ticket?

I lay in bed on the last day of 2017 and asked God to take over, asked my body to let go, coaxed myself to breathe. I'd done everything I could do, everything that the experts and the lawyers and the FBI and my own heart had dictated.

The year was ending, the FBI was moving in, but how would India's story end?

Her life and her future weren't in any of our hands, and maybe not even her own.

16

A PASSAGE TO INDIA

India was set to return to Albany on January 9, 2018, and the more I thought about it, the more I slipped into paranoia. I was convinced she was being lured back for her next, and final, assignment: a suicide mission.

After she'd made plans to move back to LA and take a vacation that first week of January with her grandmother, India suddenly canceled both. It was obvious to me she'd been abruptly summoned back to the mother ship.

"It's a shame, we almost had her here," Bill said. "But without enrolling in the cooking school, she doesn't have anything keeping her here."

I wanted to shake him.

"Bill, I didn't want to enable her! But don't you see what else is going on here?!"

He still didn't get it or see the danger she was in—especially now, with this sudden trip back. But Rick Alan Ross surely did. It was a big, big red flag, he said.

"I've watched and studied this man for fifteen years, but I've never seen him escalate like this, like the way he is now," he told me, and he'd said the same thing when interviewed on *The Dr. Oz Show* six weeks earlier for a segment about the cult, comparing Keith to Charles Manson.

I'd read in Rick's book, *Cults Inside Out*, that small groups like Nxivm are the most deadly, especially when they're tightly wound around a leader who becomes progressively delusional. This puts them at a higher risk of becoming a formula for tragedy.

Raniere was far away in another country, but he was still running the show. And as far as I could see, he used India like a puppet. I was worried that his next "distraction" would be for India to commit an honor suicide, like the ones he spoke of so glowingly in class.

He'd been under a lot of pressure since all the press came out, and he'd fled to Mexico—he knew very well the FBI was after him. What Keith needed to do as soon as possible was to create a distraction as a diversionary tactic. This would feather the flock, it would create a drama that everyone would rally around, and it would take attention away from the chaos the press had caused.

I scanned Allison Mack's social media pages and saw an image she'd posted of Joan of Arc. Underneath, she'd quoted the play *Joan of Lorraine*—it was dialogue from the moments just before Joan is executed:

Every man gives his life for what he believes. Every woman gives her life for what she believes. Sometimes people believe in little or nothing, and so they give their lives to little or nothing. One life is all we have, and we live it as we believe in living it . . . and then it's gone. But to surrender who you are and to live without belief is more terrible than dying—even more terrible than dying young.

I quickly scanned other slave and master sites and saw Joan's post of a woman standing by the ocean, ready to jump in, with the title "Standing By" and these words underneath:

"We've been called to take up arms . . . Sisters, the light is dimming and we are the fire."

More red flags.

I called my lawyers and explained my fears. Keith, Nancy, Sara Bronfman (whom I learned was still India's ESP coach), Allison, and Lauren all had the rank to demand that India cancel everything and return so quickly. They implanted every idea and directive in her mind. And now, because she'd failed at her two missions at the end of 2017, I worried they were implanting a new belief in her mind: that she had no hope of a future and that she had more value to them dead than alive.

How else do you begin preparing someone to do something drastic and dangerous for a cause?

Toni Natalie had told me how Keith had had a hand in her brother's suicide, and I knew about the other two suicides linked to Keith: those of Gina Hutchinson and Kristin Snyder.

Sacrificing her life for Keith would prove India's ultimate allegiance to him and save Keith's worthy cause in one swoop. The DOS women were already convinced they were "at one" with Nxivm—that they were one collective entity. If the group died, so did they; if the group lived, so did they.

I wouldn't put it past Keith to find a way to pass around the cyanide-laced Kool-Aid, kill them all, and make it *look* like a mass suicide. At the 2016 V-week, over a hundred Espians (including children) had gotten violently ill. Keith and the other high-ranking Espians there didn't—and, strangely enough, neither did any woman Keith was having sex with. Everyone was bedridden for days, with foul stuff gushing out of both ends of their bodies. He quarantined everyone to their rooms and swore them to secrecy. A mother cannot help but wonder if this was a Jonestown-lite situation. It certainly would not have been the first time that a cult had poisoned the water supply.

It wasn't too far-fetched; it had happened in real life. The followers of the Osho cult in The Dalles, Oregon, gave food poisoning to 751 people by contaminating the *salad bars* at ten local restaurants with Salmonella, sending 45 people to the hospital. Apparently that was a test run for a bigger plan to poison the county by contaminating the water supply using a blended mixture of . . . dead beavers. (It was a plan that was never carried out.)

—

BEFORE INDIA LEFT Los Angeles, I tried to convince her that she had so much to live for. The day before she flew to Albany, she came by to pick up her sisters and take them to Casper's. I gave them a handwritten note to give to her.

"I know you don't believe me, but there is a beautiful, prosperous life waiting for you, full of opportunities when you are ready," I wrote, "and I'm here to help you."

After the plane took off the next day, I had back-to-back nightmares that I'd never see her again.

"Don't worry, Catherine," Sarah Edmondson called to say, "we won't quit until you have her back."

But we were running out of time.

If Keith or the group was in trouble, as they were now, would the DOS slaves be expected to perform the ultimate sacrifice to either save the group or die for it in one grand, apocalyptic finale?

If so, they would plan ahead to ensure the blame wasn't on the cult but on something or someone else. The current media persecution India kept talking about, for example, was an ideal target to blame as the trigger that had pushed a slave over the edge.

Or in India's case, the blame could be pinned on her celebrity mother for exposing her the way I had. Think of the publicity *that* would give them.

I felt sick.

After I talked to my lawyers, I wrote an email for them to forward to government officials, feeling that too many times people had sensed impending catastrophe and didn't speak up. I wrote:

> I believe that the likelihood of the worst-case scenario playing out is slim, but I couldn't live with myself if I didn't give voice to my fears, and if the consequence of my silence led to a tragedy.

I'd seen Kristin Snyder's suicide note, in which she wrote that because of ESP, "my emotional center of the brain was killed/turned off."

I could imagine India's: "My mother pushed me to my death."

—

BACK IN ALBANY, the setup for Keith's slaves to take the fall for him continued.

If the FBI was going to come for Keith, he would first make sure that any wrongdoing he'd done pointed to someone else.

An emergency meeting was called during the coach summit, and we had one of our moles—an ESP insider—there to report back to us. At least seventy Espians attended, including India.

At the meeting, Lauren stood up and announced that she, Allison, and Nicki Clyne were going to publicly take full responsibility for DOS.

Allison and Nicki had gotten married in 2017 and I'd heard that India had been a witness at the ceremony.

"It was our idea, not Keith's," one of them said. India was there, in apparent full support with the rest of the group.

When our mole reported all this back to me, all I could think was, *How naïve can they be?*

Their asshole leader had fled the country, leaving them all to hold the bag. Didn't they realize their actions wouldn't protect Keith from prosecution but would implicate them overtly as coconspirators?

At least they're alive, I also thought. Though taking the blame for Keith was a form of suicide, as far as I could see.

One of the topics at the meeting was that they were going to rebrand DOS and call it the Squad. It was also announced that a writer for the *New York Times Magazine*, Vanessa Grigoriadis, was working on a "friendly" article about Nxivm, so arrangements would be made for slaves to give interviews and tell the reporter how happy, healthy, and unbrainwashed they were. Grigoriadis was photographed by one of our boots on the ground together with Sara Bronfman entering Apropos during the coach summit.

When I heard about this, I panicked. Their policy was to never speak to the press, aka "fake news." Now Keith was telling them to give interviews? It meant two things: he wanted all the DOS women to go on the record to say that everything they'd done, including the branding, was consensual. And, most important, that he had nothing to do with it. The more interviews that broadcast his innocence, the better. For him.

How could an article like this be possible? After a bit of sleuthing, I found out that Clare Bronfman had hired a PR company who'd pitched the story of "inside the world of the DOS slaves" to various reporters—a rare glimpse, a scoop! And the scoop included an exclusive interview with the Vanguard himself.

After all they'd been through, and then being brave enough to come forward, a flowery story presenting DOS as a female empowerment group would devastate the defectors, I knew.

I went into hyperdrive trying to figure out how I could put a wrench in the story. But at least I had one piece of good news—law enforcement was not remotely fazed. No puff piece was going to affect the investigation.

Then more good news arrived midmonth. I got tipped off that the investigation was going to widen way beyond the DOS crimes and expand vertically and horizontally, even beyond racketeering, to possibly include a public corruption investigation. This meant more potential crimes to pin on Keith and his cronies, and hopefully an investigation of violations committed by government officials and law enforcement at the federal, state, and local levels.

I was elated to hear this. The Bronfmans had spent untold millions to feed this beast, conspired, and enabled Keith's criminal enterprise to continue—and even thrive. If Albany was as corrupt as my first attorney had said, then the only path to true justice was to include everyone who was complicit and had allowed the enterprise to continue for decades as lives and families were destroyed.

The FBI was getting closer, and my attempts to get India out of the cult and out of Albany intensified. But she'd inherited her mother's stubbornness, and the more I tried to warn her about the inevitable tragic outcome, the more defensive and resistant she became. This was the pattern all year when we spoke with or texted each other. Her wall of indoctrination was as thick and unrelenting as the concrete Berlin Wall—but even that had eventually toppled, I told myself. (I even had a piece of it. The year it went down, Bill was in Germany and had brought a piece of it to me as a souvenir.)

"A cult leader's narcissism trickles down and infects all the ranks," Rachel Bernstein explained. "It becomes a mass trickle-down of hubris. They feel above the law."

In early February Frank also had words of warning for those still in Nxivm, to get the hell out while they could:

The people left in Nxivm think, "Oh this will pass like in the past. Just bad publicity, we need to stay strong, blah blah blah."
This is nothing like the past.

Nxivm has never been under a Department of Justice criminal investigation before, and if the Eastern District of New York (DOJ) is doing it, the evidence of crimes must be really, really bad.

The prosecutor's office that extradited El Chapo, and prosecutes some of the most dangerous and complicated terrorism cases in the United States, would hardly waste the time and resources to go after a small cult in another district unless the evidence is extremely damning.

Keith Raniere knows this—he's no fool—that's why he's gone.

India's next email, however, showed she was still oblivious to the danger and that the wall had gotten thicker; it read as perfunctorily as a laundry or grocery list you might give a stranger.

Hello,

I wanted to ask you to please gather a few of my things for me and give them to Bill or Casper this Monday. At this stage, I would like to have and use those items to support myself and pay for cooking school, apply for jobs, and organize my taxes.

1. My Social Security card.
2. My bonds that you have in your safe.
3. My personal jewelry and the items my dad gave to me on your behalf, please.
4. My tax information and any mail I might have that was sent to your home address.

5. Any other material that you think would be helpful in order
   to go forward with school and my responsibilities.

   Thank you for understanding and respecting my right to
   have these things.

The personal items, including three paintings and a wooden statue
of a Burmese Buddha, had been given to me by Bill for safekeeping,
to give to India one day in the future, "when the time was right."

The time was so *not* right, I told India. But the more I said no, the
more hopping mad she got, whipping herself into a frenzied state I'd
never seen her in before. My usually calm and docile daughter then
resorted to a myriad of manipulative strategies—something else I'd
never seen her do so overtly before—and roped everyone into the fight,
shooting out texts and cc'ing her fathers and sisters to be on her side.
She attacked me and wanted them all to see me in a negative light.

Greg likened India's behavior to that of a panicked addict who
wasn't getting her fix—something he'd seen plenty of times. He
helped me stay strong and continue not to relent.

"No, absolutely not!" he advised. "Don't give her anything. You
are dealing with someone who has the mentality of a heroin addict
right now. You have to consider yourself her trustee. You want to give
her those paintings when she gets married and buys a house. The
reason she has no money isn't because of you, it's because Keith went
through all her money. One day she'll understand."

I tried to put myself in India's shoes, assuming I'd wake up one
day and get out of that cult. My future self would be thankful that

my mother didn't let go of the last remnants and small treasures of my true life. And so I didn't.

But the tantrum texts kept coming, until I had an idea:

India, this is not a text convo. I will pay for you to come home and have a face-to-face. Much faster resolution. Not to drag u through the dirt as u told your dad but bc I love u and care about ur safety above all else.

Shockingly, she agreed. I quickly bought her a plane ticket for the following week and spent the next few days preparing what I was going to say to her. I wanted to reach her, not alienate her. I wanted to love her, not enable her.

I was going to see India!

Here was my second chance after that first failed intervention to speak to her face-to-face and try to help her connect the dots that Bonnie, Yasmine, Lisa, Ava, Mark, and hundreds of others had seen and connected.

At the same time, salvaging our relationship was more important than anything else. I wanted to focus on the love between us, not on who was right and who was wrong.

Except for the brief faraway wave we'd had in November, it had been almost nine months since I'd talked to her on the phone or seen her in person—nine months since I'd hugged my daughter.

India didn't want to meet at home, so we set up a three o'clock tea on Tuesday, February 13, at our favorite Greek restaurant in Malibu. Demeter and Persephone were about to break bread.

I couldn't sleep the night before. I woke up at one thirty and stared at the ceiling for hours. She'd already landed and would be at Bill's by now, I calculated. I felt agitated and tossed and turned and couldn't figure out why, until I did. I was dreading the confrontation of having to say no to her over and over again—no to liquidating her assets, no to stopping the docuseries, no to not writing this book.

And then I realized: this was the first time since the second I'd learned I was pregnant with India that I was *not* looking forward to seeing her.

How incredibly sad, I thought.

—

I GOT TO the restaurant a minute before India, and as I took a seat at a table, in she walked.

Never mind my earlier hesitation about seeing her; as soon as I set eyes on her, my heart swelled with love. She looked beautiful and elegant in black slacks and a thin sweater. I grabbed her and hugged her tight and kissed her on her face repeatedly, and petted her hair.

"Mom!" she giggled. I couldn't help it. "You smell so good, Mom!"

I gave her a humongous bag full of girly beauty gifts: sweet-smelling soaps, lotions, powders, creams, and colorful bubble bath liquids. The Spartan cult lifestyle didn't condone all the feminine things I knew India loved, so I wanted to encourage a sensory feast. In her world, in which women were branded and used, I wanted her to reconnect with her body in a loving way and remember her beauty.

"How did you know I was a lizard?" India laughed, in appreciation.

"You're a California girl in the middle of winter in Albany!" I said.

As I ordered two pots of mint tea and an order of baba ghanoush, India admitted that she too had been nervous about our meeting.

"My heart was pounding, I kept pacing around and rehearsing what I was going to say. I felt like I was going on a first date," she said with a laugh. "And then I let it all go. My goal is reconciliation, Mom."

I'd done the exact same thing and felt the exact same way that morning—we were so much alike.

At first, we had what might be considered a normal mother-daughter conversation. She talked about looking for a job at vegan restaurants in Manhattan, and that gave me a shiver of hope—until she said she'd also applied to restaurants in Albany, and showed me her resume. Under "Work Experience," she'd written: "ESP, 2011 to present."

We were even able to laugh a bit about our troubled year.

"I told my sisters that their *cult sister* was coming to see them," India said with a smirk. "But I think it was too soon to make a joke like that. They freaked out."

I smiled and nodded, thinking, *You don't even realize what a cult is and that you're in one.*

But I let that go, as I would let a few things go during our talk that day. Because as I watched and listened to her, and we laughed and teared up at times, something more important was happening.

I was amazed and grateful to see that no matter what had gone on in the last nine months, the love between us was as authentic and undeniable as ever. We could both feel it radiating across the table like an invisible force that overpowered any cult script or agenda she'd been instructed to employ on this trip.

And she *did* come with a memorized script, and a new mission: *Shut your mother up.*

After about thirty minutes, India announced she wanted to talk about what I was doing that upset her: the book and docuseries and the interviews I was giving to the press.

"This has been the hardest six months of my life," she said. "I've been humiliated in public. I have lost friends. People have said terrible things to me, like, 'You're torturing girls, you're a disgusting person!'"

"I'm so sorry, darling, that I've contributed in any way to your pain," I said. And I *was*, of course. It tore me apart to hear her tell me in person how much hurt I was directly or indirectly causing her. But I still believed this pain was the necessary and difficult ring of fire that would deliver us from the greater pain, which was a fate worse than death: India giving up the rest of her life to this depraved cult.

I had my own practiced script ready, too. Anytime my daughter named a grievance, I was empathetic and apologized for any pain I may have caused.

"If I were in your position," I continued, "and I was part of a group, and people were saying bad things about me and the group, I would feel the same way."

"But Mom, I don't think it is fair that my private life is so public. I have the right to choose how I want to live."

"Darling, when you began recruiting people, it was no longer private. Do you understand why I went to the media?"

"Because you were desperate?"

"Exactly."

"I wish I could reassure you that I'm *fine*."

One thing was for sure, she was eating again—which I was so relieved to see. As we talked, India was inhaling the delicious toasted chunks of bread dipped in baba ghanoush with zest. I remembered Lisa telling me that one of the most difficult challenges India had in Albany was sticking to the slave diet and that she'd break it by eating cheesecake.

"India, it would help me to be more reassured if you'd be open to seeing a therapist. If there is nothing wrong with you, then you have nothing to lose. I really want to understand where you are coming from, but I need help. I'm really struggling."

"There are only two people I will not talk to: Rick Alan Ross and Frank."

Which didn't surprise me, since they were both archenemies of Keith's. But wait—was she saying she would see a different therapist?

Somehow we got onto the topic of branding, and she actually used the word *DOS* when describing the sorority group, which surprised me. It was all but admitting the master-slave setup. From this moment on in the conversation, I felt like I was falling into a black hole.

"You said the branding was a good experience for you, but how would you feel if some people found it terrifying?" I asked. "Would that concern you?"

I read her a quote from a clinical social worker named Dan Shaw—who'd treated dozens of cult victims in his practice—about Keith and Nxivm:

I've been doing this work for many years. I am nevertheless aghast at the level of contempt for women and cruelty toward women that is at the rotten core of this group. Raniere succeeds in fulfilling his sadistic need to enslave others through a kind of battering, his twisted rationales convincing followers, and not just the women, that self-torture and torture of others builds character.

In fact, what he does is utterly self-serving, exploiting others entirely to feed the delusion of his own omnipotence. Those who have been brainwashed with Raniere's hateful ideas about women will need time to free themselves from their conditioning, to be able to respect and trust themselves again.

India looked shocked and confused.

"That hasn't been my experience at all," she said in a loving tone. "Maybe it's just not for everyone. I've chosen an alternative lifestyle."

The entire time we spoke, we spoke with love, tenderness, and appreciation for each other; it didn't matter what words we were saying. Every word was couched in love—we both smiled the entire time.

"It's *weird*, darling. Creepy weird."

"I've only had a positive experience."

"I understand that, and I don't want to take that away from you. I'm just afraid that you've been taught to normalize things that just aren't okay. You've been branded with the symbol of Keith and Allison's initials!"

"It doesn't matter what I'm branded with," she replied. "That's irrelevant to me."

I was aghast.

"I am not anyone's property," she insisted. "And it's not his initials, like they are trying to sensationalize in the press. The branding was me pushing past my fears, my limitations. Besides, even tattoo parlors offer branding."

The branding talk was pointless, and we agreed to disagree—which became the refrain of the afternoon.

"Mom, you just think I'm stupid, don't you?"

"No, India, I don't. I think you are smart, and I believe that down the line you are going to figure it out. When people start getting arrested, please promise me that you will call me."

"Yes, I will."

My daughter was far from stupid. In fact, she had a prepared answer for everything.

"Why did Keith flee to Mexico?" I asked.

"Because people don't like him."

"People don't leave the country just because people don't 'like' them!" I asked her about Mark and Bonnie.

"It's okay if you want to leave," she said, "but it's not okay to destroy people's lives."

"What if Mark and Bonnie were unhappy with what the company was doing? What if that was not what they signed up for? It no longer aligned with their values. Would you be willing to think about that as a possibility?

"And what about Sarah and Nippy, you were so close to them. Would you talk to them?"

"No, I don't want to talk to anyone who has publicly tried to destroy the group. I feel defensive about anyone saying that they are a victim."

I refrained from saying what I was thinking: *Keith cornered the market on victimhood*. But I didn't want to be argumentative and push too hard.

"The point is, people are fleeing the group. Doesn't that bother you?"

"They're afraid because of the rumors that were spread."

"Rumors? You don't think that people had evidence? Do you know about the investigation?"

"Yes. No one here's been too worried about that . . ."

"Well, it's nothing compared with what's coming."

I was trying to wake her up, but all I was getting were the same blank stares I'd seen months before. My words were not penetrating; she didn't understand what I was saying.

"Are you aware that this is a *criminal enterprise*?" I asked her.

"What are the crimes?"

"Well, they could include racketeering, tax evasion, sex trafficking, human trafficking, money laundering, identity theft." I was speculating, sure, but I wanted to scare her. "That doesn't worry you?"

"Lots of people do those things."

No, India, they don't! Criminals do these things!

Her tone and delivery sounded so normal, so smooth and rational on the surface, but what she was saying was so warped and off, it rocked my internal balance and made me dizzy.

Then India took it a step further to say that *I* was the criminal, not Keith or anyone in the cult. That's why I got that legal letter from Mexico.

"You broke the law," she said.

"What law do you think I broke?" I asked. "What crime did I commit?"

"You can't just start calling people like you did and try to scare them off."

I remained silent. I couldn't believe the garbage they fed her brain, and I was amazed how much it still shocked me to see how completely brainwashed and irrational she was. Hearing it in person was ten times more jarring than reading it in a text.

After two hours of more of the same, I started to wrap things up. I knew Bill was waiting for her outside to drive her back to his place.

"Darling, I am not trying to limit your life or make it harder, and I wish I could prove that to you," I told her. "But from the moment I gave birth to you, my job was to protect you. And that's what I am doing now. It may not feel that way to you or to the group, but this is how I am showing you love. I am fighting for you because I believe you're involved with people who are harming you."

I reached across the table to take her hand.

"I've missed you, and I love you so much. You may not understand what I'm doing, and I may not understand you. But I love you, and I will always love you—with every fiber of my being."

"I—I think this is the most honest we've been with each other in a long time," India said.

When we got up and hugged, we both had tears in our eyes.

The meeting ended in a sweet, perfect way—with a magical purse mom moment. India needed eye drops. And then she needed digestive enzymes. And then she needed a mint. So I fished around in my purse and pulled out all three for her. I felt like Mary Poppins: anything she needed, I magically had for her. It felt wonderful to be able to say yes to her after so many nos, even if it was little things. It felt wonderful to have the most basic parent-child exchange in which she needed something, and I gave it.

For a minute, I felt like a nurturing mom again.

"Will I see you again on this trip?" I asked as she was leaving the table.

"I'll think about it."

We hugged and kissed, and told each other "I love you."

It had been a two-hour conversation with the two Indias: the real India and her cult persona. In the end, I think Real India won out. I left the restaurant feeling happy and hopeful, as if we'd taken a step in the right direction together—*finally*. And India seemed to feel that way, too.

But something went wrong in the hours after our meeting. I got a nasty text from Bill shortly after India and I parted, reaming me out.

Well, that didn't work out. I really wish you'd see our daughter as the beautiful woman she is rather than the way you are prepared to ridicule and destroy her life for your own ambitions.

What a lightweight move on your part. Heartless. So Sad. Such fake concern.

What the—?

Someone from the cult must have gotten to her since our meeting, and then India dispatched her father as the nearest flying monkey available. Her requests for me to stop the book and docuseries were light and smooth as silk when we talked, but they hadn't worked. So now Bill was being sent to do the bad-cop hatchet job on me—it was the only strategy left.

It was Keith's way, I knew, of showing me that no matter how hopeful I was feeling for those few hours after my time with India, my love had no effect on her whatsoever and that nothing would pierce the armor of his brainwashing, not even a mother's heart.

She belongs to me, he was saying. *Her psyche is impervious to your love.*

Evil bastard. Raniere's devious darkness was continually working below the surface, sucking up India's beautiful light like the devil possessing an angel.

This had to stop. It had to stop before it was too late.

Frank called, and after I explained the India meeting and Bill's text, he got all prophetic on me: "In her darkest hour," he said, "she stands alone."

And he meant me, not India. Frank, the snake eater, was reminding me that when you took a stand for someone or something, you sometimes found yourself on the field of battle by yourself—as he had done many times, trying to fight Keith.

He was right. And I'd made a vow to fight forever. But . . . I was desperate for something to give, for both my sake and India's.

Three days later, I got a call from one of my lawyers.

"In the next month or so, we'll have arrests," he promised, "and you'll be pleased. I can't say anything more, but I can tell you this: the charges will be huge, Catherine. Huge."

Hurry, was all I could think. *Please hurry!*

17

CAPTURED

As the saying goes, there is no rest for the weary.

Six weeks later, on March 26—after ten anxiety-ridden months—I took my very first, much-needed moment to stop and pamper myself. I lay down on a spa table to get a facial; I was so exhausted, I started to fall asleep.

Fifteen minutes into it, my phone went berserk. Beep after beep after beep until I finally couldn't ignore it. *Maybe an emergency with the kids?*

My facialist handed me my purse so I could dig out my phone. I had to adjust my eyes to the light and blink a few times before I could take in what I saw: dozens of frantic texts, emails, and voice mails marked "Urgent" from Bonnie and Mark, Toni Natalie, Frank, Karim, my various Albany spies, my various lawyers, everybody.

ART: Catherine, we received documents from the EDM that Raniere was arrested and will appear in court tomorrow in TX. I emailed you the complaint.

Congratulations for your perseverance and dedication to this cause.

I quickly called Art. "Tell me everything! What happened?!"

"Catherine! There was a raid yesterday and Keith was arrested in Mexico, near Puerto Vallarta! He did not go willingly. The Feds worked in conjunction with the federales . . . they were concerned about his connections to the Salinas family so they wanted to get him out of there as quickly as possible. We have issued a press release for you."

"Thank you so much!" I cried into the phone. "I'm so grateful for you! Arrested!!!" I screamed, bursting into tears. I hopped off the table and jumped up and down, then hugged the facialist, explaining what had just happened—and she started crying, too. The creams on my face dripped all over us. After we finished jumping and dancing around the room together, I started making calls from the spa table. The first was to Mark and Bonnie: "Ohmigod, ohmigod!!!" I laughed and cried into the phone, hyperventilating, "I can't believe . . . it actually happened . . . *ohmigod* . . . Keith . . . arrested . . ."

Bonnie and Mark were crying and laughing on the other end, too.

"Catherine, this is unprecedented," Bonnie said. "Remember what the cult recovery therapist, Rosanne Henry, told you? Over twenty-five years in her work and she'd never seen a cult leader arrested *before* the Kool-Aid scenario—never! But now . . . we did it!"

From the spa table, to the street, to my car, I dialed and texted everybody: Mom, Greg, the Expians . . . I was like the town crier banging the drum and yelling out the good news. I had to pull over to the side of the road because I was crying so much, the leftover facial cream was getting into my eyes and I couldn't see.

"You're a hero," Greg said to me. "You just saved hundreds—thousands—of people. I'm so proud of you!"

The pièce de résistance was a text I got from Bill:

It seems like you are right about Keith. Call me. Thx

From what my resident Sherlock Holmes group could gather from our inside sources, someone from the US government had called in a favor with the Mexican government, asking them to swing by and pay a friendly Sunday call on Keith at his resplendent manse in Mexico.

And not just on any Sunday, mind you, but Palm Sunday. These Catholic federales were giving up church with the family on a holy day to smoke Keith out with machine guns.

But it was so fitting, because Keith was about to be crucified. He was even surrounded by a flock of slaves, his branded apostles—Allison, Nicki Clyne, Lauren, and a Mexican DOS slave who I wasn't familiar with—who all protested as he was handcuffed and hauled away. *Where are Baby Avatar and his mama*? I wondered. There seemed to be no sign of them.

Keith was deported instead of extradited, which would have been the proper protocol. There was a worry that the Salinas family would step in and use their government ties to block extradition if they caught wind of it. The beauty of deportation was: no warning, no paper trail, no due process. All it took was one phone call: "Pick him up and toss him out!"

As it turns out, Mexico was not so keen to have a branding pedophile in its backyard.

They handcuffed Keith behind his back—a sure sign they didn't like him, I'd heard—and drove him to the US border. There they unceremoniously dumped him, squirming, into the waiting arms of the FBI on the other side, like a reluctant mail-order bride.

He didn't go willingly, Art said.

I imagined Keith begging for mercy and hanging on to the legs of furniture or curtains as they dragged him out of his beautiful hacienda. I imagined them ripping the virgin margarita, hot tamale, and churro out of his hand as he caught his last glimpse of the stunning Pacific. I envisioned him crawling under his bed to hide like a baby, scratching and biting as they yanked him out by his ankles. I visualized them chasing him through the giant house like it was a maze until he was cornered, tangled up in reams of mosquito netting.

His fake judo expertise and his phony hundred-yard-dash record were of no help to him now. He was such a coward, he probably threw his slaves in front of himself, yelling, "They did it! It wasn't me! Take them!"

It was doing my heart wonders just to imagine all this.

After he was taken away, Keith's devoted apostles hopped in a car and launched a high-speed chase following the machine-gun-toting federales as they ferried Keith from Puerto Vallarta to the border, until they ran out of gas. God forbid they should lose sight of their

Vanguard. I'd heard they were last sighted in Guadalajara, a five-hour drive from Keith's manse.

———

THE GOVERNMENT'S CASE was being handled by the office's Organized Crime and Gang Section—another clue they were going for RICO. Assistant US Attorneys Moira Kim Penza and Tanya Hajjar were in charge of the prosecution, and a new third name—another woman!—was added to the team. Assistant US Attorney Karin Orenstein was in charge of the forfeiture portion of the case—the first indication that they were going to seize assets! My lawyers sent me the official twenty-two-page criminal Complaint and Affidavit in Support of Arrest Warrant, written by FBI special agent Michael Lever, who specialized in investigations involving sex trafficking and civil rights violations. They also sent me the eight-page letter to the judge written that day by Moira and Tanya.

The first two bits of information I saw on the complaint made me laugh out loud. First, it was filed on February 14—Valentine's Day! Keith loathed Valentine's Day. In general, he had a vendetta against anyone having a day named after themselves—even a saint. He didn't like the competition. Keith particularly hated Valentine's Day because he didn't believe in (or understand) romance, devotion, and love. He used to throw anti–Valentine's Day parties during which he ordered couples to pair up with someone who was not their spouse or significant other.

The second bit that I saw at the top was this:

United States of America against KEITH RANIERE, also known as "The Vanguard."

Vanguard!

The whole country was fighting a comic-book character, a video-game super-antihero!

It was a taunt if ever I saw one.

The rest of the complaint couldn't have been more serious. As I began going through it, I could now see what the FBI had been working on so diligently over the past four months. They knew and understood everything about Keith, ESP, and DOS—all the details the slaves had told me were in there: the sashes, secrecy, money debts, and the rotating fifteen to twenty women Keith had sex with. It mentioned the slaves, collateral, branding, punishments, and diets. It confirmed that Keith created DOS and it mentioned "the Heiress" who owned a private island in Fiji (*Holy shit*, I thought, *they're targeting Clare Bronfman!*). It mentioned ESP's teaching that women had "inherent weaknesses including 'overemotional' natures." It talked about slaves feeling forced to have sex with Keith, and described his "Library" lair that had a hot tub and a loft bed (all Keith was missing was the lava lamp).

The complaint asserted that Keith, along "with others, did knowingly and intentionally conspire to recruit, entice, harbor, transport, provide, obtain, maintain, patronize and solicit persons . . . affecting interstate and foreign commerce, knowing that means of force, threats of force, fraud and coercion . . . used to cause such persons to engage in one or more commercial sex acts . . ."

Right away, I recognized Jane Doe 1 and 2—the slaves who gave the major testimony—in the complaint, but I learned new details I hadn't known before. Like that Keith had emailed a DOS slave and said, "I think it would be good for you to own a fuck toy slave for me, that you could groom, and use as a tool, to pleasure me . . ." Or that he demanded a return of expense money from another after she refused to have sex with him anymore.

And I also learned that the intimidating letters sent out by Nxivm Mexico to me and others had indeed been orchestrated by Keith and Clare, who'd also, the complaint confirmed, tried to have Sarah Edmondson charged with crimes after she defected:

"Since defecting, several DOS victims have received 'cease and desist' letters from a Mexican attorney. Emails exchanged between RANIERE and the Heiress, received pursuant to a search warrant executed on RANIERE's email account, discussed below, reveal that the Heiress and RANIERE orchestrated the sending of those letters. Additionally, the Heiress has made multiple attempts to have criminal charges brought against a former DOS slave, who has discussed her experience in the media." I immediately recognized this former DOS slave as Sarah Edmondson.

The judge's letter, written by Moira and Tanya, requested no bail for Keith ("if released, he would pose a danger to the community," they wrote) and was filled with more personal digs and a staggering emphasis on Keith's history of sexual abuse.

They wrote that "the defendant had repeated sexual encounters with multiple teenage girls in the mid-to-late 1980s and early 1990s," and detailed many of the encounters I'd read and heard about. They also wrote that Keith "posed disturbing hypotheticals as part of the

Nxivm curriculum, challenging whether incest and rape are actually wrong. He told one DOS slave that incest is not wrong if the 'victim' is sexually aroused by the experience, and he questioned whether gang rape is bad if the person being raped has an orgasm."

Reading that jogged my memory of watching Nancy coach someone through their childhood sexual abuse during one class and normalizing it. She told the Espian that in indigenous cultures it was an accepted practice for fathers, or some respected elder in the tribe, to initiate their daughters sexually at puberty. Callum and I looked at each other in horror and mouthed "WTF" to each other.

"That's barbaric!" I said. "We've learned, progressed, and evolved since then!"

But this was not only the philosophy of Nxivm's weird, perverted leader, but of the cult itself. And it confirmed what I suspected about the curriculum—that the seeds were being planted to normalize Keith's rape of young girls.

As French philosopher Voltaire once wrote: "Those who can make you believe absurdities, can make you commit atrocities."

As a zinger, Moira and Tanya once and for all put a nail in the coffin of Keith's bragging about his educational accomplishments:

"Nxivm students are also taught that the defendant is the smartest and most ethical man in the world. He frequently cited having earned three degrees from Rensselaer Polytechnic Institute, but a review of his transcript shows that he graduated with a 2.26 GPA, having failed or barely passed many of the upper-level math and science classes he bragged about taking."

Moira and Tanya intended to expose Keith and hold him accountable for every single woman, man, and child he'd ever abused, exploited, or raped—each one was represented in their narrative, not one voice was left behind. I was stunned at the power of their words, and cried tears of joy and relief. The women who were silenced for months or years had their voices given back to them.

In the press release put out by the US Department of Justice, the United States Attorney's Office wrote that "as alleged, Keith Raniere displayed a disgusting abuse of power in his efforts to denigrate and manipulate women he considered his sex slaves . . . these serious crimes against humanity are not only shocking, but disconcerting to say the least, and we are putting an end to this torture today."

That the FBI and prosecutors had connected the dots on all these issues was incredibly emotional and vindicating for me.

—

BUT SOON, MY joy turned to devastation (something I should have expected by now).

As I went back and forth, reading both the complaint and the judge's letter, I recognized Allison Mack as "Co-Conspirator 1" in the complaint . . . and then I recognized "Co-Conspirator 2"—it was India.

My heart broke into a thousand little pieces. There she was, re-duced to a criminal code—"CC-2"—even though she was a victim, which was how I and so many others saw her. I hoped law enforce-ment would perceive her that way, too.

Never in a million years, when I pushed to get this investigation opened, did I imagine India would be implicated with the others. Never. I'd stirred up a hornet's nest and, in doing so, seriously im-

plicated my precious girl—she could be prosecuted for her involvement! Keith was in custody, so one nightmare was over. But now an
entirely new one began.

I was advised that the best thing for India to do now was to go in
voluntarily and talk with them. But would she?

A few weeks earlier, one witness told me that the FBI was divid-
ing people in the investigation into three categories: subject, witness,
and target. India, she said, did not seem to be a target.

"Okay, who are the bad guys?" they'd asked this witness.

"Keith, Clare, Allison . . ."

"Not India?"

"No, I truly believe she's a caring, loving person. She never punished anybody. She's innocent, like a bunny rabbit."

The Feds agreed, she told me.

Still, I was trembling with fear and tried to reach India to let her
know she was in the complaint and in jeopardy, and I was ready to
help. The previous November I'd lined up several pro-bono lawyers
for her after the *New York Times* article came out, but she hadn't
wanted them. Now, unfortunately, their free legal advice was no
longer available. But I was willing to pay for whatever attorney she
needed as long as she was a witness for the prosecution.

Maybe the seriousness of Keith's crimes and the arrest would
finally wake her up? Or, at least, convince her to let me help her?

For the rest of the day I emailed, texted, and called her. Radio
silence. I enlisted her sisters, my mother, Stanley, and my lawyers to
try. Her response to everybody was essentially this: she didn't believe
anything serious was happening at all.

"It's not real," she texted my mother. "You're buying into the fear-mongering."

To Stanley, she wondered why people were bothering her all day; to her sisters, she complained I was bullying her.

One of our insiders reported that higher-ups at Nxivm were telling the faithful that Keith had orchestrated his own arrest as a ruse to gauge how loyal his slaves were.

I sent her another text:

Darling—I am going to email you the complaint from FBI & US Attorney. You will see the charges. The US Attorney is offering u a chance to come in immediately and it is in your best interest to do so or they will come after you. You need lawyers immediately.

Please understand how serious this is.

But it was continued radio silence for me.

The next day, Keith wore shackles and chains during a hearing in Fort Worth, Texas, where he was held without bail. Next, he would be transferred to Brooklyn, where he'd be arraigned in an open courtroom. I knew without a shadow of a doubt that I had to be in that courtroom that day.

Online, I saw a sketch of him in court wearing chains. I thought of India just two years earlier, asking for the loose diamonds from one of my rings to make a belly chain—now I realized it was part of her induction and initiation into DOS. Now Keith was blinged out, courtesy of the US government.

Now you're the slave, I thought, looking at the sketch. *Now the master is wearing the chains.*

—

YEAH, IT WAS a bad week for the Vanguard and his flying monkeys. Soon after his arrest, I heard that the cops found $8 million still in Pam Cafritz's bank account (the dead, rich, harem member he'd kept on ice) that Keith had been using.

After his arrest, the FBI, NY State Police, and IRS raided Nancy Salzman's house in Halfmoon and soon after, Keith's sex lair—aka the Library. From Nancy's, they confiscated over half a million dollars in cash stuffed in shoe boxes and envelopes. In Keith's lair, they found a book called *The History of Torture*, a DVD about sex trafficking called *Bought and Sold*, and a mysterious box of unidentified white pills. Was this what provided the promised "true enlightenment" Esther told me about once, that women found only by having sex with Keith? The pills might explain the blue light some women reported seeing during sex with him. I wouldn't be surprised if they were roofies—or maybe quaaludes, with Keith being so frozen in the eighties.

Keith was tossed in the infamous Federal Transfer Center in Oklahoma City, the hub where everyone awaiting trial goes until they're assigned a prison. It's huge, and it's the worst of the worst, people say.

"I'm glad the creep is in jail," Bill said to me. "I've heard of that FTC, it's a total dump. Good. The highlight of his week will be a bologna sandwich."

And if an MS-13 gang member demanded his sandwich, Keith would have two choices: give it to him, or get fucked—literally and figuratively.

He was surrounded by rapists and murderers there, said the friend, and as unappealing as Keith was, no one was going to be looking at his face. Now it would be Keith doing the bowing and bending over. Now he was the one being told when to wake up, when and how much to eat, when he could take a shower and for how long, and when he could sleep.

With that knowledge, a sense of balance slowly returned to the universe.

Karma's a bitch.

But there was more—much more—to come, said one of my insider flies on the wall.

On March 29, Attorney General Eric Schneiderman of New York announced that while "some dramatic steps have taken place over the past week or two . . . you should expect to see the aggressive pursuit of Mr. Raniere and some of his cronies."

More arrests were to come! And this was confirmation that multiple agencies at different levels were working in tandem to create a monumental task force from both federal and state authorities.

"Consider this as act one," said the insider. "You ain't seen nothing yet."

—

AS ALWAYS, I was both elated and afraid—ecstatic about getting the bad guys, but worried for India.

I got a call from Bill.

"Catherine!" he said in a panic. "We need to help our daughter!"

I was stunned, and felt a flush of anger rush over me. It took every ounce of self-control I had not to lash out at him.

"Bill. What do you think I've been trying to do for the past year?!"

"As far as helping our daughter," he said, "you have failed."

I tried to remain civil. At least Bill was finally understanding the severity of the situation, and maybe he'd finally help me help her, rather than work against me. He agreed she needed to be proactive with law enforcement rather than wait to see if she got arrested.

Mark was having less success trying to convince Casper of the situation, and they had a text argument that ended with Mark reproaching Casper: "Time to be a real hero, not just a movie one."

We were all angry, but the most damaging and misdirected anger was India's, because it was preventing her from focusing on the task at hand, which was to save herself. She was busy blaming me for everything, Bill told me, instead of facing the facts and taking action.

"She feels like you got her into this mess and now she's going to jail. She thinks it's all your fault."

I sighed.

"India thinks you want her to do a mea culpa," said Bill.

"I don't give a shit about a mea culpa," I yelled into the phone. "I just want her to be safe!"

"Can't you get immunity for her?" Bill asked. "You got Keith for them, practically handed him over on a silver platter. Now you want a mother's quid pro quo, tell them."

"Bill. I don't think it works that way. They are already offering India an open door to come in and talk to them, all she needs to do is go do it. As amazing as they are, I don't have the power to negotiate immunity for her."

And they were amazing. They were offering India the support, kindness, and caring I'd hoped they would. One of my lawyers told me they'd never worked with FBI and prosecutors who cared so deeply about the well-being of their clients.

"Every week they call to see how each and every woman is doing," he said.

Bill decided he was going to fly from LA to New York, get India lawyered up, and give her a hard reality check by describing the brutal facts of prison life to her. In his former life, Bill had been a "pot tradesman" ahead of his time and had his own brushes with the law and prison: "I know what the inside of a jail looks like," he said. The fantasy of being Nelson Mandela doing time was not all it was cracked up to be, he'd tell her, especially if the cause you were fighting for was a screwball like Keith.

Bill was now finally going to do what I'd hoped and prayed he'd do all year—step up and show up for his child.

—

AND SO, HE went. But within hours after arriving in New York, he was pulled back into India's web of delusion. She'd convinced him everything was just fine.

Successful day, I'm really glad I came to see her in her environment. Jury still out on which lawyers she's going to pick. This is containable. Leaving tomorrow. She's not scared right now. Looks healthy. Carving out a good life for herself. More than willing to go on and tell her story. Basically, she's moved on. The group is a thing of the past. I think she's going to be loyal to herself. Is she going to be indicted? I don't know . . . Not imminent at all.

For a moment I wondered: Could this really be true? Could Bill have pulled this off? Was India really ready to move on? Then I gave myself a pinch, and asked Bill the million-dollar question.

Me: did you see where she lives? are you aware that she lives with Alli M.?

Bill: No. It didn't come up.

There was no moving on with her life, I knew, while she was still living with Allison—aka "Co-Conspirator 1"—and living in a bubble of delusion.

—

KEITH'S APPEARANCE IN Brooklyn federal court was imminent, but I had no way to find out ahead of time what day it would be. The transferring of criminals is kept top secret so that no one tries to get to them en route and harm them or free them.

The team started making daily calls to the Oklahoma FTC see if he was still there, and I checked in with my lawyers constantly.

Finally, I had a gut feeling I had to just get on a plane and get to

New York. I couldn't miss it; I *needed* to see him in a court of law. I hoped the experience would give me a small amount of closure and help me let go of the Keith Nightmare a little bit.

On my way to the airport on Monday, April 9, I texted India.

Me: DARLING I am on my way to ny and I would love to see you. Let me know if you have time ❤

India: thank you for reaching out. Fly safe.

Me: Thank you, love.

In the kindest way possible, she blew me off—which made me sad. But I was buoyed soon after by a Facebook post from a stranger, who wrote: "Thank you for being brave enough to let her hate you by exposing the evil."

The stranger's words reminded me of my strength and resolve, and that I'd started this journey coming from a place of bravery and would conclude it that way, too.

Before I boarded my flight, I received another encouraging message: Keith was in transit! Even the lawyers and the AUSA and Eastern District of New York press office in Brooklyn didn't know this yet!

Being the supersleuth that he was, Frank called the detention center to find out what Keith was eating while in prison for a blog he was writing. He wanted to compare Keith's prison menu against the diet he'd given his slaves. Lucky for me, he got a chatty warden on the phone.

"Oh, he won't be eating anything here anymore," said the warden. "He just left."

Bingo!

Frank tried to find out Keith's mode of travel, but the warden was mum on that.

Keith would either be traveling by plane—"Con Air"—or getting his very first dose of "diesel therapy." Diesel therapy, I learned from a friend, was the nickname for transporting an inmate by bus—and it was not a pretty sight. You traveled for days, sometimes weeks, handcuffed and wearing leg irons and shackles. There was an open toilet on the bus, but most guys ended up pissing and shitting themselves because it took too long to stop the bus and get them unshackled. The driver zigzagged all over the country, like a Magical Mystery Tour from hell, stopping at various prisons along the way to pick up more passengers.

We had to know how Keith was traveling so we'd know when he'd be arriving and could try to figure out what day he'd be in court. The next day, Toni Natalie used her charm. She called up the detention center and got another chatty warden.

"I'm sorry, ma'am, we can't give you status on any prisoners," he told her.

"I understand, I understand," she said, sweetly. "But you know . . . he's a very bad man. And there are a lot of people who need to see him get the justice he deserves."

"Well . . . let me put it to you this way," the warden said. "Sometimes, there are people who *need* a little diesel therapy."

"I love you!" Toni yelled into the phone, then called me immediately: "He's on the move—by bus!"

We found out soon after that Keith's arraignment would be that Friday—Friday, April 13. It made perfect sense to me that he'd be arraigned on the day featured in a horror movie franchise.

—

I STAYED WITH Stanley all week; his apartment was only two blocks from the courthouse.

The day before the arraignment, I got word from the powers that be that they didn't want me in court unless I had a security detail—they couldn't be specific, but there had been threats. I already had my dear Stanley, who planned to stay by my side and hold my arm the entire day. For extra backup, I hired two beefy bodyguards.

The next morning, Rick joined us at Stanley's apartment for more filming and to give us a celebratory send-off.

"I remember in the summer, when Catherine said, 'That's it! I'm done being nice and it didn't work. Now I'm going to war,'" Rick said, smiling. "I was skeptical. I wondered: *Can she really pull this off?*"

"I wasn't skeptical at all," said Stanley, putting his arm around me. "I've know this girl since she was eighteen and when she wants something, she goes for it."

Rick didn't come with us to the courthouse; he'd spent well over a decade in and out of courtrooms with Keith, more than enough for one lifetime.

The first bodyguard arrived at 12:45 p.m. to drive Toni, Stanley, and me the two blocks to the courthouse. Once we got there, the second bodyguard met us across the street and they both escorted us in—past a wall of photographers, through security—while they scanned the crowds for vicious, murderous flying monkeys.

Inside, the courtroom was packed with media. I quickly scanned the room and spotted Barry from the *New York Times* and said hello, meeting him for the first time. Toni introduced me to Suzanna Andrews (the *Vanity Fair* writer who'd been sued by Nxivm). Barbara Bouchey, one of Keith's former significant others, whom he'd tortured for years in court, was there—she came up to me and we hugged.

Barbara joined the three of us as we positioned ourselves in the front row. We didn't want to miss a thing, and we didn't want Keith to miss seeing us.

I looked over at the prosecution table. It was surrounded by people whose names I knew and voices I'd heard over the months. But this was the first time I was actually seeing the army of angels that took Keith down.

From where I sat, I figured out who was who. There were Moira and Tanya, the badass prosecutors who skewered Keith and his low GPA in the letter to the judge. And there was the Mike whose name was on the criminal complaint . . . and there was the other Mike, the first FBI agent I'd spoken to—his wife had just had a baby and he was showing photos. The team consisted of Moira, Tanya, two Mikes, and a Charlie. And even though I'd never met them and was not to approach them now, I couldn't help but gaze at them from afar with boundless gratitude and love.

On the other side of the room was the defense table, and behind it sat three stooges huddled together—I assumed they were Keith's overpaid lawyers, his version of the OJ Simpson "dream team," courtesy of heiress Clare Bronfman's billions. The media commandeered the left side of the gallery, and they were essential soldiers in this army, too. If it weren't for them, we wouldn't have been in the courtroom that day. The darkness of Nxivm demanded that good people stand up and fight, and the media heeded the call by exposing the injustice and danger, and sounding the clarion for law enforcement to take action.

In my palm, I clutched my lucky bronze Archangel Michael coin like an amulet. Not only was Michael the slayer and vanquisher of evil, he was also the patron saint of law enforcement. (I usually kept the coin in my car, where he'd kept me from getting dozens of speeding tickets.) Looking out into the courtroom, it occurred to me for the first time that the two FBI agents who led the charge against Keith were also named Michael.

A coincidence? I'd like to think not. I took it as a sign that India's special angel, who had announced twenty-seven years earlier that it was my destiny to protect India, was also watching over her himself.

"I've got this covered," he was saying to me, from the heavenly realm.

—

THE JUDGE ENTERED the room, and we all rose.

Minutes later, we heard the sound of heavy, jangling chains from behind a door at the front of the courtroom. The three stooges rushed to circle an incoming Keith and escort him to their table along with a dozen big men who looked like plainclothes prison guards.

I flashed back to one of my first ESP classes, when everyone huddled together like a football team to say a mantra in unison: "WE ARE COMMITTED TO OUR SUCCESS!!"

The stooges and prison guards parted on the floor, and there he was: the Great Vanguard.

I hadn't seen him up close since the volleyball game five years earlier, when he French-kissed Allison, and Casper guessed he was having sex with everyone.

He looked shorter and wider than I remembered (no slave diet for him!) and colorless; the Mexico tan he'd sported in his backseat mug shot had faded. He wore a dishwater-brown prison-issued onesie that emphasized his stockiness and loping gait.

Keith walked to the defense table and sat down, facing forward. I had a good view of his right profile, and could see right away that three weeks in prison and several days of diesel therapy hadn't made a dent in the Vanguard. On his face was the same smug, arrogant expression he always wore—no remorse, no conscience. He wasn't going to indulge us with any of that.

As the judge spoke, Keith leaned in toward him in mock deference.

"Do you understand the severity of these charges?" the judge asked.

Keith leaned. "Yes, Your Honor," he answered in his thin, high voice.

We were inconveniencing him. He was impatient for his highly paid stooges to finagle him out of this in the same way he'd wriggled out of his previous transgressions. It was only a matter of time, he conveyed, until he'd be out again, surrounded by his fawning slaves.

Keith glanced in our direction—twice.

For a fraction of a second, he and I made eye contact. I stared him down with daggers. He looked at Toni, and there was a fleeting moment of surprise on his face. The last thing he'd said to her was "I'll see you dead or in jail."

But when he said it, he'd meant *her,* not him. Surprise, surprise.

One of his lawyers—the strutting, portly one whose other unsavory client was Harvey Weinstein—tried to save face for Keith—and for them, too. There was no way Keith was getting bail; he'd done a stellar job proving he was a flight risk when he fled to Mexico. But just for show:

"Your Honor," he said, "we're not going to request bail because our client has only been here for a couple of days . . ."

It was the lamest excuse for not requesting bail I'd ever heard. It wasn't even worth $10 of his $1,000-an-hour fee. My client has only been in this hellhole for a few days, no biggie. He can take it. I smiled: if this was how his lawyers worked, this trial was in the bag.

I looked at Keith again.

I felt a lot of emotions raging inside of me when I looked at his smug, unrepentant face, but most of all I felt validation.

In a way, this whole ordeal had put my own sanity on trial. For months I was told by law enforcement, by India, by other family members that no crime had been committed, that everything Keith and Nxivm did was consensual. But every cell in my body screamed the opposite to me—so much so that I couldn't rest until I was sitting in the front row of this courtroom on this day.

And now I was surrounded by people who knew the wrongness this man had done and they wanted to hold him accountable.

Vindication, I thought. And justice. I had a rare, front-row seat to watch the wheels of justice turn, and it was a privilege—a miracle, even.

—

THE HEARING WAS over in just three minutes.

The Great Vanguard loped toward the same door from which he'd emerged and exited with his new posse around him. After the door shut, we heard the chains jingle-jangling again.

Toni, Stanley, Barbara, and I were in a daze. As we left the courthouse and stepped into a sea of reporters outside, I could hear one of Keith's attorneys saying something to the media like "There are two sides to this story!" and "I'm impressed by our client's stamina!"

It's doubtful, I thought—with a chuckle—*they're referring to their client's sexual stamina.*

The media swarmed around Toni and me.

"Catherine, do you have a message for Keith?"

"Yes I do," I said: "You are where you belong, behind bars, for the rest of your life."

"And what would you like to say to India?" yelled another reporter.

"I love you. Come home."

18

PERSEPHONE'S DILEMMA

Yes, I desperately wanted India safe and back home again.

But from the start—and time and time again after that—I had underestimated the all-embracing and absolute hold that Keith and the others had over her. That I had been certain my own little intervention in the bedroom a year earlier would loosen their grip was tragically laughable to me now.

I thought of the Demeter myth again.

After Zeus orders Hades to release the abducted Persephone from the Underworld and send her back up to the light and home, Demeter and her daughter finally have a joyous reunion. The mother and daughter rush to each other and have a long-awaited, emotional embrace. But during that embrace, Demeter notices that something is still amiss. She discovers that Hades had forced Persephone to swallow pomegranate seeds while in the House of the Dead, which would now tie her to him forever.

Even though she'd been "saved," Persephone was doomed to peri-
odically return to Hades's dark world for the rest of her life.

I always hated that part of the ending.

—

THE DAY AFTER Keith's arraignment, my mother arrived in New
York to help me, hopefully once and for all, rescue our girl from the
underworld and bring her back to the light.

India was sharing an apartment with Allison in Brooklyn Heights,
the same area where Stanley lived. The plan to infiltrate and invade
Brooklyn with the newfangled Nxivm program called the Source,
headed by Allison, was obviously in full swing even though their
grandmaster had been temporarily detained.

As soon as Mom arrived, we set up camp at my usual Lower East
Side hotel and she texted India, saying she was in town and hoping
to see her. I hadn't heard back from India myself after my text a few
days earlier, but I couldn't see her saying no to her grandmother. Yet
when her replies appeared, they were vague, nonsensical excuses about
being busy: "I'm making snacks," she wrote. "I'm packing my things."

I'd never seen her avoid her grandmother before, and then I realized: Alli must be back from her high-speed federales adventure in
Mexico. And as her slave, India would be busy tending to her needs.
My suspicions were confirmed when Mark spotted Alli with her
mother in Brooklyn Heights as he left a coffee shop. The two women
entered an apartment building two blocks from Stanley's—which
means the entire time I was there, India and I had been in the same
bloody neighborhood!

"Use the 'croaking card,' " I told my mother. "Tell her, 'Grandma won't be around forever so come spend time with me.' "

Two days later, Mom and I met with Art and Anthony at their offices in the Chrysler Building. Thanks to Bill's nudging while he was in New York City, India had finally met with them the week before. Their impression of her, they told us, was of a very gentle soul. This is what so many have marveled to me: no amount of brainwashing could hide India's sweet essence.

"She believes she is innocent of any wrongdoing," I said. "Will that attitude hinder her at all? Is she out of jeopardy?" I asked.

"We can't predict what direction the prosecution will go," they said. But there was some good news: the prosecution worded the complaint in a way that created an "out" if they decided *not* to prosecute India.

"They called her a 'slave,' " said Art. "Her defense would be that she was ordered to do things—that her actions weren't of her own free will. If she becomes a witness for the prosecution, it's likely she wouldn't be charged with anything."

This should have given my mother and me great solace, but it didn't. Because in order for India to accept that line of defense, she'd have to comprehend that it was actually *true*. And in order for her to see that it was true, she'd have to be deprogrammed first. But because she was brainwashed, she refused to be deprogrammed.

It was a catch-22, and the question still remained: Would India be a witness for the prosecution, or would she remain in the grip of the underworld?

This was India's dilemma, and our agony.

—

AFTER OUR MEETING, Mom and I walked two miles down to the East Village, to the vegetarian café where India was working. I could barely keep up with my mother. (Even at eighty-two, Mom considered that an easy hike. For her birthday a week before, she'd gone to Morocco to trek through the desert.)

India still hadn't answered her grandmother's text about getting together, so we decided she'd surprise India at work. I hid inside a Starbucks across the street and watched from the window while Mom went in. We had no idea if India was even working that day, or if she'd be receptive to seeing her grandmother, so this was a hit-or-miss stakeout.

I watched with my heart in my mouth as my mother walked into the café and minutes later emerged smiling with India in tow. The two walked up the street, arm in arm. Success! I felt infinitely calmer just *knowing* India was with Mom. I waited our agreed-upon half hour, then walked back to our hotel to wait for Mom there. Karim and the crew were waiting to do some filming with me for the documentary.

An hour later, Mom showed up in the lobby where we were shooting, shaken up. I've always known her as the super-stoic type—she lived through World War II, a childhood in exile, the loss of a brother, and three marriages. Nothing ruffled her. But now, my mother collapsed in my arms in tears.

"I failed," she sobbed. "I couldn't get through to her! She still thinks Keith is a nice man!"

As we hugged, a hotel manager darted toward us with his eye on the camera crew and gave us a stern reprimand, telling us to cease filming. Karim quietly went up to the front desk and pulled the "princess card," telling another high-ranking hotel employee that, "the Princess Elizabeth of Yugoslavia was documenting a very important family moment!"

A minute later, a different manager suddenly appeared and excitedly began speaking Serbian to Mom and calling her "Your Highness." A fellow countryman, he'd been scanning the guest list earlier and spotted her name, Karageorgevic, and assumed she was an imposter. He began chatting away about his exodus from the former Yugoslavia, and Mom listened to him graciously. Another minute and he might have started to bow.

He ushered us into a private dining room in the back of the restaurant, where we could film to our hearts' content, he promised. (And where half the waiters from the hotel restaurant, also from the Old Country, showed up to greet their princess.)

That night, I could barely sleep. I was haunted by the idea that India was so willing to throw her life away. I watched the clock: three a.m., four a.m., five a.m. . . . and then it struck me what day it was— April 17, a year to the day after I got that first call to save India.

———

THE NEXT DAY Mom went to see India's new lawyer in my place.

I was still apprehensive to go, fearing I was being set up in a trap somehow. I envisioned myself arriving at the lawyer's office and him slapping me with a lawsuit the moment I stepped inside. So armed with a list of questions and a stack of evidence we'd carefully compiled, my mother set off for his office near Columbus Circle.

The goal was to show him the truth so that he'd then convince India of it, and Mom did a whizbang job. This was a woman who'd enthralled Richard Burton, don't forget—and she still had the charisma and beauty that rivaled screen legend Elizabeth Taylor.

Her scene with the lawyer was like a sequel to my dramatic scene in the attorney general's office in Albany months earlier, except that Mom wore black rubber boots instead of my kick-ass thigh-highs.

She plopped the thick pile of evidence onto his table with a thud and started off by showing him the most graphic part of the complaint against Keith—Jane Doe's testimony of being tied to a table, blindfolded, and forced to engage in oral sex with an unknown person. Then, she showed him the letter to the judge from the FBI, outlining Keith's history of rape, pedophilia, and sexual abuse.

"India thinks this man is *sweet*," my mother said. "Does this seem like a sweet man to you?"

Next, she pulled out the official police report of everything confiscated from Nancy's house.

"This is evidence that over half a million dollars in cash was found in Nancy's house. India says no money was found. Can you show this to her," Mom asked, pounding his desk for emphasis, "that she is being lied to and this is to help her see the reality?"

I may have gotten my flair for drama from my mother, who could always command a room. At one point during the meeting, she stood tall in her rubber boots, put her hands on her hips, and said, "My granddaughter is brainwashed! I should know, I have known her since I cut her umbilical cord!" The meeting ended with Mom winning him over, and the lawyer saying he'd suggest to India that she see a psychiatrist. He also agreed that India's best option was to testify for the prosecution. This time, my mom was a total success.

"You may be the only voice of reason he will hear on India's behalf," I told her, as I whisked us off to celebrate her triumph with much-needed retail therapy in SoHo. After that, we took in a show— *Hello, Dolly!*—on Broadway.

Before the curtain rose, I sent another text to India:

April 18, 2018, 8:05 p.m.

Darling, I love u deeply. I'm sad u didn't want to see me. I miss u. And I hope that soon you will be open and more receptive.♥

In the musical, the heroine uses hypnosis to seduce the object of her affection. It made me think of Keith and the mesmerizing hand gestures he used on women during his three a.m. walks—which ruined it for me. Afterward, we went backstage to meet the star, the legendary Bernadette Peters, who was a friend of Stanley's.

The next morning, Mom and I were dog-tired from the emotional week. We lay in bed talking and laughing and taking ridiculous selfies together until noon. I guess we needed a bit of silliness and fun to offset the stress. Then we raced around to pack everything up and cabbed it to JFK together, dropping me off at my terminal first.

"Thank you, Mom!" I said, and gave her a big hug. She'd been my bridge to India all year—talking to her and writing to her when India had me set to radio silence. Even on this trip, I was able to get a brief glimpse of my daughter from across a busy Manhattan avenue because of Mom—a glimpse that did this mother's heart good.

"You are my hero!" I told her. "I couldn't have done this without you."

Mom returned my hug and smiled.

"Maybe we can do something relaxing next time we get together?" she yelled out as I ran to my gate.

I got there just as they were boarding.

Mom headed east, I headed west, and between us was our girl, lost somewhere in the middle.

—

THE NEXT MORNING in LA, I woke up to tremendous news: Allison Mack had been arrested and was to appear in Brooklyn court that afternoon. The Feds had struck again! I was in shock and awe at how fast and stealthily the government was moving.

They had arrived at her Brooklyn Heights apartment in the early dawn hours and cuffed her while India was there, but I didn't know any other details. I got a text immediately from India's attorney, saying that prosecutors had assured him that India was not getting arrested—not today, anyway.

I was relieved about that, and elated at Allison's arrest. But it wasn't the same as how I felt about Keith's. Allison's came with a feeling of despair and anguish; that this psychotic man had ruined this woman's life. She had everything going for her—career, beauty, and talent, and was at the prime of her life, and he stole all that from her. At the same time, this was the woman who lured my daughter into Keith's hell world, and for that she must face the consequences of her actions.

Hopefully, now with Allison's arrest, India would have her connect-the-dots moment? Maybe this time?

Diane Benscoter, the ex-Moonie, gave me a new perspective as to why it may be so difficult for India to give up the cult.

"She is fighting for the most precious part of her," said Diane, "the part that wants to be beautiful in the world and that wants to help people. That is the part they have used against her." Stanley raced to the courthouse to act as our family representative. In court for her arraignment, Allison's demeanor was a 180 from Keith's.

She looked scared and defeated as she pleaded not guilty, Stanley reported to me later. That was the difference between someone who was a born psychopath (Keith) and someone indoctrinated into sociopathic behavior (Allison).

Still, "it was horrible to look at her," said Stanley. "All I could think about was how much pain and devastation she'd caused—especially to India. All I could feel from her was evil." The unsealed indictment revealed that Allison and Keith were now eternally bound as codefendants, accused of the same crimes and facing the same penalties. The crimes were: sex trafficking, sex trafficking conspiracy, and forced labor conspiracy.

"Under the guise of female empowerment, she starved women until they fit her codefendant's sexual feminine ideal," Assistant US Attorney Moira Kim Penza told the judge.

According to court documents, during the branding ritual Allison "placed her hands on the slaves' chests and told them to 'feel the pain' and to 'think of [their] master,' as the slaves cried with pain."

The judge declined to release her on bail, saying her lawyers didn't offer a sufficient enough bail package for such serious charges. Federal prosecutors also worried that Allison might engage in "witness intimidation and tampering," since it had been discovered that high-ranking Nxivm members had been registering websites in witnesses' names and threatening to release damaging information about them there. If guilty, Allison was looking at the same amount of time in prison as Keith: fifteen years to life.

They tossed her into jail for the weekend at the Metropolitan Detention Center—to mull things over. Nothing like a few days behind bars with no cell phone, no Wi-Fi, and no contact with any members of the cult to give a girl like Allison clarity—I imagine it was like deprogramming express. I'm sure Allison would find her new role as a prisoner in *Orange Is the New Black* a little too realistic for her liking.

"I want to see her put away," Stanley told the waiting press outside. "She's dangerous. She's sick. She's evil. She's dark. And she's done harm to many people. She's a B-grade actress—beyond B-grade— and she is not in a reality show or a TV series. This is life," he said. "She has to go away."

He called me on the phone as soon as he was done with the press, singing: "Ding-dong, the witch is dead . . . the witch is dead . . . the witch is dead . . ."

The following Tuesday, Allison's lawyers offered her bank account, her house in Clifton Park, and her parents' home in California as collateral. She was released on $5 million bail and ordered to serve home detention wearing an ankle bracelet at her parents' until the trial. When I read that, I couldn't help but think with a smile: *Kinda gives new meaning to the word "collateral," doesn't it, Allison? COLLATERAL.*

I'd also read that her lawyers were working on a plea deal for her in which she'd give information against Keith to negotiate a reduced sentence.

If that was the case, so much for Nxivm loyalty and ethics and the DOS girls' pact to never go against Keith. Suddenly, a Joan of Arc sacrifice for the cause wasn't looking so glamorous after all.

I wondered if the news that her best friend might go against "the family" and Keith would have any effect on India.

The best part of Allison's bail package was that she was ordered to have no contact with anyone involved in Nxivm, and that included my daughter.

—

TEN DAYS LATER, on May 4, Toni Natalie and Stanley took front row seats again inside Brooklyn federal court. What I would have given to see this day with my own eyes.

Both Keith and Allison appeared together in court for a forty-five-minute hearing. Allison didn't look at her former master the entire time, and always arrogant Keith looked like he was unraveling, Toni told me later. He was fuming, red in the face like a tomato. He turned to look at Toni and snarled at her.

Keith's attorneys had demanded a speedy trial that would have resulted in a start date of June or July, but the judge declined— Allison's attorney had already waived it. And since they were being charged as codefendants, he had to abide by his own slave's decision. A speedy trial was Keith's only chance in hell to get out of this. It would have given the government less time to gather evidence and less time for more indictments.

The judge set the trial date for October 1.

No wonder Keith was so angry: the world that he'd created out of his sick mind was falling apart before his eyes.

His good buddy Emiliano Salinas jumped ship from Nxivm Mexico and resigned as its head honcho, and so did partner Alex Betancourt.

Dr. Brandon Porter, who'd made the slaves watch videos of women being dismembered by machetes, would be charged the next day with illegally conducting human experiments by the New York State Office of Professional Medical Conduct. Soon after, the New York State Department of Health would accuse Porter of failing to report the outbreak of disease during V-week 2016, and charge him with moral unfitness, gross negligence, and gross incompetence.

And more arrests were to come, said Moira Kim Penza in court that day—plus superseding indictments for Keith and Allison, coming in early June.

After the hearing, Toni gave the reporters outside a long list of who she thought would be indicted next: Clare Bronfman, Nancy Salzman, Karen Unterreiner, Emiliano Salinas, Alex Betancourt, Lauren Salzman, and Sara Bronfman.

"This snake has more than one head," she told them.

The evil house of cards was collapsing; the dominoes were toppling over.

The only fate no one seemed sure about was India's. What was to become of India?

I'd fulfilled my vow to take down the cult, but what about my vow to free India's mind from them and get her home?

Around the time of Keith's arrest, I had a talk with Callum Blue.

"Love, I have to remind you of something," he said. "I once asked you what your end game was in all this. Do you remember what you said?"

"Um . . . to run away?"

We laughed. We always laughed together.

"You said that your end game was to have Keith arrested."

"Did I say that? Wow!"

"You did, dummy. And all I'm saying is . . . this could never end. And it's India's journey. You brought a cult down. You did it. You win. You've got the end of the story. And now it's up to India to navigate the end of *her* story."

Nine days later, she began doing just that:

Sunday, May 13, 6:30 a.m.

India: Happy Mother's Day, Mom

Me: Thank u, precious girl. I am so proud to be your mom.

With her text, she'd attached a photo of us when India was one month old and I'm cradling and nursing her. Below that, she'd posted a portion of Dr. Kent M. Keith's "The Paradoxical Commandments":

People are illogical, unreasonable, and self-centered.
Love them anyway.

If you do good, people will accuse you of selfish ulterior motives.
Do good anyway.

If you are successful, you will win false friends and true enemies.
Succeed anyway.

The good you do today will be forgotten tomorrow.
Do good anyway.

Honesty and frankness make you vulnerable.
Be honest and frank anyway. . . .

What you spend years building may be destroyed overnight.
Build anyway.

People really need help but may attack you if you do help them.
Help people anyway.

Give the world the best you have and you'll get kicked in the teeth.
Give the world the best you have anyway.

Me: Just what I needed to read ❤

India: ❤ me too

Me: I miss you ❤

I took the poem and photo to mean that no matter what has happened between us, nothing could or would ever destroy our love for each other; we would love each other anyway, and forgive each other always. And that I should never stop fighting for her, no matter what.

Keith set out to destroy us, and he'd failed. Ours was a bond that could not be broken.

It was a beautiful, sunny day and after Maya and Celeste brought me freshly cut white roses from our garden and arranged them in my bedroom, I took them to spend the afternoon on Greg's one-hundred-foot superyacht, *Sympatico*.

Greg was throwing a Mother's Day party for his wife, Andrea, with lots of food, cake, champagne, and music. The girls and I had a great time—though when I started dancing to Guns N' Roses' "Sweet Child o' Mine," they were so embarrassed they nearly jumped overboard.

We sailed for hours, from Marina del Rey heading north up the coast until we reached Venice Beach, where my journey with India on this road began.

The journey continues. India and I are strong, defiant, stubborn women—just like our valiant, freedom-fighting ancestors before us; so she hasn't given up on the cult yet, and I haven't given up on her.

And so, we wrestle on.

But looking out to the horizon that day, something occurred to me that made me laugh out loud. It hit me that India's own stubbornness had been the cult's undoing—her strength had been Nxivm's Achilles heel.

Had my initial intervention been successful, she and I would have walked away arm in arm without ever looking back and Keith would still be recruiting, abusing, exploiting, and branding innocent women.

Had she not been so resistant, I wouldn't have been so moved to expand my mission and help so many more needful victims through my foundation.

Every time India resisted, my heart broke—and then expanded, and my desire to help others increased.

So I want to thank her for that. I want to thank India from the deepest part of my heart for teaching me how to be a better person.

Far from the shore and surrounded by the tranquil waters of the Pacific, I felt at peace.

I didn't know how much longer it would take, but I knew now that India would find her way back to herself again, and we'd find our way to each other; the original, inseparable duo.

Until then, I would be there to help her and love her as always, with arms open as wide as the ocean.

ACKNOWLEDGMENTS

I want to thank all the brave warriors who dared to speak out against the evil ways of Nxivm over decades—even though many of you sustained terrible scars in battle, I hope you can all feel some peace in your hearts that justice is finally being served.

For helping me tell this story, I am grateful to my literary agent, Yfat Reiss Gendell at Foundry Literary + Media. You are a treasure and without doubt the best agent on the planet; thank you for hand-holding me through every stage of the process.

To my collaborator, Natasha Stoynoff, for your sensitivity in sharing some of my family's most private and harrowing moments; collaborating with you was pure joy.

To my editor, Natasha Simons, thank you for embracing my vision wholeheartedly and for your absolute brilliance. And to my wonderful team at Gallery Books—Natasha's right-hand woman, editorial assistant Hannah Brown; publisher Jennifer Bergstrom; associate publisher Jennifer Long; editorial director Aimee Bell; director of publicity Jennifer Robinson and publicity assistant Hannah Payne; marketing professionals Abby Zidle, Diana Velasquez,

Mackenzie Hickey, and Anabel Jimenez; managing editor Monica Oluwek and assistant managing editor Caroline Pallotta; production editor Chelsea Cohen; production manager Larry Pekarek; designer Bryden Spevak; art team members Lisa Litwack and John Vairo; subrights team Paul O'Halloran and Liz Lotto; and the audio edition team, including Tom Spain. Thank you also to Ed Klaris and Alexia Bedat at Klaris Law, PLLC. Thank you for supporting this complicated project.

To Gavin Bond, Sandy Flynn at Copious Management, Paul Rao, Dale Gold, Gaelle Paul, Clyde Haygood, and Katey Denno. To my lawyer, Monika Tashman, Esq. of Fox Rothschild, LLP, for your ongoing guidance on a process fraught with land mines. And the rest of my book team at Foundry Literary + Media: Jessica Felleman, Anna Strzempko, Deirdre Smerillo, Sara DeNobrega, Colette Grecco, Sarah Lewis, Kirsten Neuhaus, Michael Nardullo, Heidi Gall, Richie Kern, and Molly Gendell.

I'm grateful to members of the media for the relentless coverage given to exposing the atrocities of Nxivm, helping to generate much needed public outrage. Thank you to Barry Meier, Liz McNeil, Brendan Lyons, Megyn Kelly, Glenn Ruppel, Elizabeth Vargas, Tim Uehlinger, Chemene Pelzer, John Filimon, Alicia Powers, Scott Thompson, and many more. And a very special thanks to Frank Parlato: because of your tireless efforts, hundreds defected and escaped the horrors of branding and slavery.

With deepest gratitude to the United States Attorney's Office for the Eastern District of New York and the New York Field Office of the Federal Bureau of Investigation for spearheading the Nxivm investigation, New York State Governor Andrew Cuomo and the

New York State Department of Health, the New York State Police, the FBI Albany Field Office, the FBI's Mexican legat, the Mexican Federal Police, the New York State Office of the Attorney General, and the United States Attorney's Office for the Northern District of New York for their assistance.

I could never have succeeded in getting the truth out about the Nxivm group without the incredible generosity, patience, and guidance of my lawyers: Art Middlemiss and Anthony Capozzolo at Lewis Baach Kaufmann Middlemiss, PLLC; Neil Glazer at Kohn, Swift & Graf, P.C.; Robert Malone; and Anne Champion at Gibson, Dunn & Crutcher, LLP. Thank you all for providing countless hours of pro bono legal advice. And of course, tremendous thanks to foundation donors Tom Bove and Tom McKissick.

With deepest appreciation to those mental health professionals and other subject matter scholars for their kindness, wisdom, and insight. This gifted group includes Greg Hannley; Rachel Bernstein, LMFT; Daniel Shaw, LCSW; Rosanne Henry, LPC; Doni P. Whitsett, PhD, LCSW; Janja Lalich, PhD; Diane Benscoter; Dr. Annie Thiel; and Rick Alan Ross.

I'm also grateful to the gifted documentarians who have helped me capture some of this story on the screen, including Karim Amer and the Vow team—I love you all! I am so grateful that our lives intersected.

Special thanks to the wonderful friends with whom I laughed and cried this past year, including Stanley Zareff, Callum Blue, Bonnie Piesse, Mark Vicente, Juliana Vicente, Toni Natalie (my bookend), Toni Zarattini, Allison Rood, Margot J. Leviton, Sarah Edmondson, Nippy Ames, Maayan Tuati Saraga, Jen Kobelt, Tom Porter, Chitra Selvaraj, Deborah Matte, Lori Christina, Randy Jackson, Chris Burbs, Robin Tenaglia, Jessica Skyler Gifford, Janice Collier, Christy W., Sam McCloud, Ann Marie Hudson, Marissa Pomerantz, Connie Troncale, Anissa, Bev, Cherokee, Bea, Liliana, Erin, and Island Angel. And to the rest of you who prefer to remain anonymous, you know who you are—dear friends and acquaintances alike. I am deeply grateful for your contributions both large and small. Thank you for your enduring love, support, kindness, and friendship.

To my mother, Elizabeth, thank you for being my lifeline. I could not have weathered this storm without your strength, love, support, and humor. And to my precious children Maya, Celeste, Grace, and Casper Robert (Cappy)—I love you just as fiercely as I love India, so please, do me a favor, and promise me that you won't ever join a cult! And I promise you I will never suggest another seminar.

RESOURCES

Books

Cults Inside Out: How People Get In and Can Get Out
Rick Alan Ross

Cults In Our Midst: The Hidden Menace in Our Everyday Lives
Margaret Thaler Singer and Janja Lalich

Take Back Your Life
Janja Lalich and Madeleine Tobias

Freedom of Mind
Steven Hassan

Combatting Cult Mind Control
Steven Hassan

Traumatic Narcissism: Relational Systems of Subjugation
Daniel Shaw, LCSW

Coercive Control: How Men Entrap Women in Personal Life
Evan Stark

Shoes of a Servant: My Unconditional Devotion to a Lie.
Diane Benscoter

Other Cult Resources

Freedom Of Mind: https://freedomofmind.com/resource-links

International Cultic Studies Association (ICSA): http://www
.icsahome.com/elibrary/faqs

Cult Education Institute: https://www.culteducation.com

Open Minds Foundation: https://www.openmindsfoundation
.org

Cult Experts: http://www.cultexperts.org

reFOCUS: http://www.refocus.org

Families Against Cult Teachings: https://www.familiesagainst
cultteachings.org

FrankReport: https://frankreport.com/

Catherine Oxenberg Foundation 501-c-3 EIN# 82-1511988
The Catherine Oxenberg Foundation is a human rights organi-
zation dedicated to reclaiming female sexuality from the cultural
shadow.

Women have the right to accurate, science-based knowledge about
their bodies, they have the right to maintain complete sovereignty over

their bodies, and they have the right to preserve the sanctity of their bodies.

Our contribution is in the realm of research, rehabilitation, and restoration.

Establish an evidence-based approach to female sexuality.
Sponsor rescue and long-term recovery for victims of sexual exploitation and trafficking in the USA.
Fund reconstructive surgery for victims of FGM.

The full freedom we aspire to as women can only become a reality in an environment where women are free from subjugation, exploitation, and abuse.

In the wake of recent developments, we have expanded the scope of the foundation to include exit counseling for defectors of extreme cults. Defectors are often in a state of acute trauma. Many are suffering from symptoms such as PTSD, paranoia of the outside world, severe phobias, and limited critical thinking. They have debilitated vocational skills; they have often been alienated from family and isolated from any support network. They are most likely financially broke and often in debt. They have fear of speaking with law enforcement, often as a result of cult indoctrination and severe intimidation. They often require a period of healing and recovery where they can unpack what has happened to them, organize their thinking, and take time to educate themselves. Education is a key component to recovery. The fact that they are financially destitute is a factor in why many remain trapped in the abusive environment of the cult. Our objective is to spearhead and craft new legislation to protect people against destructive cults. We need to lobby for stricter regulations when it comes to uninformed consent, undue influence, and coercive control. Currently the laws protect the perpetrators, not the victims.